Observations on
"The Two Sons of Oil"

WILLIAM FINDLEY

Observations on "The Two Sons of Oil"

Containing a Vindication of the American Constitutions,
and Defending the Blessings of Religious Liberty and Toleration,
against the Illiberal Strictures of the
Rev. Samuel B. Wylie

WILLIAM FINDLEY

Edited and with an Introduction by John Caldwell

LIBERTY FUND

INDIANAPOLIS

Introduction and annotations © 2007 by Liberty Fund, Inc.

Frontispiece: Portrait of William Findley by Rembrandt Peale, from
life, 1805. Reproduced by permission of Independence National
Historical Park.

C   1   2   3   4   5   6   7   8   9   10
P   1   2   3   4   5   6   7   8   9   10

Library of Congress Cataloging-in-Publication Data

Findley, William, 1741 or 2–1821.
  Observations on The two sons of oil: containing a vindication of the American
constitutions, and defending the blessings of religious liberty and toleration, against
the illiberal strictures of the Rev. Samuel B. Wylie / William Findley; edited and with
an introduction by John Caldwell.
       p.   cm.
  Includes bibliographical references and index.
  ISBN-13: 978-0-86597-667-2 (hardcover: alk. paper)
  ISBN-13: 978-0-86597-668-9 (pbk.: alk. paper)
  1. Wylie, Samuel B. (Samuel Brown), 1773–1852. Two sons of oil.   2. Freedom
of religion.   3. Religious tolerance.   4. Church and state—United States.
5. Christianity and politics—United States.   I. Caldwell, John.   II. Title.
  BV741.F5   2007
  323.44'20973—dc22   2007016790

Liberty Fund, Inc.
8335 Allison Pointe Trail, Suite 300
Indianapolis, Indiana 46250-1684

CONTENTS

INTRODUCTION

by John Caldwell

I

It was during the summer and fall of 1811 that William Findley wrote his third book, *Observations on "The Two Sons of Oil": containing a Vindication of the American Constitutions, and Defending the Blessings of Religious Liberty and Toleration, against the Illiberal Strictures of the Rev. Samuel B. Wylie.*[1] Wylie had published his *Two Sons of Oil* in 1803.[2] In this work of radical Presbyterian theology Wylie pointed out what he considered to be deficiencies in the constitutions of both Pennsylvania and the United States. *Observations* is a typical Findley response. He first lays a very thorough historical background for what he wants to discuss and then proceeds to give it a detailed, point by point, examination.

Presbyterians had begun to arrive in America before the end of the seventeenth century. By 1705 the Presbytery of Philadelphia had been organized and was providing general supervision of congregations in a wide area centering on that city. As immigration increased, especially of Scotch-Irish from Ulster, the divisions that the Scots brought with

1. The book was published by Patterson and Hopkins in 1812. Findley had previously published *A Review of the Revenue System Adopted by the First Congress under the Federal Constitution . . . In thirteen Letters to a Friend* (Philadelphia: T. Dobson, 1794) and *History of the Insurrection in the Four Western Counties of Pennsylvania in the Year 1794* (Philadelphia: Samuel Harrison Smith, 1796).

2. Samuel B. Wylie, *The Two Sons of Oil; or, The Faithful Witness for Magistracy & Ministry upon a Scriptural Basis; also, A Sermon on Covenanting: Being the Substance of Two Discourses* (Greensburg: Snowden & M'Corkle, 1803).

them to Ulster were carried across the Atlantic, chiefly to Pennsylvania.[3] In America the two principal dissenting groups, the Associate
Presbytery (the Seceders) and the Reformed Presbytery (the Covenanters), found their major difference in their attitudes toward government.
Seceders saw government as a law of nature given by God the Creator
for the common benefit of mankind. It was not, they believed, connected with Jesus Christ as Savior and thus had no religious responsibilities. Covenanters maintained that government was an ordinance
provided by God through Christ as mediator, that the scriptures provided the principles and qualifications for rulers, and that the only legitimate government was one that recognized Christ as the source of its
authority.[4]

II

William Findley, the son and grandson of Covenanters, was born in Antrim County, Northern Ireland, probably in January of either 1741 or
1742; he himself was not quite sure which. His family belonged to a
Reformed Presbyterian society.

Because the Reformed Presbytery had no regular minister, services
were usually conducted by laymen, and the worshipers referred to themselves as a society.[5] Much of his religious education he received at home.
"My father had a larger library of church history and divinity than many
of his neighbors," Findley writes in his *Observations,* "to these means I
am under great obligations for any early religious knowledge that I possessed, or impressions that I experienced."[6]

When he immigrated to Pennsylvania in 1763, Findley first settled
in the Covenanter community at Octoraro, in Lancaster County, where

---

3. Robert Ellis Thompson, *A History of the Presbyterian Churches in the United States* (New
York: Christian Literature Co., 1895), 14–21.

4. David Melville Carson, "A History of the Reformed Presbyterian Church in America
to 1871" (Ph.D. diss., University of Pennsylvania, 1964), 51–52.

5. Ibid., 6.

6. *Observations,* 307 (see p. 210, below).

some friends of his father resided and where he was accepted as being in full communion with the Reformed Presbytery of Scotland. It was probably here that he first became acquainted with John Cuthbertson, the only Reformed Presbyterian clergyman in Pennsylvania.[7] After several months he moved westward to settle in another Covenanter community in the southeastern corner of Cumberland County, near present-day Waynesboro. Here he met Mary Cochran, the daughter of a Covenanter family. He purchased a farm in 1768, and he and Mary were married on March 21, 1769. The following year, on November 11, 1770, John Cuthbertson ordained him and his father-in-law, John Cochran, to be ruling elders in their local Reformed society.[8] The delegates from the various societies met in an annual or semiannual general meeting, usually at Middle Octoraro, Cuthbertson's home base. Findley was for many years the clerk at these meetings. In 1773 Matthew Linn and Alexander Dobbin arrived in Pennsylvania to share Cuthbertson's ministerial responsibilities and with him organized the Reformed Presbytery of America.[9]

Although he refused election to the Pennsylvania General Assembly, William Findley was during the Revolution active in local government as a member of the Committee of Safety and the county board of finance. He also served two tours of active militia duty with the Cumberland Associators. After purchasing a farm along the Loyalhanna Creek in Westmoreland County, Findley moved his young family across the mountains in 1783. From Westmoreland County he was elected to serve on the Council of Censors that met in 1783 and 1784 to consider the revision of the state constitution. He was for four terms a member of the General Assembly and then of the Supreme Executive Council. As the Anti-Federalist leader in the Pennsylvania convention to ratify the United States Constitution, Findley fought for changes that later were adopted as the Bill of

7. Ibid., 305 (see p. 208, below).

8. John Cuthbertson, *Register of Marriages and Baptisms Performed by Rev. John Cuthbertson, Covenanter Minister, 1751–1791*, ed. S. Helen Fields (Washington, D.C.: Lancaster Press, 1934), 129.

9. T. C. Evans, "Octorara United Presbyterian Church," *Historical Papers and Addresses of the Lancaster County Historical Society* 34 (1930): 74.

Rights. On January 16, 1789, he was elected a member of the American Philosophical Society.[10] Along with James Wilson, in 1789 and 1790, he led the convention that wrote a new constitution for Pennsylvania that ensured virtual manhood suffrage, freedom of worship, trial by jury, and a free press. It is this constitution that Wylie attacks in *The Two Sons of Oil*.

Findley represented the western country in the Second through the Fifth Congresses and again in the Eighth through the Fourteenth. During these years opposition to Federalism was just beginning to coalesce around James Madison and Thomas Jefferson into a party that would call itself Republican. Findley was firmly allied with this group. However, his Republicanism was often outweighed by his regionalism. "At all times the westerners' champion"[11] he was a consistent advocate for selling some western land in small parcels that individual farmers could buy, rather than selling all of it in large blocks that only speculators could afford. He always opposed any extension of the excise and any import tax on salt for which western farmers had no regional source. He broke with his southern and eastern colleagues by his support for keeping a standing army on the western frontier. While most Republicans opposed it, he supported a resolution expressing thanks to General Anthony Wayne on his victory at Fallen Timbers in 1794. He broke with them again over providing indemnification to those who had suffered property damage during the Whiskey Insurrection. Although he consistently voted against domestic slavery he just as consistently supported the other policies of these two presidents. Among other things, he supported Jefferson's Louisiana Purchase and the admission of Louisiana as a state. During the War of 1812 Findley was very nearly a War Hawk for he saw the conquest of Canada as a way to end British-supported Indian attacks on the western frontier.

Because he was its longest serving member, Findley was officially designated the "Father of the House" before he retired from Congress in 1817. In 1821, in his home along the Loyalhanna, he died of tuberculosis.

10. American Philosophical Society, *Year Book, 1990* (Philadelphia: American Philosophy Society, 1991), 261.

11. Elizabeth K. Henderson, "The Northwestern Lands of Pennsylvania," *Pennsylvania Magazine of History and Biography* 60 (1936): 147.

Samuel B. Wylie was born in Antrim County, Ireland, May 21, 1773, and graduated from the University of Glasgow with a Master of Arts degree in 1797. That same year, because he had become associated with the independence movement, he had to leave Ireland. Immigrating to the United States, he settled in Philadelphia, where he was appointed as a tutor at the University of Pennsylvania. After studying theology under the direction of the Reverend William Gibson, he was ordained by the Reformed Presbytery at Ryegate, Vermont, where Gibson was pastor. On November 20, 1803, he became the pastor of the Reformed Presbyterian Congregation in the City of Philadelphia, a Covenanter congregation. The American Philosophical Society elected him a member in 1806. When a Reformed seminary was organized in 1810, Wylie was elected its first professor. Holding this position until his resignation in 1817 he was again elected in 1823 and served until 1828. The University of Pennsylvania—where he taught Hebrew, Greek, and Latin—appointed him Professor of Humanities in 1828, in which position he served until his resignation in 1845. During this period he was Vice-Provost from 1834 until his resignation.[12] Wylie died on October 13, 1852.

III

As clerk and elder, William Findley was active in the formation of the Reformed Presbytery in 1774. However, along with many others, he had become increasingly unhappy with the requirement that the covenants made in the seventeenth century between Scots Presbyterians and the British government were binding on their descendents who had emigrated to America. He was, therefore, also an active participant in the further union that brought Seceders and Covenanters together, in 1782, as the Associate Reformed Church. This merger took the position that "Magistracy is derived from God as the Almighty Creator and Governor

12. Reformed Presbyterian Church (Covenanted), "Samuel Brown Wylie: Biographical Sketch," http://www.covenanter.org/Wylie/samuelbrownwylie.htm (accessed November 6, 2006); American Philosophical Society, *Year Book 1990,* 282; and University of Pennsylvania Archives and Records Center, "Penn Biographies," http://www.archives.upenn .edu/histy/people/1700s/wylie_saml_brown.html (accessed December 15, 2006).

of the world, and not from Christ as Mediator." From this statement the Associate Reformed Church drew the conclusion that as government derives directly from God it is not essential that it be overtly Christian. Therefore as long as the government of the United States did not impose anything sinful on the church, it was its "duty to acknowledge the government of these states in all lawful commands." The merged organization further agreed that the matter of adhering to the covenants be "referred to the councils and deliberations of the whole body."[13]

Not all of the Covenanters accepted this union. Various local societies, chiefly in Pennsylvania and South Carolina, repeatedly requested a minister from the Reformed Presbytery in Scotland and for instructions on what they should do in the meantime. They were advised by the Scots to avoid participation in the American governments. Between 1790 and 1797 several Covenanter ministers from Scotland served for varying periods in America. It was not until the arrival of James McKinney in 1793 and William Gibson in 1797, both Covenanters from Ulster, that permanent pastoral leadership was obtained. On February 21, 1798, in Philadelphia, McKinney and Gibson reestablished the Reformed Presbytery in America.[14]

IV

In *The Two Sons of Oil,* Wylie denied the authority of both state and national government in America and declared them to be immoral because they did not recognize the necessary bond between the ministry and the civil magistracy. Basing his argument on Zechariah 4:1–14, concerning the restoration of the Hebrew nation under Zerubbabel and Joshua,[15] Wylie contended that the Law of Moses thus established was

---

13. "The Basis of Union of 1782, on which the Associate Reformed Church Was Formed," in *A History of the Presbyterian Churches in the United States,* ed. Robert Ellis Thompson (New York: Christian Literature Co., 1895), 347.

14. Carson, "A History of the Reformed Presbyterian Church," 53–59, 64.

15. The Babylonian exile of the Jewish nation ended when Cyrus of Persia, having conquered Babylon in 538 B.C., proclaimed that the exiles were free to return to their homeland, and that they should, with Persian assistance, rebuild the temple in Jerusalem that the Babylonians had destroyed. The chronicle of the return and rebuilding is told in

still applicable and that any government that did not honor it was immoral and not to be obeyed.

Wylie concedes that the American government is "the best now existing in the Christian world," but he insists that Covenanters, that is, members of the Reformed Presbyterian Church, cannot, for conscience's sake, yield obedience to it. He sums up, in the form of nine objections, his reasons for rejecting government as it exists in the United States.

1. The federal constitution "does not even recognize the existence of
   God."

"Ought not men, in the formation of their deeds, to consider their responsibility to the moral Governor, and this obligation to acknowledge his authority? . . . That a national deed, employed about the fundamental stipulations of magistrates, as his ministers, should nowhere recognize the existence of the Governor of the universe, is, to say nothing worse of it, truly lamentable. . . . Did not the framers of this instrument act, not only as if there had been no divine revelation for the supreme standard of their conduct; but also as if there had been no God?"[16]

Even worse, Wylie says, the American government recognizes the wrong god. In a treaty made with the Bey of Tripoli in 1797, it was specifically declared that "the government of the United States of America is not, in any sense, founded on the Christian religion." This is to deny Christ's holy religion and "to count kindred, or at least deny enmity against Mahomet, the vile impostor."[17]

---

two Old Testament books written by the contemporaries Haggai and Zechariah. There was no immediate great surge of return, and the serious rebuilding of the temple did not begin for eighteen years, when Joshua was High Priest and Zerubbabel, as the governor appointed by the Persians, exercised civil authority in Jerusalem. Both prophets make the civil and religious leaders of coordinate importance. Haggai (2:20–23) had, in veiled language, announced that Zerubbabel, the grandson of Jehoiachin, the last pre-exilic king of Judah, was Yahweh's Anointed One, the Davidic Messiah. Zechariah, in a series of visions, reinforced the hope for restoration of the Jewish state under the coleadership of the High Priest and the Davidic prince. In one of his visions Zechariah (4:1–14) sees a large golden candlestick topped by a golden bowl, from which seven lamps are fed. On either side of the candlestick stand two olive trees that represent Zerubbabel and Joshua—the civil and religious leaders in Jerusalem—who are identified as "the two anointed ones."

16. Wylie, *The Two Sons of Oil,* 39–40 (see note 2, above).

17. Ibid., 48–49.

2. Most of the state constitutions contain "positive immorality" in rec-
   ognizing the rights of conscience in worship.

American ideas about freedom of worship, Wylie contends, are immoral:
"Witness their recognition of such rights of conscience as sanction every
blasphemy which a depraved heart may believe to be true. . . . The recognition of such rights of conscience is insulting to the Majesty of Heaven,
and repugnant to the express letter of God's word."[18]

"Civil government does not, as some modern politicians affirm, originate either in the people, as its fountain, or in the vices consequent
upon the fall. . . . Magistracy flows immediately from God Creator, and
is predicated upon his universal dominion over all nations."[19]

3. The government gives a legal security and establishment to gross
   heresy, blasphemy, and idolatry, under the notion of liberty of
   conscience.

Wylie points out that the Pennsylvania constitution "recognizes and un-
alterably establishes the indefeasible right of worshipping Almighty God,
whatever way a man's conscience may dictate; and declares that this shall,
for ever, remain inviolable. We believe that no man has a right to worship God any other way than he himself hath prescribed in his law." This
sanction of any kind of worship, he asserts, amounts to the establishment
of a religion. The question then is "Whether the religion of Jesus alone,
should be countenanced by civil authority? Or every blasphemous, heretical, and idolatrous abomination, which the subtle malignity of the old
serpent, and a heart deceitful above all things, and desperately wicked,
can frame and devise, should be put on an equal footing therewith?"[20]

4. Civil officers are sworn to support the constitutions, which sanction
   gross immorality.

The Pennsylvania constitution, Wylie points out, requires that "Members of the general assembly, and all other officers, executive and judicial, shall be bound by oath or affirmation, to support the constitution
of the commonwealth. If, therefore, the constitution of Pennsylvania . . .

---

18. Ibid., 40.
19. Ibid., 9–10.
20. Ibid., 40–41, 43.

supports, and legally establishes gross heresy, blasphemy and idolatry, it necessarily follows, that those who swear to support it, are bound by solemn oath to support the above principles and practices."[21]

5. The governments make no provision for the interest of true religion. "The civil magistrate," Wylie asserts, "ought to defend and protect the church of Christ." Citing Isaiah 49:23, "Kings shall be thy nursing fathers and their queens thy nursing mothers," he concludes that civil magistrates "are bound to exercise all the influence, which in the providence of God is conferred upon them, in promoting the religion of Jesus."[22] He goes on at great length to demonstrate from Scripture and history that as the civil magistrates have no authority in ecclesiastical matters they "ought to use every lawful endeavour to promote purity, unity, and reformation, in the church."[23]

6. The governments are in a state of national rebellion against God. "God, in mercy, has been pleased to send us a written transcript of his will. . . . If we refuse to receive it, and obstinately prefer the obscure shattered fragments, revealed by nature's light, to the rejection of divine revelation, do we not pour contempt upon the Legislator, and hoist the signal of rebellion?"[24]

7. Deists and even atheists may be chief magistrates. "A belief . . . in the existence of a Deity, is not, by the Federal constitution, either directly or by implication, made a necessary qualification of the first magistrate."

8. Most of the states recognize the principle of slavery. "Is it not strangely inconsistent, that the constitution, the paramount law of the land, should declare all men to be free, and the laws pretended to be constitutional, doom a certain portion of them to hopeless bondage, and subject them to the wanton barbarity of savage and

21. Ibid., 44.
22. Ibid., 22, 46.
23. Ibid., 24.
24. Ibid., 47.

inhuman masters, who, in many instances, treat their brutes with more tenderness?"[25]

9. "A last reason why we reject these constitutions is, that we are bound by the moral law, as subjects of the God of Heaven, to obey his will; and whatever is contrary thereunto we are obliged to reject."
"This obligation necessarily flows from our relation to God, as the Moral Governor. See Exod. xx. 1, 7, where we have an epitome of his laws, and by this we hold ourselves indispensably bound."[26]

In a sermon published with *The Two Sons of Oil,* Wylie argued that the Solemn League and Covenant established between the Presbyterians of Scotland and the English Parliament in 1643 should be applied to the church in America. This because the taking of the covenants by their forefathers in Scotland continued to make them binding on their posterity in America.

V

After living in the United States for more than thirty years, Wylie modified his opinion of the American government. At the Reformed Presbyterian Eastern Subordinate Synod meeting in April 1832, Wylie led a movement to reverse the position that he had previously championed. He chaired a committee whose report to the meeting concluded that it is not immoral for Christians to support the government of the United States. "It is susceptible of demonstration," the report asserted, "that since the commencement of Christianity, no Government on earth has had a fairer claim to recognition, as the ordinance of God, than that of these United States. . . . We do claim for our beloved country, the character of a Christian land, whose institutions are worthy of recognition, and active support." In its published report the Synod deleted the paragraphs that included these references to the government. Wylie responded by restoring the deleted material and publishing the report as *The Original Draft of a Pastoral Address from the Eastern Subordinate Synod*

---

25. Ibid., 49–50.
26. Ibid., 50–51.

of the Reformed Presbyterian Church.[27] This publication was answered by a twelve-page pamphlet entitled *Sentiments of the Rev. Samuel B. Wylie, A.M. in 1803, respecting Civil Magistracy and the Government of the United States Contrasted with Sentiments of the Rev. Samuel B. Wylie, D.D. in 1832.*[28] This publication contrasted selections from *The Two Sons of Oil* with selections from *The Original Draft* to demonstrate how Wylie had fallen from grace. "The Doctor," the anonymous author remarks, "has evidently lowered, in great degree, the standard by which he once thought civil government should be tested. . . . On viewing the direct contradictions . . . between *Mr.* Wylie and *Dr.* Wylie we cannot help saying, with the Patriarch Jacob, 'Unstable as water,' and with the Apostle James, 'A double-minded man is unstable in all his ways.'" In his history of the church, David Carson notes that, because of Wylie's new position, "a division in the church was created and never healed, each side claiming to be the true Reformed Presbyterian Church." The nicknames "old lights" and "new lights" developed to distinguish the two positions.[29]

The following work was an important contribution to the early debates about the nature of the American constitutional regime. How should people of faith relate to the national and state governments? What ought the relationship of church and government look like? What are the foundations of religious liberty in America? Given the persistent interest in this subject throughout the political history of our republic, Findley's commentary offers an informed and salutary reminder of the early historical context that first defined our constitutional traditions.

27. *The Original Draft of a Pastoral Address from the Eastern Subordinate Synod of the Reformed Presbyterian Church* (New York: W. Applegate, 1832), 10, 29.

28. *Sentiments of the Rev. Samuel B. Wylie, A.M. in 1803, respecting Civil Magistracy and the Government of the United States Contrasted with Sentiments of the Rev. Samuel B. Wylie, D.D. in 1832* (Montgomery, N.Y.: Press of Thomas & Edwards, 1832), 4, 8.

29. Carson, "A History of the Reformed Presbyterian Church," 99–102.

PREFACE

It appears proper to inform the reader of the occasion that called my attention to the book called "*Sons of Oil,*" and why I considered it as a duty incumbent on me to offer the following Observations on that work; and also why it has been so long delayed, after it had been expected. With respect to the first, though I had seen the Sons of Oil advertised in the newspapers for sale, yet being possessed of other approved commentaries on the symbolical vision of the prophecy of Zechariah, on which it is founded, I had not curiosity enough to purchase it, and did not, for some years, hear of its singular import and effect.

It was, I believe, in the year 1808, that a very respectable and intelligent neighbour, who, in a public company, where the government and laws of the state, and United States, had been very rudely misrepresented; and while he was endeavouring to explain and vindicate them, he was told by some of the company, that if they should kill him that instant, we had no law to punish such murder, &c. He informed me of it, and consulted me about the propriety of taking surety of the peace of such boasters of the impunity with which they could commit wilful murder. Neither my neighbour, nor myself, having seen the Sons of Oil, from which it was said they had their authority, I was of the opinion that they had mistaken the author, and that these boasts were but an ebullition of folly and ignorance, and would have no dangerous effect. I advised, therefore, to pass it over without further notice. Not long after this, however, I heard the poison had a more extensive influence in different quarters where the book had spread—but my attention was particularly called to the subject by an intelligent magistrate, in a distant county to the westward, who, being attacked in the same manner that my neighbour had been, endeavoured in vain to convince them of their error, by explaining the law of the state respecting murder; but he found that the doctrine of the Sons of Oil was too powerful for his statement, or explanation of the law. He procured a perusal of the book itself, and carefully took notes of it, with which he furnished me a copy, accompanied with a request, to turn my attention to the subject. This was not the first advice that was given me to that purpose; but, though astonished at the notes, without having the least doubt of their correctness, yet I could not, on the notes alone, proceed to make observations on the book itself. In the mean time, however, the intelligent farmer who took the notes, published, while on a journey, a very small pamphlet from them, called the "*Plough-Boy,*" which, it afterwards appeared, had the good effect of putting a stop to the wicked boasting of the impunity with which they could commit wilful murder. Those of Mr. Wylie's church, who did, on different occasions, boast in this manner, I am persuaded, must have been the most ignorant and vicious of the society—for I am acquainted with such of them as would be very far from disturbing the peace of society; but why should such a disposition be promoted by a professed minister of the gospel, at the expense of truth?

The books having been taken away from the office at which they had been advertised for sale, I had difficulty to find a copy—and when I did procure one, I found that the half of the mischief, which it was calculated to promote, had not been told me; that it not only grossly misrepresented the government and laws of the United States in general, but more particularly that of Pennsylvania. The encouragement given to people so disposed, to kill their neighbours with expectation of impunity, and for slaves to kill their masters, are but a few, out of numerous instances, of the insidious slanders which his book contains. If teaching to resist the ordinance of legitimate civil government, to refuse to obey the magistrates, for conscience sake, from whom they receive and claim protection; if despising dominion, speaking evil of dignities, and stirring up sedition, are contrary, not only to the moral law, but also to the precepts of the gospel, the Sons of Oil is certainly so. On a first perusal of it, I thought these, together with the numerous inconsistencies it contains, must, to every dispassionate enquirer, be so harmless, as to render an antidote unnecessary. But when I considered the artful sophistry, tinselled over with spurious religious zeal, equal at least to that practised by the most bigotted popish missionaries, set off with an unusual number of notes of astonishment, supported by the most unprincipled declamation; when I also considered, that besides the influence it has had in drawing a number of people into such gross immorality, as to think and boast of the impunity with which they could murder their neighbours, and besides being mostly aliens, as he says (p. 76) having drawn away many respectable citizens from their allegiance to the government, and from discharging the duties of citizenship, and attending on gospel ordinances as formerly, in such churches as do not promote the same excesses with themselves—I say, on considering these things, I became convinced that it was a duty to endeavour to prevent the delusion from taking such deep root as to draw many into its vortex, and disturb the peace of society, to preserve which, civil government was instituted, with the divine approbation, among men.

It would have been desirable that some other person, younger in life, and having more leisure than me, should have undertaken it; but it so happened, that I was pointed out for that purpose before I had seen the book, or was informed of the extent of the mischief it was likely to produce. There were, indeed, some reasons for this. I was the oldest man known to be alive, or at least in a capacity to undertake it, that was educated by the old dissenters, and under the inspection of the reformed presbytery of Scotland (there being no reformed presbytery in the north of Ireland when I left it.) I was likewise one of the oldest men living, who associated with, and was a member of the conferences of those who had, in this country, sought for and obtained a supply of ministers from that presbytery; and also one of the few survivors of those, who, more than forty years ago, promoted the revision of that testimony in this country, and with the presbytery, when such was constituted, rejected all local and traditionary terms of communion, founded on human fallible authority, and took the scriptures and the doctrines of the

Westminster Confession,[1] &c. agreeing with scripture, as the terms of their communion; and the only survivor of that reformed presbytery, who, a few years afterwards, assisted in bringing about the union with the associate presbyteries, which constituted the associate reformed synod, designed as a step towards a union of all the presbyterian body who professed the same faith of the gospel. My personal knowledge of these things pointed it out as my duty, to vindicate them from the doctrines contained in the Sons of Oil. Having been also engaged in the early committees, &c. which promoted the independence of the United States, and in making or ratifying the constitutions of this state and of the United States, and, for a long period, in legislating on the one or other of them, it appeared to be my duty to engage in their vindication, when they were so grossly traduced. These reasons had such weight in my own mind, as to induce me to make observations on this extraordinary work, notwithstanding that my other engagements, and time of life, might have afforded a strong apology for declining it.

The old dissenters, from whom I am descended, were a very pious people, exact in their morals, and so inoffensive in their deportment, that they were treated with great respect and sympathy by their neighbours; but when they came to have ministers, and their numbers increased, their respectability had not a proportionable increase; they began to make some deviations, seemingly inconsistent with their testimony; they began to consider paying tithes to the episcopal clergy, whom they did not acknowledge, as compounding with a robber—as Mr. Wylie does with paying road and county taxes, of which he and his people receive equal benefit with others. But though, because of the rescinding of the covenants, the establishment of episcopacy, and the king's headship over the church, the reformed presbytery of Scotland disowned the authority of the civil government; they did not like those who assume that name in this country, claim its protection; they did not apply to courts or magistrates for the recovery of debts, damages, &c. or the protection of constables to their presbytery, as those assuming that name do in this

---

1. The Westminster Confession of Faith is a statement, in English, of Calvinist doctrine. It is the basic statement of belief in Presbyterian and Congregational churches.

country. Doing so, was there esteemed highly censurable; they did not
act so inconsistent a part as to claim protection where they refused allegiance. They, indeed, laboured under mistakes by trusting to tradition.
They believed that not only the solemn league and covenant,[2] but even
the national covenant of Scotland,[3] neither of which were ever taken by
the kingdom of Ireland, or their representatives, were binding on that
nation. They appear to have been led into this mistake by reading the
title of the solemn league, affixed to it by the committees of Scotland
and England, who prepared that instrument, but to which Ireland never
acceded; and also by the local testimonies of the sufferers in Scotland,
of those who laboured under the same mistake. They also believed that
those covenants were legally taken in England, agreeable to the constitution of that nation—whereas the solemn league was only taken by
authority of an ordinance of parliament, which never became a law, and
for which the clergy of England, which were deprived of their livings,
and persecuted under Charles II. to more than five times the number
of the clergy of Scotland, who were deprived, on the same occasion, and
persecuted also for not complying with prelacy, never during that persecution, nor after it ceased, claimed the legal obligation of that covenant
on England. With the national covenant, England and Ireland never
had any concern. Upwards of fifty of the English presbyterian ministers, many of them very eminent divines, whose works yet praise them,
outlived the persecution, and afterwards enjoyed protection; but none
of these ever set up a claim to the solemn league, as of legal or moral

2. "A Solemn League and Covenant for Reformation and Defence of Religion, the
Honor and Happiness of the King, and the Peace and Safety of the Three Kingdoms of
Scotland, England, and Ireland" was an agreement made in 1643 between the English
and Scots, by which the Scots agreed to support the English Parliament in its disputes
with the king, and both countries pledged to work for a civil and religious union of
the three countries under a Presbyterian-parliamentary system. It was adopted by the
Church of Scotland, the English Parliament, and the Westminster Assembly. The Scots
considered it a guarantee of their religious system. The English regarded it as a civil
agreement and disregarded it whenever it was not to their advantage.

3. The National Covenant of 1638 was based on the King's Covenant of 1580. It was
largely a rejection of Roman Catholicism and especially of episcopacy in church government. It was for the most part signed by the Scottish military powers.

obligation, or as a term of christian communion, as the old dissenters in Scotland did.

They were also under a mistake in believing, that any act of a human fallible legislature could be in its own nature unchangeable, thus setting human authority on an equal footing with the unchangeable God; or that one legislature had not equal authority to revise or repeal a law, as another had to make it; or that either law-makers or subjects had a moral right to engage, by oath, to make rules of conduct unchangeable, which were, by the providence of God, rendered changeable in their own natures. Into this mistake they were led by the unhallowed union of church and state, and the misapplication of the Sinai covenant.[4] The old dissenters being few in number, and left without a minister, when they commenced their testimony in Scotland against the establishment of church and state, in 1689, had not the opportunity of correct information— correct records respecting them not having been then published, and they themselves being strongly prepossessed in favour of national churches. They never, however, pretended that the obligation of these covenants extended to the American colonies (now United States) nor did their presbytery, when they obtained one, as is evident from their judicial testimony, apply it to them. Nor did they ever teach, that civil protection could be claimed, where allegiance was not due. They claimed, indeed, the right of native born citizens of Britain, but not of the colonies. The new presbytery which has assumed that name in this country, however, has, by its own authority, transferred these local, and, in their own nature, changeable obligations, to the United States, which they might, with equal justice, have done to any other nation. They have also taught the immoral doctrine, that protection and obedience to the lawful commands of the civil government are not of reciprocal obligation, and Mr. Wylie has supported this doctrine solely from a misapplication of the judicial law of Moses, and the decrees of emperors and councils; and he has appealed to the reformers and approved commentators for the support of his doctrine, without giving extracts from any of them.

In my Observations I have shewed, from the prophets, apostles, and

---

4. The Sinai Covenant says that God covenanted to bring the Hebrew people into Canaan and the Hebrews covenanted to worship no other God (Exod. 34:11, 14).

approved commentators and reformers, that the Sinai covenant, including the judicial law, is not only abolished, but that it never was intended for any people but Israel, nor for any country but the typically holy land; and that even there it did not authorise persecution for what has been since called heresy, &c. That the christian religion authorises no persecution, by the civil magistrate, for religious opinion; and that civil magistrates are not church officers, nor have any law-making power in, or over the church of Christ, &c. I have also endeavoured to shew the true moral foundation of civil magistracy. For these purposes I have inserted a few extracts from approved commentators, reformers, and church history, out of many that I had prepared; and have also endeavoured to refute his numerous mistaken charges against the governments and character of this country, some of which are truly slanderous, and to correct and explain some of the objections which he supposes we make to his doctrine, and the conduct which he patronizes.

The sixth chapter chiefly relates to the rise and progress of the numerous divisions of the presbyterian church, while they all profess the same faith of the gospel, &c. wherein it is shewn that they all, directly or indirectly, have originated from the union of church and state, viz. political establishments of certain modes of religion, enforced by civil penalties and rewards; and I am endeavoured to demonstrate the impropriety of so many different sects holding the same faith, worship, government, discipline and order, and, at the same time, holding separate church communion, and several of them treating each other as if they were enemies to the gospel of Christ. This indeed I have considered as a great evil, and have shewn that it is contrary to the practice of the primitive church, and of the reformers, and of the spirit of christianity.

I have used the word sect instead of *denomination,* not as a term of reproach, as it is applied to those who separate from a religion established by human authority, which happily has no place in this country, but as a term of distinction, as it is used in the New-Testament. In this country all denominations are equally sects. In Britain all are sects or sectarians, who separate from the establishment.

In page 21, I have commenced some observations on a manuscript "concerning toleration," and in the last chapter I have mentioned a second reformed presbytery in this country. This manuscript was writ-

ten several years since, by a respectable elder of that communion, and
sent to me for an answer, which, as it had not a tendency to disturb the
public peace, like the "Sons of Oil," I then declined—but in as far as it
is connected with that work, I have taken notice of it in the following
Observations.

As these Observations were expected to have gone sooner to press, it
may be proper to offer some reasons for their delay. As soon as I could
procure and peruse the Sons of Oil, I commenced my Observations on
it. But as he has appealed to the reformers and approved commentators, boasts of being surrounded with a great cloud of witnesses, and,
throughout the whole, states himself as the advocate of the reformation,
and holds up all who do not agree with him, as enemies of that blessed
work, I thought it necessary to examine and give extracts from the writings of the reformers and approved commentators, and also from the
history of the christian church in the fourth and fifth centuries, which
he introduces as the period of the greatest perfection. I also thought it
proper to introduce the doctrine and example of the primitive apostolic
church, which he has wholly passed over, except in so far as he has given
such a gloss or comment on the doctrine of the apostles, as is in direct
contradiction to their own practice, and the obvious meaning of the
words, and to the sense in which they have been taken in all the protestant Confessions of Faith, and by all protestant commentators to which I
have had access. From these I took such numerous extracts, as, with my
own observations, would have made a volume much larger than I had
intended. In this state the work was, when I was called abroad on public business during the winter, and also during several of the summer
months, and the winter following. Some family distresses also occupied
my attention.

Besides the above reasons for delay, I was informed that the presbytery (of which Mr. Wylie was a member) was employed in preparing a
testimony against the sins and errors of the times, and I was certain, that
if they held the same principles with the reformed presbytery of Scotland, they must testify against at least a number of Mr. Wylie's extravagant errors, and from his books being so withdrawn from sale, as that
there was not a copy left, I thought it probable that he himself would
make such retraction or explanation, as would render my observations

unnecessary. I had heard, above two years ago, that this testimony was in some hands, but never saw it advertised for sale, and I did not suppose that such a candle was lighted to be put under a bushel. However, when on a journey after harvest, 1810, while I lay by to rest, I had an opportunity of the perusal of that testimony, and found that the author of the Sons of Oil was still sustained as a regular member of that presbytery, and observed that no censure was passed on his book of errors—I then justly considered that presbytery as responsible for them, and, on my return home, set about revising and making an abstract of the work, which, in the first draught, was too extensive for the design. Numerous extracts from approved commentators, &c. were withdrawn, and so many only retained as carried the doctrine of protestants down from the commencement of the reformation, to the present day. Observations on many positions in the Sons of Oil, of minor importance, were also suppressed, and the printing engaged—but the printing press was not set up till a few months since.

My object was, to promote truth and peace in both church and state. In the church, it was to bring christians to the acknowledgment of the scriptures, as the sole rule of their faith and practice, and the sure foundation of their hope, and to oppose terms of holding communion with Christ, in the ordinances of his own institution, imposed by human authority, whether that authority bears the name of papist or of protestant; and in the state, to promote a scriptural and reasonable obedience to legitimate government and equal laws, so that all men might be protected in leading quiet and peaceable lives in godliness and honesty, and the government itself protected from slander and sedition.

WILLIAM FINDLEY
November 1, 1811

Observations on
"The Two Sons of Oil"

CHAPTER I

The text explained—Of the moral law of nature—Of positive laws—Penalties to be executed by man, belong to positive law—Civil government founded on the law of nature—Peculiar law of Israel, positive and abolished—Christ's delegated power examined—The magistrate's power to ratify and sanction the laws of the Most High God examined.

The Reverend Author of "*The two Sons of Oil, or the faithful witness for ministry and magistracy upon a scriptural basis*," introduces the subject by a text from the prophecy of Zechariah, chap. 4, ver. 14. "Then said he, these are the two anointed ones, that stand by the Lord of the whole earth."

Of his analysis of this text, and his premises drawn from it, I will only observe here, that he makes it the foundation of his system, viz. That the gospel ministry, and civil magistracy, are not distinct governments, but component branches of one government. To this purpose, page 8, he says, "This universal dominion committed to him, (Christ) as it respects the human family, in its administrations, consists in two great branches, namely, the magistracy and the ministry." As he afterwards more fully explains and applies this doctrine, I will take no further notice of it in this place, than just to observe one error in his statement. The church of Christ, and the gospel ministry are not, as the author says, *committed* to Christ. The gospel ministers are appointed to feed the church of Christ, which he hath purchased with his own blood. The church is his purchased possession. It is the body of Christ, of which believers are members. It is his kingdom, which is not of this world, &c. We read of the word of reconciliation, and a dispensation of the gospel of Christ, being committed to the ministers of Christ, as ambassadors from him; but not of the church being committed to him. It is his own house, in which Moses and the apostles were servants. It is not committed as a trust. It is, by virtue of union, his body, his spouse.

The real meaning of this text, on which the author erects such a visionary superstructure, I will offer in the words of the learned and judicious Scott, in his notes on the place.[1]

"The prophet was still ignorant of the meaning of the two olive-trees, especially of those branches from which the oil was immediately conveyed to the lamps; and on enquiry he learned, that they were the two anointed ones, which stood before the Lord of the whole earth. Zerubbabel and Joshua, the anointed ruler and high-priest of Judah, who stood before the Lord, and were his instruments in the work of the temple, were *the anointed ones* intended: but they were only types and shadows (as the temple itself was) of him that was to come. They therefore typified Christ, as anointed with the Holy Spirit without measure, to be the king and high-priest of the church, and to build, illuminate and sanctify the spiritual temple. As the anointed high-priest, he purchased those gifts by the sacrifice of himself; and through his intercession in heaven, they are communicated by him as the anointed king of his church. From the union of these two offices in his mysterious person, both God and man, this inexhaustible fulness of grace is derived and conferred. Thus the olive branches of themselves distil the golden oil through the two golden pipes into the bowl: and from his fulness all receive that grace which they require for their several places and services, through the means of grace, as the seven pipes fed the seven lamps of the candlestick. It is plain, that the candlestick is the Jewish church, both civil and religious; and the oil with which the lamps were supplied, is the Spirit of God: and is it not equally plain, that Zerubbabel and Joshua were in

---

1. Thomas Scott (1747–1821), Bible commentator, *The Holy Bible with . . . Notes*, 4 vols. (1788–1792).

these transactions typical persons, types of Christ our king and high priest." See also the venerable Henry to the same purpose.[2]

The vision was for the encouragement of the Jewish church and nation, then newly emerged out of captivity, and was suited to that symbolical oeconomy under which they were placed during the continuance of the theocracy, or immediate government of Jehovah, in another and more peculiar manner than other nations were, and which was to continue until Christ the antitype should come and fulfil all that was prefigured of him by that typical oeconomy, and introduce the new covenant, or gospel dispensation. When Israel was brought out of Egypt into the waste and howling wilderness, they were constituted a peculiar and holy nation. "And ye shall be unto me a kingdom of priests, and an holy nation." Exod. xix. 6. This was the divine proposal; and after they had been ceremonially sanctified, and had heard the law of the ten commandments, which is a compend of the moral law of nature, pronounced with an audible voice, from the top of Sinai, with tremendously awful accompaniments, and had publicly announced their cordial acceptance of the divine proposal, the peculiar national covenant, whereby they were constituted in their national character, a kingdom of priests and a holy nation, was wrote in a book, and consecrated by the shedding of blood. See Exod. xxiv. and Heb. ix. 15. 22. Many ordinances were added to this covenant, which were received by Moses in the mount, and afterwards in the tabernacle, and all was again ratified about forty years after. See Deut. v. No permanent additions were afterwards made, except for the building of the temple instead of the tabernacle, (2 Sam. vii. 18.) and adding psalmody and music, both vocal and instrumental, to the stated worship, by express divine authority. 2 Chron. xxix. 25.

In this covenant, a standing, hereditary priesthood and numerous symbolical rites were added to the ancient sacrificial worship, as well as the sanction of temporal rewards and punishments, and the immediate divine presence in the sanctuary, to deliver oracles when sought in difficult cases, according to the due order; and a succession of prophets,

---

2. Matthew Henry (1662–1714), English Nonconformist divine and commentator, *Exposition of the Old and New Testament* [through Acts], 5 vols. (1708–1710).

until the great prophet should come with power to change the system, was engaged. A civil magistracy, of very limited authority, was instituted, and of a peculiar form. It was not sovereign; it had no legislative authority: and it is in this that sovereignty consists in all civil governments. They could not add to, or diminish from, the code of laws, without immediate divine authority. Even David, a king according to God's heart, and a prophet by whom the Spirit of God spake, could not add stated singers and psalmody to the worship, but by special authority from God, delivered by other prophets. The civil government therefore, under this covenant, was wholly executive and judiciary; and in all important instances, connected with the priesthood, a decision in judgment could not be given in the last resort, except in a court where the priests and Levites were essential constituent members. They could not go to war without a priest to make the proclamation of the law, in that case provided. A leprosy could not be cured, a case of jealousy between a man and his wife could not be decided, nor uncertain murder expiated, but by the priest. The priests and Levites were the repositories of the laws—they were wrote in a book, and laid up with them. Even when it pleased God, after severely reproving them for the attempt, to tolerate them in having a king, the king was not permitted to exercise legislative authority; that is to say, to be a sovereign. He was directed to take a copy of the laws deposited with the priests and Levites; and he could not add to them. Though the Israelites held their lands in fee simple, to them and their heirs, they were not permitted to eat of the fruit of the fields or vineyard, until the priests had received their first fruits. In short, to use the words of the justly celebrated H. Witsius, D.D.[3] speaking of the Jewish laws, "They were subservient, for the greatest part, to the levitical priesthood, with which almost the whole policy was interwoven."

I admit that the reverend author might, without great impropriety, have said, that the magistracy and ministry, under the immediate government of God, viz. the peculiar theocracy of Israel, were two great *branches* of that symbolical government, if he had explained what he meant by

---

3. Herman Witsius (1636–1708), *The Economy of the Covenants between God and Man, Comprehending a Complete Body of Divinity* (orig. publ. Utrecht, The Netherlands, 1677).

branches. He certainly could not wish to impose on his people so far, as to induce them to believe, that the word branches, thus applied, is a scriptural term. Under the Jewish polity, priests were instituted to conduct the symbolical worship, and to decide in courts of justice; whereas, in former times, every worshipper, such as Noah, Abraham, Job, &c. were priests for their own families. Melchizedec is the only person recorded, as by office, the priest of the most high God, before the institution of the Aaronic priesthood; and before that priesthood was established, Moses, the most eminent type of Christ, as mediator and lawgiver in his own house, acted the part of both priest, prophet and civil magistrate, and was a type of Christ in all his offices. But after this institution, the administration under Jehovah, their peculiar king, was distributed into different parts or portions, of which the priesthood took the highest hereditary rank, and the Levites the next; but wholly distinct in their offices, except that they were equally connected as constituent members in the supreme court of civil justice, and in being the official repositories of the laws.

Every city was enjoined to appoint local judges, from whose decision an appeal lay to the supreme court, composed of priests and Levites, assisted by such chief judge as Jehovah their king should appoint; which was sometimes a priest.

When kingly government was introduced, against the approving will of Jehovah their king, and of Samuel his prophet, they, as was expressly foretold by Samuel, became, in a great measure, despots, and usurped every power but that of the priests; and even from them the judiciary power in many cases, which was protected by the immediate divine interposition, as in the case of Uza and Uziah. Nor did the pious kings usurp the power of making laws. Zerubbabel, of the royal line of David, like his great ancestor, was honoured with being a very distinguished type of the Saviour. In the vision therefore, Joshua and Zerubbabel are very properly represented as types of Christ, in his priestly and kingly offices. Zerubbabel was the legal representative of Cyrus, king of Persia, at that time the sovereign of all the countries formerly subject to Babylon, as Ezra and Nehemiah afterwards were; and while he was honoured so far as to be the representative of the king of Persia, he was still more highly honoured with being proclaimed, by the prophet, a type of a greater than Cyrus, but whose kingdom was not of this world.

The author, surely, will not pretend that Zerubbabel, though of the stock and lineage of David, and the last of the royal race that enjoyed civil distinction, governed in right of hereditary succession from David. He was a subordinate and temporary governor, subject to the control of the governors on that side of the river, and the supreme direction of the king by whom he was appointed.

Artaxerxes, the most favourable to the Jews, for the greatest length of time, of all the Medio-Persian kings, (probably the same as Ahasuerus) appointed Ezra, a priest, to be governor of Judea; and after him, Nehemiah, once and again: both excellent appointments, but none of them of the royal line. In short; Zerubbabel, as the representative of Cyrus, in restoring the Jewish church and nation, which had been scattered abroad throughout all the nations of the east, was a very fit type of Christ, who came to restore and build up the dispersed tribes of Israel from all nations, tongues, and kindred. Melchizedec, who was a Gentile, and not after the order of Aaron, was selected as a very striking type of the Redeemer. Cyrus himself is selected by the prophet Isaiah, to prefigure the Saviour. "I have raised him up in righteousness, and I will direct all his ways: he shall build my city, and he shall let go my captives, not for price or reward."—Isaiah iv. 15, &c. [Findley meant xlv. 13.]

I have heretofore believed, that it was generally admitted by christians, that the typical priesthood of Melchizedec, and the typical redemption wrought by the Medio-Persian kings, prefigured, and was a prelude to, the calling of the Gentiles. Surely, the reverend author will not pretend that Zerubbabel was the actually anointed king of Israel, or exercised sovereign power. Even Joshua could not have been anointed and inaugurated into the priesthood, according to the law of Moses, in the sanctuary, and with the holy oil. There was no sanctuary, and the Urim and Thummim, the fire which first descended from Heaven, the ark of the covenant, and other precious arcana, were lost; therefore the anointing of Joshua and Zerubbabel was not such a ceremonial anointing as that of Aaron, Saul, David, &c. but a providential designation to those offices, in such circumstances as rendered them suitable types of the Saviour. I may here be permitted to add that the loss of those precious arcana, the visible symbols of divine presence and glory, while it was an awful correction for the breach of the national covenant, indicated the final abrogation of that system, which, being only a shadow of good things to come, was seen to vanish away; and also prepared the minds of believers to expect the new covenant dispensation, foretold by the prophets, and the greater glory of the latter temple also foretold.

Though these two typical anointed ones represented the kingly and prophetical offices of the Saviour, they were not constituted such by the law of Moses. Cyrus was the sovereign, in a much more extensive sense of that term, than any king of Judah ever could have been under, or agreeable to, the Mosaic law. Zerubbabel was his honorary servant, acting under his instructions, and solely by his authority; and by the same authority, the progress of the work was stopped, and renewed, or suspended, viz. at the discretion of the Persian kings; so that the building of the city was not completed till about ninety years after the proclamation of Cyrus, and long after the death of Zerubbabel. I only add, in this place, that facts must not be permitted to bend to fanciful theories. Admitting, but not granting, that Zerubbabel had even sat on the regal throne of his great ancestors, David and Solomon, possessed of their independence and surrounded with all their splendour, it would have made no difference, as to the general argument, respecting civil government, as instituted under the moral law of nature. Every thing in the law of Moses, superadded to the moral law of nature, is positive or voluntary; and, therefore, changeable, according to circumstances and the will of the supreme legislator; and even while they continued, they were only applicable to the cases, place, and circumstances, for which they were intended and enacted. Their example may be further applied, but their authority cannot.

The reverend author has, throughout his whole book, made the support of the union of church and state, or, in other words, tyranny over both the souls and bodies of men, his grand object; and (very unwarrantably indeed) laid the foundation of his system on the symbolical text just examined. I have, therefore, on mature deliberation, thought it best to examine the nature and obligations of the peculiar law, or covenant of Israel, on all mankind, or on all christians, and at all times, before I proceed to other observations on his system.

As a clear and exact knowledge of the moral law of nature is peculiarly important, in order to understand the whole system of revealed religion, I will state, that it pleased God to deliver, on Mount Sinai, a compendium of this holy law, and to write it with his own hand, on durable tables of stone. This law, which is commonly called the *ten commandments,* or *decalogue,* has its foundation in the nature of God and of man, in the relation men bear to him, and to each other, and in the duties which result from those relations; and on this account it is immutable and universally obligatory. Though given in this manner to Israel, as the foundation of the national covenant, then about to be entered into, it demands obedience from all mankind, at all times, and in all conditions of life; and the whole world will finally be judged according to it, and to the opportunity they had of being acquainted with it, whether by reason and tradition alone, or by the light of the written word. This law is spiritual, reaching to the thoughts and intents of the heart. It is necessarily the foundation of all transactions, between the Creator and his rational creatures; and, in this case, was very properly revealed, as the foundation of the covenant of peculiarity with Israel. See Scott on Exod. xx. This was incorporated in the judicial law, as far as divine wisdom thought proper, and is explained and applied by the Saviour, and by the prophets and apostles.

There is an evident distinction between moral precepts, and positive or voluntary appointments. The first have their foundation in the nature of God and of man, and are unchangeable; the second in the free will of the lawgiver, and might not have been, or might have been otherwise, as the lawgiver thought proper, and are liable to be changed or abolished, at the discretion of the lawgiver; but while they continue, are of equal obligation with moral precepts, except where they come into competition: in that case, a positive institution must yield, in some cases, to the unchangeable law.

Of this kind were all the additions made to the moral law, by the Mosaic institutions. Yet it is upon these, almost exclusively, that the author builds his system; he substitutes them for the moral law; he makes little use of the prophets, and none of the New Testament, except to pervert it. The New Testament has been generally understood to contain the religion of Christians. The apostles declare, that the christian church is built *on the foundation of the prophets and apostles, Jesus Christ himself being the chief corner stone;* and that the law of peculiarity, *old covenant, or testament, is abolished, taken out of the way,* &c. The author declares that it is still in full force, as far as it is necessary to support his system, but not further: he admits the rest to have been abolished. Christ himself has given the most excellent summary of the moral law, and the most spiritual and perfect exposition of it, and declared its perpetual obligation. The apostles have incorporated the ten commandments into their epistles, and enforced their obligations by the most powerful arguments and motives; but neither the Saviour nor his apostles have made any use of the law of peculiarity, except to shew that its requirements were fulfilled, and that it was abolished, except in a few instances, for illustration. The apostles no where enforce obedience to its peculiar precepts or penalties, after it was abolished by the death of Christ, but declare it to be disannulled.

Positive or voluntary laws have no obligation, further than the lawgiver intended that they should have, because all the authority they possess, is derived from his will and intention; where this stops, the law must stop with it. Now the intention of the Sinai covenant does not appear to have extended beyond the Israelites themselves; it was addressed solely to them, and calculated to operate within bounds expressly prescribed, and could not be put in operation elsewhere. It is sanctioned with numerous and severe temporal penalties, several of which were to be executed by the civil magistrate and the witnesses, after the sentence of the court, and some of them by Jehovah himself, as their peculiar king; and obedience to it was encouraged by numerous temporal rewards, and by miraculous protection. They were assured of success in war, of fruitful seasons, that nothing should cast their young, or be barren among them, &c. &c.

The moral law was addressed equally to all men in their individual character, and in the singular number: "Thou shalt have no other gods before me"—"Thou shalt not make unto thee graven images"—"Thou shalt not take the name of the Lord thy God in vain"—"Honour thy father and thy mother," &c. The lawgiver also reserves the sanctions, or rewards and punishments of this law, solely in his own hand. "I will not hold him guiltless"—"I will visit the iniquity," &c. "Thy days shall be long," &c. This law required the obedience of the heart, with a view to a judgment to come; but a fulfilling of the letter of the law satisfied the national covenant—it only required circumcision of the flesh; the moral law required circumcision of the heart. This distinction the prophets, the faithful expounders and zealous enforcers of obedience to the moral law, frequently inculcated. The Pharisees were zealous of the law, but added their own traditions. The Sadducees were zealous of the law, and opposed the traditions. Both of them were character-ised, by the Saviour, as very immoral and erroneous; yet neither of them could be excluded from communion, under that law.

The penalties enacted by the national law could only be executed within the bounds prescribed—Numbers, chap. xxxiv. Within these bounds, idolatry was not only a sin, as in other places, but it was, if committed by an apostate Israelite, treason against Jehovah, as their peculiar king. The iniquity of the devoted nations being full, they were to be destroyed; but no authority was given to punish idolatry out of those limits, nor even to carry their own worship out of the typically holy land. In their dispersions, they taught the law in their synagogues; but do not, till this day, put in practice the worship enjoined by the law of Moses—the place being an essential part of the institution.

The moral law is equally calculated for, and applied to, all persons, in all places, and at all times; and equally authorizes the worship of God, in all places, by all men, in all situations; and enjoined a respect to every discovery of his will, and institution of his appointment: but it prescribes no penalties to be executed by man for the breaches of it. None but God, that knows the heart, can judge of the demerit of sin; because it does not consist so much in the physical act, as in the will and intention, of which none but God is judge. Fallible judges must have recourse to overt acts, declarations and circumstances, to prove the concurrence of the will, or intention of the heart, and may be often mistaken. The innocent may sometimes suffer, but the guilty more frequently escape punishment. God only is the unerring judge.

This being the case, it follows of course, that human penalties for breaches of the moral law, are no part of that law itself, as it relates to God; he will not give this glory to another—nor is any creature, man or angel, competent for the exercise of it.

Penalties to be executed by men upon their fellow men, arise from the state of society, they being necessary for the peace and happiness

thereof; they, therefore, vary in every society, agreeable to the circumstances of the society itself, and the prevalence of vices, by which its
safety is most exposed to danger, or upon its competency to execute
such penalties.

In a state of nature, before the existence of civil society, no such penalties could have been executed; every man's rights were equal. Men
being, after the first pair, introduced by natural generation, parental
authority was sufficient, until they became capable to act for themselves.
After this period, we know, by the awful example of Cain killing Abel
his brother, that it was not sufficient. We know, likewise, by the same example, that no human penalties for crimes against society then existed:
indeed it was not sufficiently numerous to enact laws or execute penalties; therefore God took the case of the infant state of society into his
own hand, and inflicted such punishment of the murderer as he judged
suitable to that state of society, but spared and protected his life; yet, for
the safety of others, set a mark on him, and banished him; or, from the
influence of fear, he banished himself. When men multiplied on the
earth, oppression and other crimes prevailed to so great a degree, as
to have rendered human laws and penalties very necessary; but how far
such were enacted or executed, we are not informed. The degeneracy,
however, being so great as to be incurable by ordinary means, it pleased
God, in an extraordinary manner, to inflict the penalty of death on the
whole human race, with the exception of one family.

In this second infant state of the human race, too few in number to
form a civil society, capable of enacting and executing penal laws, it
pleased God himself, among other precepts, to prescribe death to be
inflicted by man, as the penalty for murder; and as there were not, at
that period, civil courts, or officers for public prosecution, he enjoined
the brothers (explained to include others near of kin) of the deceased,
to execute the sentence, under the penalty of God himself requiring his
brother's blood at his hands, as he had formerly done the blood of Abel
at the hand of Cain. This precept, given to the family of Noah, then
containing the whole human race, is still in substance equally applicable to all nations, and at all times. It is the only punishment adequate
to the offence; but the appointment of the brother, or near of kin, to be
the avenger of blood, arose from the then state of society, and pointed

out the expediency of civil government, when men became sufficiently
numerous for that purpose. The avenger of blood would not distinguish
sufficiently between the different kinds of homicides; and this would
produce other revenges, as it still does where it is practised, and did in
the feudal times in Europe, while the heads of families or clans exercised the right of avenging their own wrongs, or that of their relations,
and increased the shedding of human blood.

Before the death of Noah, and long before the death of Shem, we find
numerous civil societies were instituted in comparatively small territories;
that property was divided; and that, consequently, life and property and
civil order were protected. The division of languages, about 101 years after the flood, necessarily promoted the division and settling of the earth
by small civil societies. We find them very numerous in the days of Abraham, 433 years after the flood, and while Shem was yet alive.

About 857 years after the flood, when it pleased God to constitute the
Israelitish branch of the family of Abraham, (to whom he had long afforded special protection, and given special promises) a distinct nation,
and to become their peculiar King, and give them a code of laws peculiar to themselves as a nation and government, distinguished from all
the nations of the earth; he having, after long striving with them, determined to give up the rest of the world, in a great degree, to ignorance,
idolatry and licentiousness, and to wink at the prevalence of these evils
till the desire of all nations should come, this church and nation, (for
both were one, and all were symbolically holy) was the repository of the
lively oracles, first given by Moses, and continued in the sanctuary, or
added by the prophets, till Christ came. This church and nation were to
keep up a testimony against the prevailing idolatry of the world, but not
to overturn or suppress that idolatry, except within their own territory.
But to preserve them from the prevailing contagion of idolatry, their
peculiar laws were calculated to prevent their communion with the nations around them, not only in their religion, but in their manners, their
marriages, their clothing, their ploughing, sowing and reaping, and in
the preparation, and in many instances, in the substance, of their daily
food. They could not so much as eat with those of other nations.

In this peculiar code of laws, the precepts given to Noah were adopted; but the penalty respecting murder was revised. The power of the

avenger of blood was not abolished, but modified. Courts of justice were erected to decide between wilful murder, with malice aforethought, and less criminal or innocent homicides, and cities of refuge provided. The master who killed his servant, whether wilfully or not, was, for some special reasons, exempted from the power of the avenger of blood, or from being banished to the city of refuge. There were no servants or slaves when the precepts were given to Noah. We are not well informed how this law was construed in the execution; but when the government was permitted to be so far changed as to have hereditary kings, we know that the best of these kings dispensed with the punishment of murder. David dispensed with it in the case of Absalom, and also in the case of Joab in two instances; all of them wilful and malicious. It pleased Jehovah himself, as King of Israel, to dispense with, or change, the punishment of murder and adultery, in the very aggravated case of David and Uriah. Joab was afterwards put to death by Solomon for treason, as Shemei also afterwards was, without any hearing or trial before a court of justice, as enjoined by the law of Moses. And Abiether, in the same manner, thrust out of the priest's office.

The above examples contribute to demonstrate, that temporal penalties, to be executed by fallen man on his fellow sinners, are no part of the moral law of nature. If they were, they could not be dispensed with or changed: for the essential character of the moral law is immutability; it is unchangeable like God its author, a transcript of whose divine perfections it is. The sum of this law is declared by an infallible interpreter to be, *To love the Lord our God with all our heart,* &c. and *to love our neighbours as ourselves.* This law never was, nor ever will be, changed, mitigated or dispensed with. It never can yield to policy or expediency. If it could have done so, the martyrs, who loved not their lives even unto the death for Christ, were fools. That martyrs died for positive institutions, arose from the authority of the moral law, obliging to obey them.

It may be objected, that the conduct of David and Solomon, in the instances above mentioned, was probably wrong, therefore not suitable precedents to follow. They are not only not censured in scripture, but David is expressly justified in all his conduct as king, except in the case of Uriah. He is also justified in using the shew-bread, equally contrary to that law, by Jesus himself, the most perfect judge of the relative obligation of laws. Positive laws in their own nature, must yield to more powerful laws; therefore, are changeable agreeable to circumstances. No one code of penal laws can apply equally to all nations, at all times.

When Judge Blackstone wrote on the laws of England, there were 162 penalties of death.[4] The Judge laments the number, and the impropriety of many of them. The change of manners, modes of life, and property, require a change of penal laws. In Scotland, though part of the same island, and subject to the same king and parliament, there are not that number of penal laws; nor are there as many capitally convicted there in one year, as in the county of Middlesex, which contains the city of London. In all the seventeen United States, the criminal laws vary less or more from each other. In all of them they are less sanguinary than generally in the nations of Europe. In Pennsylvania they are less so, perhaps, than under any other civilized government; and in no government is the public peace better preserved. But this improvement in favour of humanity could not have been accomplished, if the legislature of that state had not been in a capacity, and willing to be at the expense of providing a suitable prison, labour, workshops, &c. for those who, under other governments, would have been hanged. By this wise institution, human blood is spared, the criminals are well clothed and fed, and contribute to their own support, while society is protected from their depredations. Thus, by the laws of that state, the detestation of shedding human blood, so laudably and strongly expressed in the precept to the sons of Noah, and in the law of Moses, is more strongly and effectually provided against than could have been done in the early stages of society, when there was yet not the means of establishing and supporting the criminal code of Pennsylvania, which provides for putting the wilful, malicious murderer to death, and preventing the effusion of human blood, by otherwise securing such other criminals as were put to death under the former government, and still are put to death under other governments.

The penalties of the judicial law were not of moral and universal obligation, because they were not from the beginning. Sixteen hundred and

---

4. Sir William Blackstone (1723–1780), English jurist, *Commentaries on the Laws of England,* 1765–1769.

fifty six years had passed away, before the precepts were given to Noah that were equally applicable to all mankind; and 2513 years, before the Israelitish Theocracy was instituted; which only continued to operate in a small territory, during 1491 years; and never was applied to, or intended for, other nations. It could not be administered, but at the place, and by the judges, appointed by God, as the peculiar king of Israel.

The moral law of nature was the same before man revolted from God, that it was afterwards; and will continue to be the same for ever. There was no place or use for temporal penalties to be inflicted by man on his fellow men, before that revolt: consequently, they are not the moral law, but were necessarily introduced because of transgression, for the protection of civil society, that men might be enabled to live peaceable lives, in godliness and honesty. It was for this purpose that men instituted civil government itself, agreeable to the will of God; and hence it is, that penal laws *are not made for the righteous man, but for the lawless and disobedient.*

The law of nature consists of the eternal and immutable principles of justice, as they existed in the nature and relation of things, antecedent to any positive precept; and describes the immutable principles of good and evil, to which the Creator himself, in all his dispensations, conforms; and which he has enabled human reason to discover, so far as they are necessary for the conduct of human actions—such, among others, as these principles: that we should live honestly, hurt no body, and render to every one his due. And he has, in the usual course of his dispensations, made it our interest to pursue this line of conduct, so far as that our self-love comes frequently in aid of our duty.

The law of nature being coeval with mankind, and dictated by God himself, is of course superior to, and the foundation of, all other laws. It is binding all over the globe, in all countries, and at all times. No human laws are of any validity, if they are contrary to it; and such of them as are of any validity, derive all their force, and all their authority, mediately or immediately, from their original: but it is necessary to exercise human reason in the application of the laws of nature to particular cases. If our reason was always, as in our first ancestor before his transgression, clear and perfect, unruffled by passions, and unclouded by prejudice, we should need no other guide but this: but every man now finds the contrary in his own experience—that his reason is corrupt, and his understanding full of ignorance and error.

This state of things has given manifold occasions for the benign interposition of Divine Providence, by which God, in compassion to the frailty, the imperfection, and the blindness of human reason, hath been pleased at sundry times, and in divers manners, to enforce his laws by immediate and direct revelation. The doctrines thus delivered, Christians call the revealed divine law, and they are to be found only in the holy scriptures. A law made by man, or penal laws to be executed by man, could have no application to men individually, in a state of nature; because the law-making power is always in such as possess supreme authority over organized society. Men in a state of nature are all equals: but man never existed long in that state. The elder brother murdering the younger, while in that state, was an awful lesson in favour of union in a state of civil society, able to afford protection to its component parts. From the fears, the wants, and the crimes of individuals, civil society originated; and from the same source has it been supported, throughout all successive ages. Anarchy has never appeared but with such destruction in its train, as soon obliged men to resort to civil society for protection. Numerous examples of this have been produced in our own day: so that it is a settled maxim, both with expositors of the bible, and politicians, that even a bad government is better than none.

It is universally admitted, I presume, that it is the will of God that all his reasonable creatures should pursue their own happiness, in a way consistent with the happiness of creatures of the same common nature; and that this is, in so far, the moral law of nature. Men must first associate together, before they can form rules for their civil government—When those rules are formed, and put in operation, they have become a civil society, or organized government. For this purpose, some rights of individuals must have been given up to the society, but repaid many fold by the protection of life, liberty and property, afforded by the strong arm of civil government. This progress to human happiness being agreeable to the will of God, who loves and commands order, is the ordinance of God mentioned by the apostle Paul: and being instituted by men, in the exercise of their natural reason, for their protection, it is the ordinance of man, and as such to be obeyed, as mentioned by the apostle Peter.

After the call of Abraham, and the gracious manifestation of the covenant of grace to him, he and his family enjoyed the special protection of God, and communications from him. This gracious dispensation accompanied the promised seed, viz. Isaac and Jacob; who, with the name of Israel and his family, enjoyed the blessing and promised protection. They enjoyed it, when in the house of bondage in Egypt. Even during this horrid slavery, they preserved the order of their tribes, and had their elders, or heads of families. The name *elder* is of Egyptian origin—The first we hear of it is in Gen. l. 7.; but it came to be much used in Israel. It was the elders of Israel that Moses addressed by the commandment of God, when he returned to Egypt; but they had no magisterial or judicial authority. Moses was the first and only magistrate, until subordinate magistrates were appointed agreeable to the advice of Jethro. When the Sinai covenant was made, a permanent magistracy was established, of which the priests and Levites were constituent members.

Preparatory to the Sinai covenant, the people voluntarily engaged to obey all that the Lord had spoken, after having received the promise of being thereupon constituted a peculiar nation. See Exod. xix. The next preparatory step was the giving of the ten commandments, viz. a transcript of the moral law of their nature; which, as it equally related to all mankind, was delivered with an audible voice, from the top of a mountain, with such tremendously glorious and awful accompaniments, as testified the presence of God omnipotent. This law was also wrote by the finger of God, on tables of stone—a fit emblem of its unchangeable perpetuity. This the people engaged by covenant to obey, as God had commanded them. See Deut. iv. 13. Thus, under the immediate divine direction, they formed a society before they became an organized body politic.

These solemn preparations being made, it pleased God to propose the terms of the covenant of peculiarity, whereby Israel was constituted a nation separate and distinct from all other nations. Rules whereby their courts of justice and magistrates were to be guided in deciding on crimes, damages, &c. were prescribed. Exod. xxi. 23. In the 24th chapter, Moses declares these laws to the people, who *answered with one voice, and said, all the words which the Lord hath said we will do. Moses wrote all the words of the Lord, and rose up early,* &c. Next follows the solemn consecration of the national, commonly called the Sinai covenant, or law of peculiarity, because it originated at Sinai, and was only applicable to Israel. The law of the ten commandments was an abstract of the moral law of nature, which was from the beginning, and is equally applicable to all mankind.

The typical consecration described in this chapter, as ratifying the Sinai covenant, is mentioned in the epistle to the Hebrews, when the apostle is demonstrating the abrogation of the Sinai covenant, and the introduction of the new covenant, viz. the gospel dispensation. Heb. ix. after shewing that the consecration of the Sinai covenant with blood, typified the death of Christ, for the remission of sins, by his own blood, he states the consecration of the Sinai covenant as emblematical of the blood of the new testament, by which Christ *put away sin by the sacrifice of himself.* He says, in chap. x. 9. "Then said he, Lo, I come to do thy will, O God." He taketh away the first, (viz. the first covenant) that he may establish the second, (viz. the second covenant, or gospel dispensation) which took place of the old covenant or testament. See Heb. ix. 18. In the 8th chapter, the apostle appeals to the prophet Jeremiah, for proof of the abolition of the Sinai covenant, who testifies that the new covenant is not according to the covenant made with their fathers, viz. the Sinai covenant, made when he brought them out of Egypt. The apostle argues from the prophet, that, in that he saith a new covenant, he hath made the first old. Now that which decayeth and waxeth old, is ready to vanish away; and in Gal. iii. 17. the same apostle, speaking of the covenant of grace, that was confirmed to Abraham by God in Christ, the law, (viz. the Sinai covenant) which was 430 years after, cannot disannul it; and Eph. ii. 15. speaking of what Christ has done by his death, he says, "having abolished in his flesh the law of commandments contained in ordinances;" and thus, as he says in the former verse, "he hath made both Jew and gentile one, by breaking down the middle wall of partition between them."

Proofs, to the same purpose, from the prophets and apostles, might be multiplied, were it necessary; but I will only add one from the evangelists—John i. 17. "For the law came by Moses, but grace and truth came by Jesus Christ." For a further contrast between the old and new covenants, I refer to Deut. xviii. 15, 19. and to Ezekiel xvi. 6, 62. In all these scriptures, and more that might be named, the Sinai covenant is abolished; not in part, but wholly abrogated, disannulled, &c. If, therefore, the Scriptures tell truth, no part of it remains obligatory on christians; and those who maintain it to be so, act, in so far, in direct opposition to the prophets, the evangelists, and apostles. This is confirmed by approved commentators.

The learned Scott, on Exodus xxiv. 3, 4. says, "When Moses had set before the people the substance of the judicial law, which he had received with the moral law of the ten commandments, delivered from mount Sinai; and the promises made to them of special blessings, while obedient; they unanimously and willingly consented and engaged to be obedient. Accordingly, he wrote in a book, the four foregoing chapters, as the conditions of the *national* covenant, which was now about to be solemnly ratified. For such it certainly was: seeing that the covenant of works has nothing to do with altars, sacrifices, and the sprinkling of blood, and the covenant of grace is not made with whole nations, or collective bodies of divers characters, but only representatively with Christ, as the surety of the elect, and personally with true believers. But whilst this covenant was made with the nation of Israel, in respect to their outward blessings, it was a shadow of good things to come."

That this covenant was abrogated, when the intention, for which it was instituted, was accomplished, is stated by the same judicious author, in his comment on Jeremiah xxxi. 31–34. "The national covenant," made at Sinai with Israel, when brought out of Egypt, is here contrasted with "the new covenant." Notwithstanding the tender and compassionate love of Jehovah to Israel at that time, when he espoused the nation to himself, they proved unfaithful, and broke the covenant, by apostacy, idolatry, and iniquity; and at length, by rejecting the Messias, they were cast out of the church, and expelled from the promised land. This covenant was distinct, both from the covenant of works, of which Adam was the surety, and under which, every unbeliever, in every age and nation, is bound; and from the covenant of grace, mediated by Christ, of which every believing Israelite received the blessing. This promise of a new covenant, as St. Paul hath shewn, implied the abrogation of the Mosaic law, and the introduction of another and more spiritual dispensation. See the same learned author on Heb. viii. Also on Zech. xiv. 4, 5. where he says, "In consequence of his (Christ's) ascension, and the commission granted to his apostles, the gospel was sent to the different regions of the earth. The ceremonial law, and the whole Mosaic dispensation, which obstructed the admission of the gentiles into the church, as the surrounding mountains did their entrance into Jerusalem, were removed."

On the prophecy of Haggai ii. 69. the author says, "Then the Lord would shake the heavens and the earth, &c. Various convulsions and changes would take place in the Jewish church and state, which would end in abolishing the ritual and whole Mosaic dispensation, the disannulling of the national covenant, the subversion of their constitution, the destruction of Jerusalem, and the ruin of their civil government." See also the venerable Henry to the same purpose, on the above and similar texts, in both the old and new testaments. I know of no approved commentators, but what are in unison with the above.

That this covenant, or national constitution, was local, viz. confined to a particular country, is evident through the whole transaction. The devoted nations are expressly described in different places, and the geographical boundaries defined with precision, Num. xxxiv. 1–15. and the administration of the national law expressly limited to the land within those boundaries. Deut. iv. 14. "And the Lord commanded me at that time to teach you statutes and judgments, that you might do them in the land whither you go over to possess it."

The time meant was after giving the moral law as the foundation of the Sinai covenant, containing these statutes and judgments. The land was that of the devoted nations, which they were going over to possess. Those statutes and judgments were not to be administered in other lands. Through their own fault, even those nations were never all subdued or possessed. They never possessed the land of the Philistines, nor the Sidonians. Though David at last overcame the former, he did not dispossess them. Edam, Moab and Ammon, adjoining Arabia and the Red Sea, Syria of Zaba, and Damascus, extending from Palestine to the Euphrates, were subdued by David; and they, as well as Arabia on the south, yielded a willing obedience to Solomon, thereby fulfilling the promise to him, as a type of the Messiah, that his large and great dominion should extend from the Mediterranean, then called the Great Sea, to the great river Euphrates on the east, and to the Southern Ocean, from near which the queen of Sheba came, and beyond which there is no continent;

emblematical of the kingdom of the Messiah, to extend over the whole world. This, however, was a dominion of peace. The people were not dispossessed, nor brought under the national law of Israel—it could not be administered there. This is the opinion, and agreeable to the practice of the Jews in Babylon, and in their dispersions, to this day. The schismatic Jews, who erected a temple in Egypt, and those who erected another at Samaria, did so in direct violation of the Sinai covenant.

Mr. Wylie, page 23, states, that "it is the magistrate's duty to execute such penalties of the divine law, (meaning the peculiar law of Israel) as are not repealed or mitigated;" and several years ago, an intelligent and pious gentleman sent me a copy of a manuscript volume, of thirty one folio pages, very closely written, entitled *"Observations concerning Toleration,"* in which he adopts and supports the same principles respecting divine laws, &c. that are advocated in the Sons of Oil. From it I will now insert the following quotation, p. 3. "I plead—the laws and examples of the Jewish nation, and that upon this ground, that all the laws and precepts contained in the Old Testament, that are not repealed in the New, either by express precept, approven example, or by necessary consequence, are still binding—a law being once given, until it is repealed by the same authority, is still binding."

The above is so much less exceptionable than the Sons of Oil, that it does not include the idea of *mitigating divine laws.* Where either of them got the idea of repealing or mitigating divine laws, they have not informed us; certainly, however, they did not get it in their bible. It is necessary that imperfect and short-sighted men should repeal or revise their laws. Revision is a repeal in part; but to apply the term mitigation to laws, whether human or divine, is a near approach to nonsense. In most governments, provision is made for mitigating the sentence of a court, arising from the law and the fact, or for remitting the sentence wholly. Thus, in England; the king frequently mitigates the sentence of death, by substituting transportation and servitude, or pardons, either with or without conditions; but neither repealing nor mitigating can be applied to any law of God, without an approach to blasphemy.

That none of these can apply to the moral law of nature, it being unchangeable, has been already stated; nor can it be maintained, without, at the same time, maintaining, that God himself is changeable. They

cannot be applied to positive or voluntary laws, without admitting that
the Almighty was short-sighted, like fallen mortals; that he did not know
the end from the beginning; that causes, or changes, had taken place,
which he had not foreseen, when he made the law, which rendered the
future repeal or revision necessary. These are the causes why human
laws are repealed or revised. I never read of a law for the mitigation of a
law, but in the Sons of Oil. Positive laws have frequently been passed for
special and local purposes, that ceased when the purposes were accomplished for which the legislature intended them; several of these I have
mentioned already. I will only add, that the laws regulating the march
of Israel in the wilderness, the gathering of the manna, &c. the command to the disciples, by the Saviour, when he sent them out to preach
the gospel and work miracles, not to go to the cities of the Gentiles or
the Samaritans—ceased, when the object intended was accomplished;
so did the whole additions to the moral law, contained in the Sinai covenant of peculiarity, when their object was accomplished, and the intention of the legislator fulfilled. They ceased, or were abrogated, but not
repealed or mitigated.

Divines have very commonly, for the sake of illustration, spoken of
the peculiar law of Israel, under two distinct views, viz. as ceremonial,
enjoining and regulating religious rites, and as judicial, regulating the
courts of justice, &c. This distinction is often made without any injury
to the subject; but having no foundation in the law itself, a precise line
of distinction cannot be drawn. The learned Dr. Witsius has well stated,
after an accurate examination, that all their polity was so connected
with priests and Levites, that no such precise line could be drawn. The
reverend author of the Sons of Oil, though he builds his system on this
distinction, has not condescended to mark the line. The author of the
manuscript has been more candid. He says, p. 9. "*The ceremonial law* was
a system of positive precepts about the external worship of God, chiefly
designed to typify Christ as *then to come,* and to lead to the way of salvation through him. *The judicial law* was that body of laws, given by God,
for the government of the Jews, partly founded on the law of nature,
and partly respected them as a nation distinct from all others. The first
respected them as a church, the second respected them as a nation, distinct from all others. This distinction is so easy understood, that it will
require a great deal more than what I have yet seen to overthrow it."

The author has been candid enough not to lay the support of this distinction on the scriptures, where, indeed, he could not find it, but gives it as *"he finds it stated by authors."* And it is as well defined as is desirable; for it is, as he says, easy understood, which is the excellence of a definition; its only loss is, that it is not supported by scripture, and is impracticable. It puts me in mind of the theories of the creation of the earth, published by Whiston, Burnet, Buffon, &c.[5] They all tell a very pretty story of how they would have made the earth, and, therefore, how God should have done it. But they all differ in opinion from each other, how they would have made the world, but agree in objecting to the method in which it actually pleased God to create it. Just so it is with those, who idolize, and attempt to reduce to practice, among christians, the peculiar law of the Israelitish theocracy, which has been fulfilled and abolished by its divine author. They all claim the authority of that law to patronize their own opinion, or justify their tyranny; yet none of them pretend to revive and execute the whole of that law; but though they all have miserably perverted it in their application of it, yet they have never agreed on defining how far it is applicable to christians, and how far not. How then shall the weak christian know, which of its precepts he is obliged to obey, and which to refuse—all of them being equally *divine laws*. The definition of the author of the manuscript, which I admit to be one of the best, he will himself, upon trial, find to be wholly impracticable, because it leaves it wholly to the private judgment of every christian to decide, what precept respected Israel, as a church, and what respected it, as a nation, distinct from all others. If applying this rule to all particular precepts was too difficult a task for the author of the manuscript, or of the Sons of Oil, what must it be to weak but well meaning christians. The difficulty to them must be the greater, from the circumstance, that the New Testament, which contains the religion of christians, having declared that this law is wholly abolished, has given no directions for making a discrimination of its precepts.

---

5. William Whiston (1667–1752), English divine and mathematician, *A New Theory of the Earth* (1696); Thomas Burnet (d. 1750), English divine, *The Argument Set Forth in a Late Book Entitled "Christianity as Old as the Creation" Reviewed and Confuted* (1730); and Georges-Louis Leclerc, comte de Buffon (1707–1788), French naturalist, *Historie Naturelle* (1749).

Divine wisdom has so intimately connected those precepts together, that they could not be separated. They, as a system, being the symbol or type of the New Testament church, were, like it, one body with many members. To this the whole language in scripture, applied to this institution, agrees that Israel was a holy nation, a kingdom of priests, a peculiar people, all ritually sanctified and holy; their kings were equally types of the Saviour, as their priests were. Mount Zion, the city of the king, was equally typical, as Mount Moriah, where the temple stood; the land was holy and symbolical of the heavenly rest. Joshua, the chief magistrate and military commander, who introduced Israel into the land, was an illustrious type of the Saviour, in that very act. The author must mark out his line of discrimination more distinctly, before he can build a system on it. For illustration, it may do well enough, if not carried too far; but it is always to be kept in mind, that it is without foundation in scripture; neither prophets nor apostles have made it.

On examining the law itself, we find it composed of a number of different ordinances, each of them called a law, such as the law of the trespass offering, the law of the meat offering, the law of the passover, and the law for leprosy, &c. but when they are spoken of as a system or code, all are mentioned as one law; there are no such expressions to be found in the Old or New Testament, as the ceremonial law, or the judicial law; all are thus intimately mixed and connected together, as if done on purpose to prevent separating what God had so joined together.

I have not slightly examined this question, to support an argument, but strictly for edification: and I find the law of Moses above fifty times expressly named or alluded to in the Old Testament, and as often, at least, in the New Testament, always as one law, and in no place with the distinction of judicial and ceremonial laws. The distinction, however, between moral and positive laws, is easily traced: but I agree with Dr. Owen,[6] in his saying, that Christ in fulfilling all righteousness in the room and place of sinners, fulfilled every law that man had broken.

That I am not singular in rejecting this distinction, it might be sufficient to state, that neither the Saviour, nor his apostles, have made it.

---

6. John Owen (1616–1683): Puritan theologian and voluminous author.

But it is also rejected by human authorities of the highest character, as the most able advocates of the truth of the christian religion. I shall only in this place insert a quotation from Locke, whose name, along with Bacon, Boyle, Newton and Addison, is the boast of christians, in opposition to the unfounded boasts of deists, claiming learning and talents, as belonging to their ranks.[7] Those great men, while they opened the gates of science to Europe, or demonstrated the extent and use of human reason, were at the same time, the ablest advocates for the truth of christianity, and set the brightest example of its power on the heart and life.

Locke says, "the law of Moses is not obligatory upon christians. There is nothing more frivolous than that common distinction of moral, judicial and ceremonial law. No positive law can oblige any but those on whom it was enjoined. 'Hear, O Israel,' &c. restrains the obligation of the law to that people.—By a mistake of both Christians and Mahometans, it has been applied to other nations. The Israelitish nation themselves never did so, nor do the dispersed Israelites yet do so."

Though the Westminster divines make the distinction, they state it in such a manner, as perfectly to agree with the above.[8] Chap. xix. after stating, that the law of nature was revealed in the ten commandments, delivered by God on Sinai, they say, sect. 3. "Besides this law, commonly called moral, God was pleased to give to the people of Israel, as a church, under age, ceremonial laws, containing several typical ordi-

---

7. John Locke (1632–1704): English political and educational philosopher; Roger Bacon (c. 1214–1294): English scientist and philosopher; Robert Boyle (1627–1691): English natural philosopher and chemist; Sir Isaac Newton (1642–1727): English scientist, mathematician, and philosopher; and Joseph Addison (1672–1719): English poet, essayist, and diplomat who, along with Richard Steele, published *Tatler* and *Spectator.*

8. The Westminster divines were members of the Westminster Assembly (1643–1652). The assembly was called by the English Long Parliament to reform the Church of England. They wrote the Larger and Shorter Westminster catechisms, the Westminster Confession, the Directory of Public Worship, and the Form of Government. The assembly was made up of 30 laymen (20 from the House of Commons and 10 from the House of Lords), 121 English clergymen, and a delegation of Scottish Presbyterians. Although all were Calvinists in doctrine, the assembly represented four different opinions on church government: Episcopalian, Erastian, Independent, and Presbyterian. Its works were generally accepted by Presbyterians everywhere.

nances; partly of worship, prefiguring Christ, his graces, actions, sufferings, and benefits; and partly, holding forth instructions of moral duties.
All which ceremonial laws are now abrogated under the new testament."
Sect. 4. "To them also, as a body politic, he gave sundry judicial laws,
which expired together with the state of that people, not obliging any
other now, further than the general equity thereof may require." The
general equity of this, or any system, is in so far, the moral law; which, in
the next section, those divines declare binds all men for ever.

Thus, those venerable divines agree, with Locke and the apostles in
opinion, that Christians are wholly set free from, the law of Moses, or
peculiar law of Israel; and this opinion was adopted by the church of
Scotland, in what has been reputed her purest times; and is still the
opinion of all the now divided branches of the Presbyterian, and also of
the Independent, churches, who adhere to the Westminster Confession.

Among the very numerous and respectable authorities, that might be
added, I insert the following extracts from the very learned, orthodox
and pious Dr. Witsius, in his oeconomy of the divine covenants.

In his first volume, the author shews that the moral law was unchangeable, and that it was the foundation of all God's other solemn transactions with fallen men, and totally distinct from positive or voluntary
laws, which had relation to men as fallen. In vol. 3, chap. 14. entitled
Of the abrogation of the Old Testament, meaning thereby, as the apostles
did, Heb. ix. 18–20. the Sinai covenant, consecrated with blood, typical
of the New Testament, purchased with the blood of Jesus, the testa-
tor of the new testament, for the redemption of transgressors, but not
including the prophets, &c. which we, perhaps improperly, call the old
testament. The Saviour and the apostles called them the Scriptures. It
is to be noticed, that he also spoke of the Sinai covenant wholly as ceremonial; because all the civil administration of it was so intimately interwoven with the ritual, that it could not exist without it; and because
all was contrived so as to be a shadow of good things to come. These
observations are necessary for the right understanding of the following
extracts:

"To begin with the first: The foundation of the moral laws, whose
perpetuity and unchangeableness is unquestionable truth, is of quite a
different nature from the ceremonial institutions, as appears from the

following considerations: Because the former are founded on the natural and immutable holiness of God, which cannot but be the examples to rational creatures, and therefore cannot be abolished, without abolishing the image of God: but the latter are founded on the free and arbitrary will of the lawgiver; and, therefore, only good because he commanded; and consequently, according to the different nature of times, may be either prescribed, or otherwise—prescribed or not prescribed at all. This distinction was not unknown to the Jewish doctors," &c. p. 320. v. 3.

"But let us proceed to the second head, namely, that God intended they should cease in their appointed time. This is evident from the following arguments: First, the very institution of the ceremonies leads to this: for since they were given to one people, with limitations to their particular state, country, city and temple; the legislator never intended, that they should be binding on *all,* whom he favours with saving communion with himself, and at all times and in all places. But this was really the case. And the Jews have always boasted of this, that the body of the Mosaic law was only given to their nation, *even to the inheritance of the congregation of Jacob,* Deut. xxxiii. 4. and God confined it to their generations, Gen. xvii. 7. Lev. vii. 36. and xxiv. 3. But as their generations are now confounded, and the Levites by no certain marks can be distinguished from other tribes, or the descendents of Aaron from other Levites; it follows, that the law ceases, that was confined to the distinction of generations, which almost all depended on the tribe of Levi, and the family of the priests. God also appointed a certain country for the observation of the ceremonies. Deut. iv. 14. vi. 1. and xi. 31, 32." p. 323.

The learned author, after shewing at large the typical consecration of the Sinai covenant, and writing it in a perishable book, distinct from the moral law wrote on tables of stone, in reply to such as, with Mr. Wylie, maintain that part of it remains binding on Christians, viz. what is not expressly repealed or mitigated in the new testament, observes,

"From these things, however, it is easy to conclude, that the new covenant was not promised to stand together with the old, and be superadded to supply its defects; but to come in place of the former, when that, as obscure and typical, should be entirely removed; which is plain from the words, *Not according to the covenant that I made with their fathers,* &c. *In that he saith a new covenant,* he hath made the first old: now that which decayeth and waxeth old, is ready to vanish away. Heb. viii. 13."

In answer to the objection, that it does not necessarily follow, that the mention of a new covenant altogether removes the old, &c. he says,

"It is begging the question. A direct contradiction to God's word. God says, I will make a new covenant, not like the former, which was made void. Men venture to answer, It is not an establishment of a new covenant, but a repetition of the old; and so far confirms the old. Yet, at the same time, this was its abrogation. We say, here is no promise of a new law, because none can be better or more perfect than that of the ten commandments. The new covenant is opposed to the old covenant, and is substituted in its place, and completes it, so as likewise, as we have shewn, to put an end to it." p. 236, 237.

"The laws of the covenant, of which the ark was the symbol, were not only the ten commandments, but all the laws of Moses: accordingly, the book which contained them was placed in the side of the ark. That symbol, therefore, of the covenant, being thus abolished, both the covenant itself, and the laws, as far as they comprised the condition of that covenant, are abrogated. The case of the laws of the decalogue is different from the rest: for they were engraven on tables of stone, and laid up in the ark, to represent that they were to be the perpetual rule of holiness, and perpetually to be kept in the heart, both of the Messiah and his mystical body: while the others were only written on paper or parchment, and placed in the sides of the ark; seeing their being engraven on stone, and kept in the ark, signified their indelible inscription on, and continual preservation in, the hearts of believers." p. 342.

The learned doctor, treating of the benefits of the new testament or covenant, and abrogation of the old, says, "Immunity from the forensic or judicial laws of the Israelites, not as they were of universal, (moral law) but of particular right or obligation, made for the Jews, as such, distinguishing them from other nations, adapted to the genius of the people and country, and subservient, for the greatest part, to the levitical priesthood, with which almost the whole polity was interwoven." p. 370.

In page 7, Mr. Wylie proves, in several premises, that all moral, physical, and delegated power, &c. is necessarily and independently in God, and that all should be done for his glory. This, none but atheists, if there are such, deny. Practical atheists, who live as if there were no God, are numerous; but atheists in theory, I never was personally acquainted with. Many, indeed, have been burned for atheism and blasphemy, who were neither atheists nor blasphemers. This was the lot of the primitive Christians, and also of the Waldenses[9] and other martyrs, under the tyrannical union of church and state, in the apostate christian church. However Vanini and others have publicly taught atheism, Spinala, and even Hume and others have taught doctrines that evidently lead to it, though they have denied the charge.[10] An atheist in opinion, must believe miracles of a more extraordinary kind than any that are recorded in the scriptures. They must believe that every thing created itself in the order and connexion in which it is found. To this purpose, it was well observed by one condemned to be burned for atheism by the inquisition, who, when going to the stake, lifted a straw, and holding it up, said, *That if he denied the being of a God, that straw would condemn him, for it could not make itself.* The Hussites, &c. were burned for blasphemy—They blasphemed the church, by denying her infallibility.[11] They blasphemed the Blessed Virgin, by not worshipping her as the immaculate mother of God.

Thus much I observe by the way, with a view to the numerous charges of atheism, blasphemy, &c. interspersed through the Sons of Oil, accompanied with an unusual number of notes of astonishment, to supply, it is presumed, the want of argument, of which I design to take no detailed notice.

In page 8, after having stated what, in his opinion, is the extent of Christ's power, he says, "This universal dominion committed to him, as it respects the human family, in its administrations, consists in two great branches; namely, magistracy and ministry."

9. The Waldenses dissented from the Roman Catholic Church. The movement originated about 1179 through the teaching of Petrus Waldus, a merchant of Lyon, France. He sought to revive the primitive pureness of living.

10. Lucilio Vanini (c. 1583–1619), Italian philosopher, was burned at the stake in Toulouse, France, for atheism and witchcraft; Spinala is perhaps Baruch Spinoza (1632–1677): Dutch philosopher; and David Hume (1711–1776): Scottish philosopher.

11. The Hussites followed the teachings of Jan Hus, the Czech reformer.

He then proceeds to show, in eight particulars, wherein these branches differ; and again, in seven particulars, wherein they agree, to the 30th page. In page 15, he says, "They agree in this, that God the Father, Son and Spirit, is the original fountain from which they flow. To suppose any power or authority whatever not originating from God, essentially considered, would necessarily lead to *atheistical* principles. It must therefore emanate from him. Rom. xiii. 1. 'There is no power but of God.' To the same purpose is 2 Cor. v. 18. 'All things are of God.' Civil power was already shewn to originate from God, as Creator, and to be founded on his universal dominion, as the King of nations. Jer. x. 7. And though all ecclesiastical power flows immediately from Christ, as Mediator, yet it is radically and fontally in a three-one God. All the right and authority of Christ, as Mediator, is originally derived from God, as well as civil power."

If this had not been laid down as a fundamental principle of his system, it might have passed unnoticed. The scripture texts which he applies to support this theory, were revealed for another purpose. Rom. xiii. 1. is expressly applicable to civil power. Of this the apostle says, "Let every soul be subject to the higher powers; for there is no power but of God: the powers that be are ordained of God." In Cor. v. 18. the apostle is treating of the hope of glory, walking by faith, the terrors of the Lord as an excitement to be reconciled to him through Christ, and of the constraining love of Christ, as a reason why those that are in Christ, should be new creatures; and the apostle assures them that all these things, of which he is there treating, *are of God,* who had reconciled them to himself, and committed to the gospel ministry the word of reconciliation. There is not a word here about a civil branch of Christ's kingdom, of which he himself testified that it was not of this world.

Man can have no competent knowledge of God, nor render to him any acceptable worship, but agreeably to the discoveries he has given of himself. To man, in his state of innocence, God revealed his divine perfections and his will, so far as was necessary for the worship and obedience required in that state. Even after man had revolted from God, so much of his divine perfections and of his will, are revealed in the works of creation and providence, and particularly, in the relation in which men stand to God, and to each other, as renders them without excuse in not knowing and worshipping him as the true God. This the apostle calls the law written in the hearts of the gentiles, by which their reason and judgment, viz. their conscience, was regulated in approving or condemning their own conduct. Rom. ii. 15.

After man had revolted from God, in addition to former discoveries, he revealed himself as merciful, as a God pardoning iniquity through a Mediator; but did not so clearly reveal the Deity, as subsisting in three distinct persons, as to render the belief of it a condition of holding communion with him in his ordinances, until by the coming of Christ in the flesh, by whom life and immortality, and particularly the doctrine of the trinity, the spiritual nature of Christ's kingdom, and the resurrection from the dead, were more fully brought to light, and henceforth became, fundamental articles of the faith of christians: consequently, whoever being favoured with the christian scriptures, worship God in any other way than he has therein revealed himself, worship a false God, and are, in so far, idolaters, however they may declaim against idolatry, superstition, popery, &c. in others.

The whole old and new testaments, and even the works of creation and providence, reveal the object of worship to be one God; but the new testament has not only clearly revealed that one God to subsist in three persons, but that christians, in the exercise of faith and worship, hold distinct communion with these three adorable persons. With the Father in love. "God so loved the world, that he gave his only begotten Son," &c.—John iii. 16. With Christ in grace—John i. 14, 17. "The only begotten of the Father, full of grace and truth—Of his fulness have all we received grace for grace—Grace and truth came by Jesus Christ." And with the Holy Ghost in comfort—John xiv. 16, 26. "He shall give you another Comforter to abide with you—But the Comforter, which is the Holy Ghost, shall teach you all things." That well known text, commonly called the christian doxology, 2 Cor. xiii. 14. "The grace of the Lord Jesus Christ, and the love of God, and the communion of the Holy Ghost, be with you all," is full to the purpose, and is used to conclude the public worship in most, if not all, christian churches, however they may differ otherwise. It is so used even by the church of Rome.

In order to support his system, the author unites what God has most explicitly kept separate. Page 8. "This delegated power is most conspicuous in the person of the Mediator. Into his hands universal dominion is committed. Matth. xxviii. 18—"All power is given unto me in heaven and in earth." From this he deduces what I have quoted above, viz. "This universal dominion committed to him, as respects the human family, consists in two great branches; namely, magistracy and ministry." Again, "though both these branches are put under the Mediator's controul, yet they are so under different regulations," &c.

Here it is to be observed, that the author confounds the administration of providence given to Christ, by the Father, whereby he rules over men, angels and devils, in consequence of the Father having given all power in heaven and earth unto him, with that kingdom *"which he purchased with his own blood;"* Acts xx. 28. and which is, Eph. i. 14. called *"the purchased possession,"* viz. the church, called a peculiar people, &c. 1 Pet. ii. 9. and in Eph. i. 23. "His body, the fulness of him that filleth all in all;" and that this evident distinction might be left without a shadow of doubt, the apostle says. Col. i. 24. *"For his* (viz. Christ's) *body's sake, which is the church."* The church, in contradistinction from the kingdom of this world, is frequently called the kingdom of God.

That Christ's purchased kingdom was specifically distinct from the general kingdom of Providence, the administration of which was given to Christ, is evident from the whole doctrine and practice of Christ and his apostles. They absolutely declined interfering with the government of nations, or the relations among men, otherwise than by expounding and applying the moral law to the conscience. They had recourse only to spiritual armour, and engaged only in spiritual warfare. The Saviour's solemn dying testimony, however, ought to be conclusive with every sober enquiring mind. When he was brought before Pontius Pilate, by whom he was asked, "Art thou the king of the Jews?" To this the Saviour answered: *"My kingdom is not of this world. If my kingdom were of this world, then would my servants fight, that I should not be delivered to the Jews; but now is my kingdom not from hence."* This the apostle calls the good confession which Christ Jesus witnessed before Pontius Pilate. On this precious, but much neglected text, the learned Dr. B. Hoadly, bishop of Bangor, preached a celebrated sermon, which procured the resentment of his high church brethren, but having the testimony of Christ and the apostles on his side, he succeeded in an arduous controversy, occasioned by that excellent sermon, a few lines from which I will insert.[12]

"The laws of his kingdom, therefore, as Christ left them, have nothing of this world in their view; no tendency either to the exaltation of some in worldly pomp and dignity, or to the absolute dominion over the faith and religious conduct of others of Christ's subjects. It is essential to it, that all his subjects, in what station soever they may be, are equally subjects to him; and that no one of them, any more than another, hath authority, either to make laws for Christ's subjects, or to impose a sense of their own on the established laws of his kingdom, which amounts to the same thing as making new laws."

If the laws of Christ in their principles, as well as in their extent, are perfect, with respect to the rules and orders of his own house, which all the different denominations of presbyterians profess to allow; the author's system is contrary to this profession: for neither in the fourth chapter to the Ephesians, nor in the twelfth chapter to the Romans, nor in any other portion of the New Testament that treats of the officers or orders of Christ's house, do I find kings or civil magistrates of any kind of political governments, enumerated. They, therefore, can have no legal authority in the church, much less can they have any legislative authority over it. This I take to be a fair conclusion.

I object to the use of the phrase *"delegated power,"* as applied by the author to the Saviour, with respect to his kingdom. It is not used in scripture. A *delegate* is of the same import as a *deputy*. The power of deputies or delegates among men, is always subordinate, and subject to the instructions and controul of the superior, and likewise liable to be removed; this is implied in the very term. This can by no means apply to Christ's spiritual kingdom. The apostle does not call Christ a delegate, *"but a son over his own house, which house are ye,"* viz. the church. Nor can it be, with propriety, applied to him as administering the kingdom of

12. Benjamin Hoadly (1676–1761) was named bishop in succession of Bangor, Hereford, Salisbury, and Winchester. A voluminous author and controversialist, Hoadly was leader of the "low church" faction in the Church of England.

providence. It is properly a given kingdom *committed* unto him, if we are contented with the Saviour's own words. Mat. xxviii. 18. "All power is given unto me in heaven and in earth." John v. 22. "The Father judgeth no man, but hath *committed* all judgment to the Son of Man."

In pages 9 and 10, he says, "both these branches are put under the Mediator's controul, yet they are so under different regulations;" and in p. 15, he says, "and though all ecclesiastical power flows immediately from Christ as Mediator, yet it is *radically* and *fontally* in a three-one God. All the right and authority of Christ as Mediator, is originally derived from God, as well as civil power." I find no ground for saying, that in Christ's administration of his church in this world, it is put under him; that applies to his enemies, whom be rules with a rod of iron, and who are obliged to submit, and to the general administration of providence. After he hath put all his enemies under his feet, and the last enemy, death, the mediatory administration of the visible church on earth will be finished; but it is the present administration of which we now speak. Under it, the church is not said to be put under Christ, but united to him as branches to the vine. His admitting only "some different considerations or regulations in the administration," but no essential difference in the source from which they flow; and his leading the whole, with respect to the present administration, up to God, fontally considered, looks very like a species of Socinianism.[13] There are such as consider all the doctrine of the trinity to be only figurative descriptions of the various dispensations of the one true God, or modes of acting, viz. In one character he is represented as the Father; in another character as the Son, and in a third as the Holy Ghost, agreeable to the different energies that are manifested. This doctrine I have heard taught with as much ingenuity and confidence as the reverend author inculcates his theory.

Through the weakness of our capacity, and the imperfection of language, we are under the necessity of speaking of the things pertaining to God, in words adapted to the affairs of men, which, however, must always have a very limited application, especially when they relate to the being and operations of Jehovah; and with respect to which, it is wrong

---

13. Socinianism is the rationalist religious system of Faustus Socinus (1539–1604) that rejected belief in the Trinity.

to make a man an offender for the wrong or doubtful application of a word. A word also may safely be applied to the things of God for one purpose, which would be erroneous when applied for another. With respect to the doctrine of the trinity, &c. the same terms are frequently used on both sides of the Socinian controversy, but with different views.

The term delegated power, so frequently and indiscriminately applied to the Saviour by the reverend author, has been applied to Christ by some orthodox commentators, but by none that I know of for the same purposes, or in the same indiscriminate manner.

Christians, agreeably to the example of the apostles, not only worship Jehovah one God, but they worship that God in three distinct persons, each being God; and they worship and hold communion with each of these adorable persons, as they are distinguished by the personal properties ascribed to them in the New Testament; and with each of them as God. Christ had power, even on earth, to forgive sin; and it was admitted by his enemies, that none but God can forgive sin. He was prayed to as God, not only for the healing of diseases, but for grace to believe: "Lord, I believe, help thou mine unbelief." "Lord, if thou wilt, thou canst make me clean." "Only speak the word, and my servant shall be healed." These were expressions of independent, and not of deputized or limited powers. This is confirmed by the apostles, who, when they wrought miracles, declared that it was not through their own power and holiness, but through the power of Christ, then risen from the dead. How the act of one adorable person of the trinity is ascribed to the whole trinity; and how, in worshipping and holding communion with one, we worship and hold communion with all the adorable trinity, is not now to my purpose to describe.

The power of the apostles to preach the gospel and to work miracles, was truly and properly a delegated and limited power. They declare themselves "Embassadors of Christ," 2 Cor. v. 20. And "messengers of the churches," 2 Cor. viii. 23. The power with which Moses was invested, was a delegated or deputized and limited power. It was *the power of a servant,* and as such contrasted with the power of Christ, *which was that of a Son over his own house, whose house is the church.* Heb. iii. 5, 6. Consequently, by taking delegated or deputized power in the sense in which the author has applied it, we put the authority of Christ, and of Moses, and the apostles, on an equal footing. This did not the Holy Ghost in the scriptures.

In doing this, however, he is not without company. All the Socinians will join with him. They will worship God through his deputy or delegate, Jesus Christ. They will even admit him to have more extraordinary powers than Moses, &c. though of the same kind. They will admit any thing of that kind, short of supreme deity, and independent power in and over his own house. Not only so, but he will find associates in the Mahometan camp.[14] They teach that Jesus had a delegated power to work miracles, &c. On this principle he might receive the right hand of fellowship from the Muslem church; with respect to which, I agree with the learned Faber, and many other divines, that it is an apostate branch of the christian church, and not strictly heathen.[15]

The reverend author agrees also with the Mahometans in the method of propagating and enforcing religion, by the sword of the civil magistrate; but they would on just grounds deny that ever Jesus, or his apostles, authorised such a method, and would claim it to their own prophet. In this controversy, the reverend author must fail; for he certainly can produce no authority for propagating the christian religion by the sword, or lesser punishments, from the new testament; nor, as I have shewn elsewhere, even from the peculiar Sinai covenant. Having thus brought himself, in so great a measure, in unison with the Mahometan church, he and they may be left to settle what differences remain. Before we have done, we will find him in as near a connexion with the other apostate christian church, viz. of Rome, in which the blood of the saints is found. For the principles of Mahomet, and the propagation of that extraordinary delusion, I refer to the first volume of the Modern Universal History; and for a compend of it, to the Abbe Millot's Elements, and to the Encyclopaedia.[16]

---

14. The "Mahometan camp" refers to Islam and its believers.

15. George Stanley Faber (1773–1854), *A Dissertation on the Prophecies that have Been Fulfilled, are now Fulfilling, or Will Hereafter be Fulfilled Relative to the Great Period of 1260 Years, the Papal and Mohammedan Apostacies, the Tyrannical Reign of Antichrist, or the Infidel Power, and the Restoration of the Jews: To which is added, an Appendix,* 1st American, from the 2nd London ed. (Boston: Andrews and Cummings, Greenough and Stebbins, 1808).

16. Claude François Xavier Millot (1726–1785), *Elements of General History,* trans. from the French of Abbé Millot, first American ed. (Worcester, Mass.: Isaiah Thomas, 1789).

The author, however, intermixes his mistakes with some great truths. Page 10, he says, these two great branches, as he calls them elsewhere, "differ in their *immediate* origin, as already hinted. Magistracy flows *immediately* from God Creator, and is predicated upon his universal dominion over all nations. And as it flows from God Creator, the common Parent, and Head of all, the law of nature, common to all men, must be the immediate rule of all its administrations. A *relation* common to all, should be regulated by a *rule* common to all. All stand in the same relation to God, considered as Creator and Moral Governor. The standard for regulating this relation, must, of course, be common. This standard is the law of nature, which all men necessarily possess. Revelation is introduced as a rule, by the requisitions of the law of nature, which binds men to receive with gratitude, whatever God is pleased to reveal; and to adhere to it, as the perfect rule, under pain of condemnation, and being treated as rebels against his moral authority."

Page 11. "Magistracy respects things external, relating immediately to the outward man." And again, "The magistratical power is lordly and imperial. It belongs to its functionaries to exercise dominion, as the vicegerents of God; use compulsory measures with the disobedient, and enforce obedience to the laws, of which they are the executors." And again, page 12, "The immediate and proper end of all civil power, is, that the good of the commonwealth may be provided for, their temporal safety and civil liberty secured upon the footing of the moral law." Page 13. "Civil power may be vested in one or more. This is left to the discretion of the body politic, and is hence called '*an ordinance of man.*' 1 Pet. ii. 13. Whatever the particular form be, whether monarchical or republican, it is legitimate, and entitled to obedience, provided the constitution be agreeable to the moral law." Again, page 14, "The civil power extends to all persons resident within the realm, be their estate, character or condition, what it may. Rom. xiii. 1. *Let every soul be subject to the higher powers.*"

The above is extracted from the particulars wherein he states that his civil and ecclesiastical branches differ; and to these I cheerfully agree. I am sorry that I cannot agree with some other positions on this subject.

In page 9, the author says, speaking of civil government, "It existed previously to the fall, and would necessarily have existed, even had we never revolted from God." "Civil government does not, as some modern politicians affirm, originate either in the people, as its fountain, or in the vices consequent upon the fall. Among the angels, who retained their primitive rectitude, we find certain orders, suggested by the denominations of Archangels, Thrones, Dominions, Principalities and Powers. Col. i. 16. This testifies regular subordination among them, agreeably to the constitutional laws of their nature."

Why did the reverend author adorn, exclusively, the angels who retained their primitive rectitude, with privileged orders? Did he not know that the new testament, Matt. ix. 34. dignifies Beelzebub with the honorary title of prince of devils—and John xii. 34. the Saviour dignifies him with the title of the prince of this world, and in Eph. vi. 12. believers are represented as having to contend with principalities and powers; and that in Col. ii. 15. Christ is represented as having spoiled those principalities, and as having made a shew of them openly? Why did not the author admit the honour of privileged orders among the fallen angels, as well as those who kept their original rectitude? This was an unauthorised insult on the fallen angels, such as Michael the archangel did not think it proper to make.

This affords, however, a reason in addition to such as he has afterwards given, why he cannot homologate, that is, acknowledge the government of the United States. They have no principalities; they have no archangels, nor archbishops; they have no hereditary dominions, nor honorary titles, but they believe they have acted agreeably to the law of their nature, which brought them all into the world with equal rights, though not with equal capacities to maintain those rights. The author is requested to explain what the law of the nature of angels, to which he appeals in support of privileged orders, was. Were they propagated by one pair, and did they pass a long probation, before they were in a situation to institute civil governments and privileged orders? Or, were they created together and at once, and their government and order instituted immediately by their Creator, suitably to the place and station in which they were to be employed? Till the author answers these questions, we are not bound to apply the government of angels to the government of men; because we believe the laws of their nature are not the same. He speaks of modern philosophers, &c. He himself is the only modern, or at least, novel philosopher, I have met with on that subject.

If, as the author asserts, civil government existed previously to the fall, he is requested to inform us, who were the privileged orders, principalities or powers, that exercised the government, and who were the subordinate officers and subjects. The scripture informs us of only one man and his wife, of the human family, existing before the fall. Does the author believe, with some others, that a numerous race was created before Adam, and that he was created to be their sovereign? or, does he mean that civil government existed in the Divine decree before the fall? To the last I agree; but at the same time, and in the same manner, I believe that the reverend author and myself existed.

It appears, in examining the Sons of Oil, that at least one great object of civil government, in the opinion of the author, is the execution of penalties, viz. to stone, burn, hang, or otherwise punish, such as did not believe or worship agreeably to his own opinion of the will of God, or, at least, the opinion of the civil magistrate. He is seriously asked, what crimes, heresies or unbelief, took place before men revolted from God, for which such penalties could be executed!

The reverend author has, in the prosecution of his work, treated of ecclesiastic government in connexion with the civil, as branches of the same government; thus connecting what the Saviour and his apostles, with the greatest care, kept separate. But as every thing respecting the church of Christ in the new testament, is equally addressed to every hearer of the word, in that plain, yet dignified language, which is the peculiarity and ornament of the scriptures of truth, I will not intrude my observations on his thesis on that subject, unless it is thrust in my way. Therefore, I pass over without notice, seven particulars wherein he says his two great branches agree, and come to his fourth head, page 20, which he says is "to shew what concern the civil branch should take with the ecclesiastic, or enquire how far the civil power, *circa sacra,* reaches."

This power, *circa sacra,* not being mentioned nor defined in the new testament, nor invested by Christ or his apostles in the civil magistrate, christians have nothing to do with it. I know it is a term used in the scramble for power, which has often taken place in national churches. The church of Christ is the same in all nations. *It is built on the foundation*

of the prophets and apostles, Jesus Christ being the chief corner stone. Eph. ii.
20. *For other foundation can no man lay, than that is laid, which is Jesus Christ.*
1 Cor. iii. 11. National churches, as such, being founded on human fallible authority, are not, in their national character, churches of Christ.
I agree, however, with the learned Bishop Hoadly, (himself a dignitary
of a national church) that they may be schools of instruction, and may,
as well as several other denominations, contain Christ's disciples within
them.[17]

The author attempts to support his unscriptural power, *circa sacra,* by
a quotation from Deut. vii. 5. "Destroy their altars," &c. This, and every
part of that law of peculiarity, all the requirements of which have been
fulfilled, and the law itself abolished after it had served the purposes
intended by the divine Lawgiver, having been fully spoken to already, to
that I refer, and pass it over at this time, and every other quotation from
that law, though I know in it the author's great strength lies; for he carefully avoids the authority of Christ and his apostles in their decisions.

In page 27, he says, "Thus, the civil authority is concerned, in sanctioning and ratifying the laws of the Most High God," &c. Again, "As it is
his duty to ratify the law of God, in like manner he ought to sanction, by
his civil authority, the decrees of ecclesiastical courts, when agreeable
to the law of God," &c.

In page 30, he says, "He (the civil magistrate) hath a right to judge
of the decrees of ecclesiastical assemblies, whether they are agreeable
to the law of God, the supreme law of the land." Again he says, "Before
he gives his sanction to any church deed, he must bring it to this sacred
touch-stone; if it agrees therewith, he ought to ratify it, if not, he has not
only a right to reject it, but he is also *bound* to stamp his negative upon
it." Thus the magistrate's discretion is, with him the test of truth.

"This ratification of it is solely *civil,* and similar to his sanctioning of
civil ordinances."

"If this power is denied him, he must be considered as a being of
no discretion, and, consequently, unfit to be a civil magistrate. To suppose him bound to ratify whatever the church might decree, without

---

17. See Hoadly, note 12, above.

previous examination and conviction of its propriety, would make him a mere tool, fit for nothing but propping up the crazy chair of the man of sin."

In the above quotations compared, in order to come at their true meaning, we have the reverend author's principles fully developed. In my first view of his book, I had a favourable opinion of the author as a pious christian minister, though probably, like other christians, mistaken in some points. But when I found him talking about the civil magistrate sanctioning and ratifying the laws of the Most High God, I was a little alarmed, but consoled myself with the opinion, that he did not understand or mean what he expressed; that he only meaned that he should ratify or sanction laws agreeable to the laws of God: but when I read, in page 30, that this ratification of it is solely civil, and similar to his sanctioning civil ordinances, I was so astonished, that I would have laid the book down without reading further; but reasons existed which induced me to proceed, though with reluctance.

Before we proceed further, it is proper to examine, by the strictest rules, the terms made use of by the reverend author. The term *ratify* as explained by Johnson, the great lexicographer of the English language, and others, means to *confirm* and *settle*.[18] The term *sanction*, means the *act of confirmation*, which gives to any thing its obligatory power, or a law or decree ratified. This sense of the word, I find, is confirmed by numerous authors of the greatest name, and must be conclusive on the author, who was educated in a British seminary. It is, in fact, agreeable to common usage.

In this country, laws are passed, with, or without, a *sanction*, or *penalty*, as the legislature think proper. If a *penalty, or sanction*, is annexed, to enforce the execution of a law, it is a part of the law itself. A law may exist without such a sanction; but, it is presumed, in no country, can any thing be a law until it is *ratified* by the authority prescribed by the government. A clerk, or a chairman of a committee, may write, or a legislative branch may pass a bill, but it is not a law, until it is ratified in due

18. Samuel Johnson (1709–1784), English lexicographer, *Dictionary of the English Language* (1755).

form. So also it is with a patent for land, &c. I am ashamed of dwelling so long on so plain a case.

Christians had usually thought that *the law of God was perfect* and fully *sanctioned* and *ratified,* as it came to the first of men, and as a new edition of it was given on Mount Sinai, and also as explained and applied in the New Testament. They have now to learn, from the reverend author, that it is not a law until it is *ratified* and *sanctioned* by the civil magistrate. Common sense dictates, that nothing can be a law till it is ratified, and that it must be ratified by the highest authority: the reverend author says this is the civil magistrate; thus making the civil magistrate superior to God.

When Thomas Paine's *Age of Reason* was first presented to me, I read a few pages of it and laid it aside.[19] A gentleman near me rallied me, on the account of my (as he supposed) delicacy; he took it up, and said he would read it throughout; but he soon laid it past, not on account of the reasons it assigned, but on account of the indecency of the language: with this book my feelings were somewhat hurt, but nothing in comparison to what they were on reading *the Sons of Oil,* where the author says that "*the civil magistrate's ratification of the laws of the Most High God, is similar to his sanctioning of civil ordinances; that this ratification was solely civil,*" &c. Thomas Paine was a professed deist—the reverend author is a professed christian, and yet on this point he has equalled even Thomas Paine in deism.[20] Civil ordinances, indeed, have no force until they are ratified according to the forms prescribed; and according to the author, the laws of God stand in need of this ratification, before they have the force of laws; for nothing can be a law till it is ratified. This, however, is too plain a case to be dwelt longer upon. I had, not long since, left the author, among the Muslems, to contend about their respective claims for the authority of hanging, burning, &c. I have now found him encamped with deists, we will pursue his meanderings a little further, perhaps we may find the reverend author in some safe retreat. He has,

19. Thomas Paine (1737–1809), American patriot, deist/atheist, was author of *Common Sense* (1776) and *The Age of Reason* (1795).

20. A deist rejects all supernatural revelation but believes that God exists as first cause while having no further interest in his creation.

perhaps, taken shelter under the expansive shade of human infallibility, though he may not acknowledge the refuge he has taken.

In page 8, the author states, as before quoted, the dominion of Christ to consist of two great branches, namely, *magistracy* and *ministry,* or as he afterwards explains it, *civil* and ecclesiastic *branches,* of which he says, p. 9. "Ecclesiastical power is delegated to him," &c. Of this delegation I have spoken already, and shewed that Christ is the head of the church, which he *purchased with his own blood,* and that the ministers of the gospel are his *delegates* or *deputies,* not to enact *laws* for Christ's house, but to execute the *laws* which Christ, the church's lawgiver, has already made and published in the New Testament, which concludes with a prohibition, under the most severe penalty, pronounced against such as add to, or diminish from, his law. This solemn conclusion is worthy to be inserted at large. *"If any man shall add unto these things, God shall add unto him the plagues that are written in this book; and if any man shall take away from the words of this prophecy, God shall take away his name out of the book of life."*

I agree with Dr. Owen, and other learned Puritan divines, that no such ecclesiastic authority (or branch, as the author is pleased to call it) as has been instituted by national churches, or even by churchmen in the third century, when they assumed a law making power over Christ's house, and the falling away foretold by the apostle commenced, was instituted by Christ or his apostles. It was an addition to the laws of Christ, and God added to them all the plagues which the church underwent, through the long and dark night of the grand apostacy.

To prevent being misunderstood, I explicitly declare my opinion, that neither church nor state have any law-making power in the church of Christ. That the state has a legislative authority to prescribe rules of civil life to all its citizens or subjects, not contrary to the moral law of nature, but has no authority to interfere with the worship of God, further than to afford protection in the exercise of it, so that christians *may lead a quiet and peaceable life in all godliness and honesty.* 1 Tim. ii. 2. This was all the apostle enjoined Timothy and the church to desire or pray for. The power of the ministers of the gospel extends no further than to declare what the will of Christ is, as revealed in his word, and to administer his ordinances. They have no power to institute new ordinances, nor to annex new qualifying conditions, to entitle believers to the enjoyment of such ordinances as Christ has instituted; therefore, the power of the gospel ministry is not improperly said, by some, to be only ministerial and declarative; and by others, to be executive.

Even in national churches, except the church of Rome, the clergy are not admitted to exercise a legislative authority. This is claimed and exercised by the state: and even in England, which, with respect to church government and ceremonies, made the least remove from the church of Rome of any of the reformed churches, the state does not profess to make decrees to bind the conscience, with respect to the worship of God. In the 20th article of that national church, it is said, "The church hath power to decree rites or ceremonies, and authority in controversies of faith;" and it concludes by saying, "it ought not to decree any thing against God's word; and besides the same, it ought not to enforce any thing to be believed of necessity to salvation." Even with respect to general councils, in the following article it is said, "Wherefore, things ordained by them as necessary to salvation, have neither strength nor authority, unless it may be taken from the holy scriptures:" yet they persecuted such as did not approve their rites and ceremonies.

The learned divines and gentlemen appointed by the two houses of Parliament to meet at Westminster, in order to give advice on such questions as Parliament would propound to them, with respect to a proposed revision of the establishment of the national religion, in the 31st chapter say, "All synods and councils since the apostles' times, whether general or particular, may err, and many have erred; therefore, they are not to be made the rule of faith or practice." In the revision of the 39 articles of the church of England, by that assembly, scarcely any change is made.[21] The words are, "The holy scripture containeth all things necessary to salvation; so that whatsoever is not read therein, nor may be proved thereby, is not to be believed as an article of faith, or necessary to salvation."

All who are acquainted with the nature of government, must at once see the absurdity of considering civil government, and the government of the church of Christ, as different branches of the same government.

---

21. The Thirty-nine Articles is the basic statement of belief of the Anglican communion. It was written during the reign of Elizabeth I.

In all free governments, the governing power is separated into different departments or branches, such as, the legislative, the executive, and the judiciary. These three being exercised by one person, or by one body of men, is, in the opinion of the celebrated Montesquieu, *the definition of tyranny*.[22] In most free governments, in order to secure mature deliberation, the legislature is divided into two branches, viz. senate and representatives. The concurrence of both is necessary to pass a law. In Britain, the king has a complete negative on passing the laws, and so have his governors in the colonies. In several governments in the United States, the executive has a qualified negative, that is, so far as to send it back for reconsideration, and to require the concurrence of two thirds. This is the case with the federal government; but all is one government, under one fundamental law, and that varying in different states agreeable to that discretion which the author himself, page 14, says they have a right to exercise: "Whatever the form be, whether monarchical or republican, it is legitimate, and entitled to obedience." Now, I enquire, what place or department, in this machine of government, has he left for the ecclesiastical branch, wherein to operate? It could not act in passing laws—that belongs to the legislature. It could not execute laws—that belongs to the executive. It cannot be employed in applying the law to cases as they arise—this belongs to the judiciary. Ecclesiastical government, as instituted in national churches, by human authority, is in so far, the ordinance of man; but few of these governments give that branch much share even in its own government. In England, the bishops in parliament do not sit as clergymen, but as Barons, in right of the barony attached to the diocese. They have no ecclesiastic branch; and the church of Rome has no civil branch.

On the author's own principle, laid down page 12, viz. "But ecclesiastical power is altogether *ministerial*," it is well known that ministerial power is necessarily a subordinate character under the government, and not a component part or branch of the government itself. Ministerial characters are agents of the executive power, whether they act

22. Charles-Louis de Secondat (1689–1755): baron de la Brède et de Montesquieu. French political philosopher.

at home or abroad; therefore cannot be a branch of the government itself. Hence, in scripture language, it always means one who serves, and not one who commands, or makes laws. Indeed, in this instance, the reverend author has in so far defined ecclesiastic power agreeable to the gospel; it being altogether ministerial. It cannot be at all legislative; that is to say, have power to make laws. How then can he call it a great branch of any government? Of a political government it is evident it cannot be a branch; and it is still more evident that it cannot make laws for the government of the church of Christ. Even the apostles were only "able ministers of the new testament, approving themselves as the ministers of God." 2 Cor. iii. 6. and vi. 4. When they wrought miracles, or prescribed laws to the church, they did so solely by the authority of Christ, the church's head and lawgiver. They did not claim, or attempt to exercise the authority of a branch of the government of either church or state. They disclaimed "being lords over God's heritage," 1 Pet. v. 3. or "having dominion over the faith of the church." 2 Cor. i. 24.

I admit the originality of the author's idea, page 8. "This universal dominion committed to him, (Christ) as it respects the human family, in its administrations, consists in two great branches, namely magistracy and ministry." I say, I admit the thought to have the credit of originality, but not of prudence. He ought to have explored the ground with care, before he ventured to invite his friends to travel on it. I have already demonstrated, that the apostles disclaimed it. Constantine, an unbaptised christian, attempted something like it; but when he thought proper, exercised the power of both branches by his own authority. Finally, the ecclesiastic branch wrested it from the civil, and disposed of kings and kingdoms at their discretion, and made slaves of the souls of men.

The authority which the author gives to the civil magistrate, to ratify the laws of the Most High God, p. 27, and his asserting that this authority is similar, that is, equal to his sanctioning power of civil ordinances, (that is to say, they cannot be ordinances, or have any obligation, till they are ratified and sanctioned by the civil magistrate) is perfectly in unison with the learned Hobbes' public conscience, viz. "that the only test of right or wrong is the laws of the commonwealth."[23]

---

23. Thomas Hobbes (1588–1679): English philosopher.

To this it may be objected, that he is only to ratify the laws of the Most High God, "acting as a terror to evil doers, and a praise to them that do well," and in like manner, "to sanction, by his civil authority, the decrees of ecclesiastical courts, when agreeable to the law of God, and calculated to promote his glory," page 27; and page 30, "Before he gives his sanction to any church deed, he must bring it to this sacred touchstone (the divine law); if it agrees therewith, he ought to ratify it, if not, he has not only a right to reject it, but he is also bound to stamp his negative upon it." This, indeed, looks plausible; but when qualified with what immediately follows, it will appear hollow. "He (the civil magistrate) must be considered as a being of no discretion, and, consequently, unfit to be a civil magistrate," if he has not the power of ratifying the divine law, and the decrees of the church, similar to his ratifying civil laws. "To suppose him to ratify whatever the church might decree, without previous examination and conviction of its propriety, would make him a mere tool, fit for nothing but propping up the crazy chair of the man of sin." This language applies equally to the laws of God, as to the decrees of the church, as in his opinion, both require the ratification of the civil magistrate; and they cannot be laws or ordinances, until they are ratified; and the magistrate, if he has the authority, and it be his duty, to ratify them, I admit that he must exercise his best judgment and moral discretion. Unless this is the case, it could not be a moral act, nor be obligatory.

It is proper to enquire, wherein does this differ from the doctrine of the church of Rome? Only in one particular. That church places the ratifying and sanctioning power of the law of God, in the Pope, the head of their church, to whom they openly ascribe infallibility, and the inspiration of the Holy Ghost. The author places this very important and sacred trust, both with respect to the laws of God, and the decrees of the church, in the civil magistrate, to whom, by necessary implication, he must ascribe infallibility: for this is essential to the trust which the author reposes in him.

In another important particular, however, the author and the Pope more cordially agree. The creed of Pope Pius, declares its approbation of the scriptures, agreeable to the sense affixed to it by their church. The author approves of it, agreeable to the sense assigned to it by the ratifying and sanctioning discretion of the civil magistrate. Both of them agree, however, in applying the authority of scripture in support of this anti-christian claim. Protestants have long charged the church of Rome with arguing in a circle, which they call sophistry. For instance, the church of Rome appeals to the scriptures for the infallible authority of their church, and they also appeal to the church for the authority of scripture, agreeable to the sense assigned to it by itself. Agreeably to this, the reverend author attempts to prove the ratifying and sanctioning power of the civil magistrate from the scripture, and the authority and sense in which the scripture and church decrees ought to be received under civil penalties, is, according to him, to be determined by the civil magistrate's discretion. Yet as the pope claims this power to the church, the author calls him Antichrist, and the *man of sin with his crazy chair;* and for claiming it to the state, papists call him an *heretic,* while, at the same time, they agree about the fundamental doctrine on which their respective systems are built, viz. that the scriptures are the law of the most high God, in that sense only in which it is ratified and sanctioned by human authority.

As the author professes to support the reformation testimony of the church of Scotland, it may be of use to examine what that testimony was. In doing this, I am at some loss for want of Calderwood's history of that church, which I have not had an opportunity of examining for thirty years past, and of which a new edition ought to be encouraged; however, I have an opportunity of examining the *Hind let loose,* by the Rev. Alexander Shields, recognized and recommended by the reformed presbytery in Scotland, about fifty years since, in their judicial testimony.[24]

On period iv. p. 31. that reverend and acute author says—"Hitherto the conflict was for the concerns of Christ's prophetical and priestly offices, against Paganism and Popery, but from the year 1570, and downward, the testimony is stated and gradually prosecuted for the rights, privileges, and prerogatives of Christ's kingly office, which has been the peculiar glory of the church of Scotland, above all the churches

---

24. David Calderwood (1575–1659), Scottish Presbyterian minister and historian, banished by James VI, *A True History of the Church of Scotland, from the Beginning of the Reformation, until the End of the Reigne of King James VI* (1678); and Alexander Shields (1660–1700), Scottish dissenter, *A Hind Let Loose, or An Historical Representation of the Testimonies of the Church of Scotland for the Interest of Christ with the True State Thereof in All its Periods* (1687).

of the earth," &c. The witnesses of that day made such great account of it, that they encouraged one another to suffer for it as the greatest concern. In support of this being the testimony of the church at that period, he inserts a number of testimonies of reformation divines of the greatest note for talents and integrity, which that age produced, such as Forbes, Welch, Knox, Bruce, the two Melvins, Lindsay, Black, the famous Mr. Davidson, &c. men who were ornaments to that church and nation.[25] I can, however, insert but a few extracts.

Mr. Knox, by many called the apostle of the Scottish reformation, was the disciple of Calvin,[26] denounced anathemas against the civil government (branch in the reverend Mr. Wylie's language) interfering with the church of Christ. The general assembly remonstrated to the king "that he had taken on him a spiritual power, which properly belongs to Christ, as king and only head of the church." Mr. Andrew Melvin protests "that they were too bold (viz. the civil government) to take upon them to judge of the doctrine, and to controul the ambassadors of a greater than was there." Mr. James Melvin wrote "that they had not only set up *a new pope, and so became traitors to Christ, and had condescended to the chief errors of papistry, upon which all the rest depended; but further, they had granted more to the king, than ever the popes of Rome peaceably obtained.*"

25. Patrick Forbes (1564–1635), Laird of Corse, was ordained at age forty-eight, and appointed Bishop of Aberdeen, in Scotland, in 1618, and chancellor of King's College; John Welch (c. 1570–1622), Scottish Presbyterian minister, was convicted of high treason for his religious practice, banished from Britain in 1606, and lived most of the rest of his life in France; John Knox (1505–1572) was a leading Reformation figure in Scotland; Robert Bruce (1554–1631), Bruce of Kinnard, was a Scottish theologian, preacher, and statesman, who, for his opposition to James VI's arbitrary proceedings and Episcopal leanings, was banished from Edinburgh; Andrew Melville (1545–1622), Scottish reformer who introduced Presbyterian organization into the Scottish churches, was confined for four years in the Tower of London by James I; James Melville (1556–1614), Scottish reformer and nephew of Andrew Melville, was exiled from Scotland in 1606; Sir David Lindsay of the Mount (1486–1555), Scottish poet and reformer, was a colleague of John Knox; Robert Black (1752–1817) served as a Presbyterian minister in Ireland; and John Davidson (c. 1549–1603), Scottish minister, stood as an antagonist to King James VI of Scotland.

26. John Calvin (1509–1564), French theologian, was the leading figure in the Reformed segment of the Reformation.

The above is perfectly in unison with all I have advanced, in opposition to the reverend author's idol, viz. the civil magistrate's authority to sanction and ratify the laws of the most high God, and the decrees of the ecclesiastic branch, the qualification and ordination of ministers, &c.

The commissioners of the general assembly, in support of the declinature of the Rev. Dr. Black, say, "there are two jurisdictions, the one spiritual, the other civil; the one respecting the conscience, the other respecting externals," &c. The famous reformer, John Welch, while a prisoner, giving this testimony in favour of the independence of Christ's kingdom, on the kingdoms of this world, viz. (the author's civil branch) says, "These two points [1] that Christ is the head of his church, [2] That she is free in her government from all other jurisdiction except Christ's—are the special causes of our imprisonment, being now convicted as traitors for maintaining thereof." Again in 1606, the ministers offer a protestation to parliament, in perfect conformity to the above. There is much more to the same purpose in this period, testifying that Christ's kingdom is not connected with, or dependent on the kingdoms of this world. How flagrantly opposed is the reverend Mr. Wylie to the church of Scotland, in the reformation period! Why did he appeal to the reformers and martyrs for Christ during the reformation, while his avowed principles were in direct opposition to theirs? They submitted to imprisonment, and banishment to foreign lands, in preference to ever appearing before the king and council to give account of their doctrine or ordination. The ordination of the precious Robert Bruce was questioned by king James and his council.[27] These pious and zealous reformers of the church of Scotland, testified, in direct opposition to the new fangled doctrine of the reverend Mr. Wylie. How can he have the confidence to appeal to the reformers and martyrs! whose principles were so directly opposite to his own?

---

27. James VI (1566–1625), son of Mary Queen of Scots, reigned as King of Scotland from 1567 to 1603 (from 1583 without a regent), then as James I, King of England, from 1603 to 1625.

CHAPTER II

A historical review of the author's standard period of the church, and of his emperors and councils—A vindication of the constitution of Pennsylvania, with respect to the rights and liberty of conscience, and of the federal government, from the author's charge of atheism—A vindication of the treaty with Tripoli.

In page 23, the author introduces the examples of Asa, Hezekiah, Josiah, &c. pious kings of Judah, who called the people back from their apostacy from the national covenant propounded by God, whom they had agreed to obey as the peculiar king of their nation, and from whom, on condition of their obedience, numerous temporal blessings were promised; and as a punishment for disobedience, temporal curses, equally numerous, were threatened.

It is presumed that no christian believes that eternal salvation was promised in the Sinai covenant; or, in other words, that it was the covenant of grace. The Abrahamic covenant was, indeed, a most gracious manifestation of the covenant of grace, such as the apostle testifies that the Sinai covenant could not disannul. The blessings of this covenant descend to all true believers, in right of which they are called the children of Abraham. The Sinai covenant, as has been shown before, was symbolical or typical of the kingdom of Christ, through which, as through a glass darkly, true believers saw Christ's day and rejoiced. The author, however, takes no notice of the divine antitype, who fulfilled every law that man had broken, and made atonement for transgressions, nor of the spiritual kingdom which he had instituted, and of which he had expressly declared that it was not of this world; but with a gigantic stride overleaps the examples of the church of God for a thousand years, viz. from good Josiah, king of Judah, till the reign of Constantine.

After, from the example of those pious kings who had no authority to make laws civil or ecclesiastic, nor even ever attempted to do it, he attempts to prove the authority of kings to convoke synods and councils, consisting of ecclesiastic persons, to consult how the church may be purged from corruption, and the truths of God most effectually propagated, he says,

"Moreover, the four ecumenical councils were called by christian magistrates. Constantine called the first Nicene council: Theodosius the elder, the first council at Constantinople: Theodosius the younger, the first Ephesian council: Marcian the Chalcedon council."

All christians who are acquainted with the history of the age which the author has fixed upon as the purest period of the christian church, and of the emperors, who, in his opinion, copied the virtues of pious Asa, Hezekiah, &c. can decide on the correctness of his estimate. To such as are not, I recommend the perusal of the histories of both church and state during the fourth and fifth centuries, the period in which the author's standard councils were held, and his pious emperors reigned.

The church of Christ had, before this period, fallen from her first love, and, like Israel of old, played the harlot; the shepherds of his flock had usurped a lordship over it; but in his standard period, the fourth century, they had transferred that lordship to the kingdoms of this world, or rather parted it between them, and to this day have never fully agreed what share of it each should possess. In proof of this, such extracts from national and church history might be given, as would fill a volume; for the professed kingdom of Christ having become a kingdom of this world, the civil history of every nation, where christianity prevailed, is also a history of the church. Gibbon's History of the decline and fall of the Roman Empire,[1] which is in many hands, is full on that

---

1. Edward Gibbon (1737–1794), English historian, *The History of the Decline and Fall of the Roman Empire*, 6 vols. (1776–1788).

subject; he was a deist, and records the corruption and tyranny of those councils and emperors, with an insidious triumph, and applies it to destroy the credibility of the christian religion, not considering that the facts which he truly records of the corruption of the church, were at the same time testimonies to the truth of prophecy.

The Abbe Millot's Elements of Universal History, give ample testimony to the truth of the facts, accompanied with judicious observations. He was a Catholic, and historiographer to a Catholic prince, and rather disposed to apologise for, than to expose their corruption, but does not conceal the facts.

The History of the Christian Church, by that reverend and learned Lutheran divine, Mosheim,[2] is full on this subject, and his facts are carefully selected from the best authority; and though he was an Erastian,[3] viz. believed that the external government of the church ought to be regulated by the civil magistrate, yet on this subject, he is justly esteemed an impartial historian. This valuable work is in many hands.

Milnor's church history,[4] though the author, being a rector of the English church, and of what is known there by the name of the high church party, and an avowed advocate of the union of church and state, and of the persecution resulting from that union, yet admits the facts, and particularly, the very rapid increase of corruption, after the council of Nice; but attempts accounting for it from other causes. From these historians I intended to have inserted large extracts; but when I had them prepared, I found they would swell the work too much. I will chiefly substitute extracts from the *History of the Rise, Declension, and Revival of the Church of Christ,* by the Rev. T. Haweis,[5] Rector of All Saints, (who was of the low church party) for those I had prepared from Mosheim, &c. not because

---

2. Johann Lorenz Mosheim (1694–1755), *Historical Commentaries on the State of Christianity During the First Three Hundred and Twenty-five Years from the Christian Era,* trans. of *The Commentaries on the Affairs of the Christians before the Time of Constantine the Great* (1741).

3. Erastianism is a doctrine named for Thomas Erastus (1524–1583), a Swiss theologian, although he never personally embraced it. The doctrine holds that the state is superior to the church in ecclesiastical matters.

4. Joseph Milner (1744–1797), *The History of the Church of Christ,* 5 vols. (1795–1809).

5. Thomas Haweis (1734–1820), *An Impartial and Succinct History of the Rise, Declension and Revival of the Church of Christ: From the Birth of Our Saviour to the Present Time with Faithful Characters of the Principal Personages, Ancient and Modern,* 3 vols. (1800).

they are more full to the purpose, but because they are less minute, and therefore more concise. For the truth of my general statements, I appeal to all the before-mentioned historians. I had proposed extracts from Parker's[6] edition of Eusebeus, Theodorate, &c. to shew the ignorance and credulity of that age, and the ridiculous miracles wrought by unlearned monks and hermits, which are still believed by the great mass of the catholic church, though treated with contempt by those better informed: but I found they also would swell the work too much. My object was, to bring Christians to be better acquainted with the state and character of the church in that period, held up by the church of Rome, her council of Trent, and the Rev. Mr. Wylie, as the standard of perfection; and taken as a model for imitation, in a less or greater degree, by all the advocates of national political churches, and of persecution. I presume, pious well-meaning christians, when they know the character of the church during the period of the author's standard councils, and his reputed pious emperors, they will not choose to be considered as in communion with it, especially now, when the terror and punishment of schism are no more. If, however, they do, and at the same time keep separate from the communion of either the Presbyterian or Episcopal protestant churches, now in being, they will be justly chargeable with straining at a gnat, and swallowing a camel, at a bar where the reverend author will not be admitted as their advocate.

Christians, who take the instructions of Christ and his apostles, as the rule for the edification and the conduct of the new testament church, and the promises of Christ to be with it to the end of the world, for their assurance of its support, may do pretty well, with little knowledge of church history: but such as consider, with the author, (pages 24, 27.) that the laws of the Most High God, and the decrees of ecclesiastic courts, stand in need of the ratification and sanction of the civil magistrate, ought to be well acquainted with church history, that they may avoid former mistakes. They having taken the government which God laid on

---

6. Samuel Parker (1681–1730) published, in 1703, an abridged translation of Eusebius, dedicated to Robert Nelson, and later *An Abridged Translation of the Church Histories of Socrates, Sozomen, and Theodoret* (1707–1712).

Christ's shoulders, (Isa. ix. 6.) and laid it on their own, have subjected themselves to a very high responsibility.

To understand the state of the church in the fourth and fifth centuries, which include the author's standard period, it is necessary to have some knowledge of the third century. Without this, we lay the saddle on the wrong horse, and set the errors of bishops to the account of kings.

Even in the second century, the presbyters, or bishops of large cities, assumed a pre-eminence, and seem to have distinguished the character of a bishop from that of a presbyter, and instituted councils with law-making power. In the third century, however, episcopacy was more exalted, and councils of the clergy assumed a higher legislative authority. "One bishop also had great pre-eminence over his fellows; summoned councils; presided at their deliberations, and usually swayed their opinions; such was Cyprian in Africa. Rome, Antioch, Alexandria, claimed a sort of pre-eminence for their antiquity, and on difficult matters were consulted: though the bounds of metropolitan, or episcopal authority fluctuated, according to the ability, reputation or ambition of the person who filled the see. The bishop of the great metropolis began to claim, and was generally now admitted to hold a certain priority of dignity above his *fellows;* for equality respecting *order* and office was yet jealously maintained by the episcopal band: And therefore, when Stephen, bishop of Rome, issued his mandate, respecting the baptism of heretics, Cyprian rebuked his insolence, with equal indignation and contempt; but whilst the bishops watched with jealousy the ambitious encroachments of their companions in office, each endeavoured to extend his claims successfully in his own church; and was supported by the spirit of the corps in his pretensions. They assumed every day more of absolute rule in their own sees, trenching upon the rights of the presbyters, and excluding the interference of the faithful. These were now taught implicit obedience, and heard the constant warnings of the deadly crime of resisting episcopal authority, seated upon the throne of God, and claiming divine right and submission. The evils necessarily resulting from such a spirit, and such abuses, must be incalculable; and appeared in the pride, pomp, luxury and carnality of many of these prelatical dignitaries. The other orders endeavoured to imitate them in lording it over their inferiors; and claiming their superior honors of sacerdotal reverence. Even the deacons usurped many

of the presbyters' offices, and, in the useless and multiplied rites and ceremonies instituted in the church, appointed beneath them a herd of inferior orders, sub-deacons, acolothists, door-keepers, readers, exorcists,
and buriers of the dead, all which strengthened the clerical army with
their subordinate functions; and were supposed to share a minor portion
of their sanctity." Haweis, vol. I. p. 223, 224. Am. Edit.

The historian further informs us, that marriage, though not prohibited to the clergy, was discouraged; that celibacy continued to acquire
a great degree of reputation; and that monkery extended its roots and
peopled the deserts, far from the haunts of men. That the sacraments,
instead of being considered as memorials, or outward signs of inward
grace, had acquired a superstitious reverence for the signs themselves,
and were thought indispensably necessary to salvation; and that the supper was administered even to infants. A warfare was carried on to a
scandalous height, by bishops and councils, about trifles. The question,
whether or not infants should be baptized on the eighth day, as circumcision had been directed, occupied the wisdom of the great saint, and
afterwards martyr, Cyprian, and a council of sixty six bishops; and for
his supposed unscriptural decision, he was solemnly excommunicated
by the bishop of Rome, whom he did not acknowledge as his superior.
The above, and other like instances, demonstrated the propriety of one
visible head or judge of truth on earth, to settle the disputes of the four
metropolitan bishops, who were each of them heads of the church of
Christ in different provinces of the empire, in right of being the vicegerents or representatives of Christ—a doctrine early advanced, and
which was a lasting curse to the church.

While the preachers had given up the simplicity of the gospel, and
substituted the Grecian eloquence, full of tropes, figures and allegory,
taken from the philosophical school of Plato, in their sermons; burning
incense on the altar was introduced from the law of Moses, as the different grades of the priesthood had been before. "The sacrament of the
Lord's Supper was celebrated with greater pomp and solemnity. Gold
and silver vessels were used in the service, with garments for beauty and
glory; supposing these would command greater reverence and respect
for the sacred mysteries. They began also to speak of the elements af-

ter consecration, in a language which laid the foundation for the gross and impious doctrine of transubstantiation, and by degrees proceeded, though after a course of ages, from veneration to adoration, and from high mystical flights, to suggest a *real* body of Christ in the eucharist.

Before admission to *baptism,* the exorcist with frightful menaces and formidable shouts, pretended to expel the prince of darkness from the candidate. The remission of sins was thought to be the immediate effect of baptism, rightly administered by the bishop or his delegate. By his subsequent prayer and imposition of hands (for his presence on those occasions was always necessary) the Holy Ghost was supposed to be given. These baptismal solemnities were reserved for the great festival of Easter, and the forty days succeeding. A solemn parade and procession of the exorcised and baptised, in white garments and crowns, in token of their victory over the devil, closed the august ceremonial. Every step we advance, betrays the growing declension, and the loss of true Christianity, in forms and ceremonies, and the tricks of jugglers to give importance to a new-invented priesthood." Haweis, vol. I. p. 226. Am. Edit.

In short, fastings, the doctrine of demons, exorcism, bodily macerations, hungry bellies to starve out the devil, &c. were introduced. In this century, the sign of the cross was supposed to administer victorious power over all sorts of trials. No christian undertook any thing of importance, without arming himself with the influence of this triumphant sign. The doctrine of the purging fire was also introduced, which, as afterwards dressed up in the form of purgatory, became a great source of profit to the clergy. Though for a clergyman to marry was not yet forbidden, it was esteemed unholy; yet many of the clergy kept concubines. The keeping of lent was introduced, and other fasts and festivals were multiplied. A superstitious reverence for the memories and tombs of the martyrs, approaching to idolatry, and also of the relics, viz. the bones of saints, and dust of places reputedly holy, was in high repute.

I have preferred giving a sketch of the history of the church during the third century; because, in the second century, superstition was but gradually commencing; and in the fourth and fifth, which includes the author's standard period of pure christianity, and from thence to the council of Trent, the change was only progressive and circumstantial, and depended on the same principles adopted in the third and fourth, viz. human invention and human tradition. The long peace and prosperity, enjoyed in the third century, was misimproved, so as to promote pride, ambition, and superstition. The ten years most cruel persecution, under Dioclesian, and two of his three associates in the empire, increased the number of real martyrs and confessors, and made very numerous apostates; but does not appear to have put a stop to the increasing superstition, or the ambition of the bishops.

On the decease of Constantius Chlorus, who governed the empire in the west, viz. Britain, Spain and Gaul, (France) and who, in protecting all men in the enjoyment of their natural rights, protected the Christians, while they were cruelly persecuted through all other parts of that widely extended empire;—the christians, then very numerous, naturally attached themselves to Constantine his son, who, with their assistance, in the hand of Providence, became sole emperor. He put the sign of the cross, which the christians had already been in the habit of using as a charm, in his military colours (laborum); and after defeating the imperial tyrant Maxentius, and taking possession of Rome, he put a stop to the persecution of christians, and accepted, of the office of high-priest or head of the church, as other emperors had done of that of Jupiter; and protected all who lived peaceably. The christians having faithfully and successfully supported him in his wars, he paid great attention to their bishops, whom he enriched by his bounty, and bestowed on them, for a church, one of the heathen temples in Rome; and they recompensed him with the seductive incense of flattery, and promises of support, which it was evidently their interest to perform.

They having, before the Dioclesian persecution, (to use the words of Mosheim) "assumed, in many places, a princely authority; and having appropriated to their evangelical function, the splendid ensigns of temporal majesty;—a throne surrounded with ministers, exalted above their equals, the servants of the meek and humble Jesus; and sumptuous garments; dazzled the eyes and the minds of the multitude, into an ignorant veneration for their arrogated authority."

Men of such influence, and held in such veneration, were well worth being courted and purchased too, by a man of the discernment and unbounded ambition of Constantine.

That the subject may be the better understood, it is proper to mention, that when Constantine subdued the tyrant Maxentius, (who was loved by none but his praetorian guards, who enjoyed his bounty) and got possession of the capital of the Roman world, and of the empire of the west; two emperors still remained on the plan of Dioclesian, for governing that extensive empire. Maximian, who reigned in Asia, was the only survivor of those who had been appointed to the government of the empire by Dioclesian, with equal authority as himself. That unwieldy empire, being attacked and pressed on all sides, Dioclesian added two Caesars, clothed with imperial authority in the districts assigned to them, and having the right of succession to the empire and title of Augustus. The title of Caesar was bestowed on Constantius Chlorus and Galerius. Chlorus, the father of Constantine, and the best of these appointments, had Britain, Spain, and Gaul allotted to his government; the second had Macedonia, Greece, &c. Maximian, as emperor, governed the west, and Dioclesian the east, a division, that afterwards proved fatal to the empire. Dioclesian was one of the best and most moderate of the Roman emperors; but after he had reigned eighteen years successfully, he, through the influence and intrigues of Galerius, the *Caesar* in most immediate connection with him, and of the pagan priests, whose altars had been forsaken through the prevalence of christianity, reluctantly issued a very severe edict for persecuting the christians. In two years after this wicked edict, he became so disgusted with the empty grandeur and excessive cares of empire, that he abdicated the sovereignty, and retired to a private life, from which he afterwards, when earnestly solicited, refused to return to empire. *"If you did but see* (replied he to those who solicited him) *the pulse which I raise with my own hands, you would never speak to me of the empire."* Galerius and his colleagues, except Chlorus, carried on the persecution with unrelenting severity for about eight years afterwards, when Galerius died (christian writers say) miserably. He, however, repealed his persecuting edict at the approach of death.

Dioclesian and the elder Maximian, both having resigned, (the last with reluctance;) he was afterwards (perhaps deservedly) killed by his son-in-law, Constantine, for the security of his own life. The two Caesars assumed the title of Augustus,—governed the empire,—and, to assist them, appointed two Caesars, viz. subordinate emperors. One of these was Licinius, who married Constantine's sister. He was made Caesar by Galerius. Maxantius, the son of Maximian, and brother-in-law of Constantine, was then emperor of the west. He hated and persecuted the christians, but was overthrown and slain by Constantine, as has been mentioned. The remaining Maximian governed the Asiatic portion of the empire;—Licinius governed Greece, &c. viz. the eastern part of Europe. Maximian, being the only survivor of Dioclesian's appointments, prepared to subdue both Licinius and Constantine. The former had, equally with Constantine, given peace and protection to the christians; he, with a very inferior force, met with, fought and subdued Maximian, who poisoned himself. Christian writers, of that age, inform us that Licinius was warned of God, in a dream, to risk the battle, and assured of success.

Thus the Roman world came to be governed by two brothers in law. Their ambition could not brook having either superior or equal. They soon quarreled. Constantine, with his hardy northern troops, defeated Licinius, at the head of his effeminate associates. Licinius, with the sacrifice of the best portion of that part of the empire which he governed, obtained peace. Constantine, whose ambition was unbounded, made his three sons, two of them infants, Caesars. The two brothers, both in blood and empire, did not long agree. Constantine had the greatest power and resources, and, from circumstances and by address, he had won the hearts of the christians, then a very powerful body. Probably on this account Licinius commenced a persecution against them. They met in battle; Constantine, with superior force, both by land and sea, defeated Licinius, committed him prisoner, with a promise of life; but he was soon after strangled in the prison. In a short time after he put to death his own son Crispen, whom he had created Caesar, and who was generally beloved; and the son of Licinius, but twelve years old; and afterwards his own wife, and many of the nobles, without a public trial; which we, in this country, would call murder, and for which, even his flatterers have never yet, from authentic documents, assigned a sufficient cause; but for which, he was in Rome spoken of as a second Nero. He left that metropolis in disgust, and erected a new one, which he called Constantinople, in a well chosen situation, to build and aggrandize which, he miserably oppressed the empire.

He had, as has been mentioned, from the first, favoured and enriched the christian bishops, who, even before he came to the empire, sat on princely thrones, to which some of them waded through blood. This was afterwards the case with Damasius, bishop of Rome, to whose infallible tradition Theodosius commanded implicit obedience to be paid, on the pain of death.

Some commentators have considered *the silence in heaven* (viz. the church) *for the space of half an hour,* Rev. viii. 1. to be applicable to the reign of Constantine. It may have been so; but could only have been so in the first twelve years of his reign, during which he put a stop to persecution, made several good and humane laws, and protected all in their natural rights. It is admitted by the best interpreters, that it could not apply to any other period of his reign. It was not afterwards silence, but war in the church.

It is generally admitted, that great courtiers, such as Eusebius then, and Laud afterwards were, are never pious ministers of the gospel.[7] With such self-seekers and flatterers, Constantine was surrounded. He not only enriched them by his bounty, but unfortunately engaged in their controversies. The same, or similar principles, to what Arius taught,[8] had been taught long before, and refuted by the force of truth, addressed to the reason and judgment of men. Constantine, who had never studied divinity, nor had received baptism, by his letters and advice endeavoured to settle the Arian controversy: this not succeeding, he by his imperial authority, convened the well known council of Nice, in which, if not formally, he actually presided. That council, after much debate, rejected the doctrine of Arius, for doing which they had sufficient authority from scripture, if they consulted it. They also decided the question on what day the festival of Easter should be held, and the Melitian controversy

7. Eusebius of Caesarea (fl. 4th century): bishop, exegete, and historian of the first four centuries of Christianity; William Laud (1573–1645), Archbishop of Canterbury, was anti-Scot and anti-Puritan. At the beginning of the English Civil War, he was convicted of treason and beheaded.

8. Arius (c. A.D. 250–336), Greek theologian, taught that God created the Son before all other things. The Son was the first creation but neither equal to the Father nor eternal like him.

about the right of ordination, then lately claimed by the metropolitan bishops, and the rank of these bishops, and the limits of their respective jurisdictions: but so far was their decision from settling any of these controversies, that it seemed to give them new life and activity. The time of keeping Easter is yet unsettled. The Arian heresy, then condemned, in a few years after, was restored through the influence of the terrors and rewards of the emperor, who, by the council of Nice, was made the head of Christ's church, which then became a kingdom of this world, and for which event it had been prepared by such carnal bishops, as the apostle Paul foretold would arise in the church, in his farewell address to the elders of the church at Ephesus. Here, at least in my opinion, the man of sin was openly revealed, who, even in the time of the apostle Paul, did *already work,* but who was to be openly revealed in his appointed time. They that *letted* or *prevented* it, in the apostles' day, viz. the heathen emperors, were then *taken out of the way,* which gave a fair opportunity for the usurper of Christ's kingdom, viz. the man of sin, to be revealed. Constantine commenced, and Theodosius completed his inauguration.

Protestant commentators have perplexed themselves in endeavouring to ascertain the beginning and ending of the *days* mentioned by the prophet Daniel, and the corresponding *times* in the apocalypse. With those I have nothing to do on this question. Probably they will never be perfectly known till the prophecy is accomplished; but the early degeneracy of the christian church is well known. It *already wrought* in the days of the apostles, and was rapidly progressive after the apostles were dead, and redoubled its progress after the conducting of it was, by bishops, transferred to a fortunate and unprincipled adventurer, like the Napoleon of the present age. Unfortunately, he had not ballast to bear, nor prudence to guide, such a degree of elevation, as never any man before him enjoyed; not only the civil government of the Roman world, but also the government of Christ's spiritual kingdom.

He did not claim divine inspiration to himself, Theodosius afterwards did; but in his circular letters, enforcing the decrees of the council of Nice, he considered them as divinely inspired. He banished Arius, and decreed the penalty of death against those who would even read his books. In a few years after, he became convinced in his own opinion, that the decision of the council of Nice was wrong; he recalled Arius,

replaced the Arian bishops whom he had banished, and commanded
Athanasius to receive them into communion: but that veteran confes-
sor refused, and Constantine convened a council at Tyre, who, as most
other councils did, obeyed their master's will, and banished Athanasius.
Constantine, after this, threw the weight of his influence against the
Nicenes, and at the approach of death was baptized by an Arian bishop,
and left his will in the hands of an Arian priest. Long before his time,
the name priest had been substituted for minister. He distributed the
empire to his three sons: the eldest and favourite son, Constantius, was
left in possession of the imperial city, Constantinople, and of the east;
his two brothers, Constans and Constantine, had the empire of the west
divided between them; and two of Constantine's brothers had ample
estates allotted to them in the east. These were soon dispatched to the
other world, except two children; one of which was put to death for
his crimes by Constantius, through whose means their father had been
murdered. The other, Julien, called the apostate, came to the empire
on the death of Constantius. He, after a short reign, was killed in the
Persian war, and the house of Chlorus became extinct. I never read the
history of that good man, Chlorus, and his numerous and promising
family, extinguished by the hands or commands of those who ought to
have been their protectors, without a tear of sympathy and regret.

Constantius, left by his father in an Arian court, by numerous councils established Arianism, and not only protected, but promoted it, by all
the powers of the secular arm. The distress and destruction which took
place on this occasion, I would rather weep over than relate. It was the
first instance of professed Christians so profusely shedding the blood of
their fellow christians for difference of opinion; but, alas! it was far from
being the last. Constantine had commenced the practice—Mr. Wylie,
himself, advocates the bloody anti-christian cause, which, happily for
mankind, he has not the power of carrying into effect.

The two brothers of Constantius, between whom the empire of the
west was divided, were discontented with their shares, and quarrelled
about the division. They protected and encouraged the Nicene faith,
which their brother Constantius persecuted. They soon fell by the hands
of assassins, and Constantius became possessed of the empire of the
Roman world, as his father Constantine had been, but governed it with

still less wisdom. He died of a fever, on his way going to fight with his cousin Julien, who was, as I have said before, killed soon after in the Persian war.

I will pass over the short reign of Javian, and the longer reigns of the two brothers, Valentine and Valens, who divided the Roman empire between them. Valentine not only protected the Nicenes, but all who lived peaceably. Valens supported the Arians, and persecuted all who differed from them. I will pass over the other emperors, who governed the Roman world and the christian church, then become a kingdom of this world, till the reign of the emperor Theodosius the Great, who was called to the throne, and to take part in the government. He was the first baptised emperor who ever sat on the imperial throne. A fit of sickness, which threatened to be fatal, induced him to go to the baptismal font; in coming from which, he, unacquainted with the principles of the christian religion, believed he was divinely inspired, and issued the following decree, over which the christian has often weeped, and the infidel, not without reason, triumphed.

"It is our pleasure, that the nations which are governed by our *clemency* and *moderation,* should stedfastly adhere to the religion which was taught by St. Peter and St. Paul to the Romans; which faithful tradition has been preserved, and which is now possessed by the pontiff Damasius, (of Rome) and by Peter, bishop of Alexandria, men of apostolical holiness. According to the discipline of the apostles, and doctrine of the gospel, let us believe the sole deity of the Father, the Son and the Holy Ghost, under an equal magistracy, and a pious trinity. We authorise the followers of this doctrine to assume the title of *Catholic* christians; and as we judge that all others are extravagant madmen, we brand them with the infamous name of *Heretics,* and declare that their conventicles shall no longer usurp the respectable appellation of churches. Besides the condemnation of divine justice, they must expect to suffer the severest penalties, which our authority, guided by heavenly wisdom, shall think proper to inflict."

Agreeably to the above imperial decree, he drove out the Arian bishops of Constantinople, who refused to embrace his creed; occupied the church with a military guard; and conducted Gregory Nazianzan, who had before kept an orthodox conventicle, to the church, with solemn military triumph, and placed him, with his own hand, on the arch-episcopal throne. The good bishop, however, was deeply affected by the consideration, that he entered the fold rather like a wolf than a shepherd; and that, while the glittering arms were around him, necessary for his protection, he was receiving the curses of the people, and not their blessing. He did not, however, enjoy it long. A council of the clergy thought that the throne of the capital episcopate should be occupied by one of noble birth, and not by the son of a poor bishop. He withdrew from it to retirement, and they elected a nobleman, who consented to be baptised and consecrated. Nazianzan was one of the few of that age, whose writings are still in esteem. In six weeks after the military instalment of Gregory, which he himself records, the city had the appearance of one taken by the arms of a barbarian conqueror. Theodosius expelled from all the churches of his dominions, such as refused to profess their belief in his own faith.

This violent and tyrannical prince did not embrue his hands in kindred blood as Constantine had done; but he far exceeded him in persecution. He made it criminal to differ, even in the slightest degree, from his own religious opinions, and enacted the most cruel pains and penalties against such as did. The christian lesson, taught him by Libenius, the heathen philosopher, *"That religion ought to be planted in men's minds by reason and instruction, and not by force,"* had no effect. Constantine introduced this system of tyranny; but it was Theodosius who completed the establishment of the bloody idol of *uniformity in religion by human authority,* at whose shrine more human sacrifices have been made, than ever were offered on the polluted altars of Moloch. It was this prince who dignified the christian church, as founded on the council of Nice, and the infallible traditions, preserved and possessed by the metropolitan bishops of Rome and Alexandria, with the honourable title of Catholic, which it still retains; and degraded those who did not agree with him in receiving those traditions, and resting their faith on the authority of the council of Nice, or, to use his own words, branded them with the opprobrious name of *extravagant madmen and heretics*—a character severely known since that day. Vigilentius, and many of that age, who had the sense and courage to lift up their voice against the prevailing superstition, and to call the people back to the scriptures, were branded and punished under that character. Very numerous sacrifices, to this idol, were made of the Waldenses, the disciples of Wickliffe, &c. John Huss and Jerome of Prague,[9] by the sentence of the ecumenical council of Constantine, (which had certainly equal authority with the council of Nice, both having the authority and presence of the emperors,) expiated the crime of heresy in the flames. The arch heretics and extravagant madmen, Luther,[10] Calvin, Knox, &c. narrowly escaped that fate; but many of their followers were not so fortunate. The laws of Theodosius were executed to effect by the massacre of Paris, and the flames kindled in Smithfield by Mary, queen of England, in which the bishops, Cranmer, Latimer, Ridley, Hooper, and many others, were consumed, for disobeying his imperial decree.[11]

Theodosius, agreeable to this law, if it could have been executed, subjected myself, and all denominations of protestants with which I am acquainted, except the Rev. Mr. Wylie, and such as adhere to his opinions, to have been burned or hanged as heretics, long before this time. Many a joyful festivity has been held in Spain, at the burning of heretics in groupes (*auto de fe.*) It was, by some of their kings, considered and practised, as the most acceptable thanksgiving to God, for victory in war. Unfortunately, when the blessed reformation took place, and the

9. John Wycliffe (c. 1324–1383), English reformer and theologian, instigated the translation of the Bible into English, and he was condemned as a heretic but not molested; Jan Hus (c. 1372–1415) was a Czech nationalist, educator, and reformer, and was burned as a heretic; and Jerome of Prague (c. 1365–1416) was a Czech philosopher, theologian, and reformer, as well as a colleague of Hus. He too was burned as a heretic.

10. Martin Luther (1483–1546), German reformer, theologian, and Bible translator, was father of the Reformation.

11. Smithfield is a district in London where executions were carried out; Mary I, or Mary Tudor (1516–1558), daughter of Henry VIII and Catherine of Aragon, was known as "Bloody Mary," reigning as Queen of England from 1553 to 1558; Thomas Cranmer (1489–1556), Archbishop of Canterbury from 1533, attempted, during the reign of Edward VI, to make the Church of England Protestant, and under Queen Mary I he was declared a heretic and burned; Hugh Latimer (c. 1485–1555), Bishop of Worcester and an English reformer, was burned as a heretic during the reign of Queen Mary I; Nicholas Ridley (c. 1503–1555), Bishop of Lincoln, publicly denounced Queen Mary I, and was declared a heretic and burned at the stake; and John Hooper (d. 1555), Bishop of Gloucester and Worcester and an English Protestant reformer, was burned as a heretic during the reign of Queen Mary I.

reformers protested against the religion and uniformity established by Theodosius, *the great,* they did not wholly divest themselves of the principle. If they did not kindle the flames, they made a pretty free use of the gallows and lesser punishments, against such as would not worship the idol Uniformity, which Constantine had set up, and the worship of which, Theodosius completely established; and which has continued, hitherto, unchanged in the catholic church.

To find the true church of Christ, after the catholic church became degenerated—the hierarchy exalted—and superstition greatly increased—I recommend the reader to the perusal of Haweis, first chapter in each century, on *The true spiritual church of Christ.* Even in the third century, it will rarely be found among the high dignitaries; but among those of low degree, and such as were declared schismatics, for not acquiescing in some decisions of the metropolitan bishops and councils, and some questions about ordination and discipline. The number of these increased after the council of Nice, when by persecution they were banished from the empire, or suffered great oppression in it. It was some of those that spread the gospel, with the bible in their hands, but without the support of wealth, or the sword of the civil magistrate, into Persia, Tartary, China and India.

They were not clear of superstition or mistakes; but they did not enjoy wealth as the means of corruption, and led lives agreeable to the gospel; and there were still some in the catholic church, who plead with their mother, but their voice was not heard. In every instance, in which human uniformity has been enforced by the sword of the civil magistrate, many of the servants of Christ have suffered persecution. It is not in the wisdom of man to make a clean riddance of the tares from the wheat; and the Saviour has forbidden the attempt.

It is not necessary to make remarks on the character of Theodosius the Younger, or of Marcian, who called the two last of the author's standard councils, viz. the Ephesian and Chalcedon councils. They pursued the same system. Marcian was not a bad man; he married the empress Pulchrea, after a solemn engagement that he should never cohabit with her; she having devoted herself to perpetual virginity. Thus a marriage took place, under a solemn engagement not to accomplish the purpose for which marriage was instituted. I only mention this to shew the

substitutes invented for real religion in those times. I will drop the emperors, whose authority was, in their own opinion, to use the words of
Theodosius, guided by *heavenly wisdom,* (Infallibility!) and insert a few
extracts of the character of the church and priesthood of that age.

On this period, Haweis says, "The church, in all the pomp of rites and
ceremonies, groaned under the load of her own trappings. Vestments,
holidays, fasts, festivals, shrines, martyrs' tombs, holy water, with all the
trumpery so happily since improved, had begun to deck out the mer-
etricious Church of Rome. The growing virtue of relics, and the supposed efficacy of the intercession of departed saints, opened a door for
the grossest superstitions. Even Augustin himself laments, that the yoke,
under which the Jews were held, was liberty compared with the bondage
imposed on Christians." Patronage was then introduced, which has ever
since been the curse of even many protestant churches. Building churches
was an atonement for sin, and entitled the builder to the appointing of
his own pastor. This right is continued even in Britain. The deserts were
then peopled with monks and hermits, to whom an uncommon degree
of sanctity, and the power of working miracles, were ascribed.

"The presbyters wholly depended on bishops and patrons: The bishops were the creatures of patriarchs and metropolitans; or, if the see was
important, appointed by the emperor. So church and state formed the
first inauspicious alliance, and the corruption which had been plenti-
fully sown before, now ripened by court intrigues for political bishops of
imperial appointment, or at the suggestion of the prime minister."

"The establishment of christianity under Theodosius, and the uniformity enforced by his decrees, seemed to have placed the Catholic Church on the summit of eminence. This, added to all the wealth
poured into it, and the patronage now enjoyed, cast a glare of splendour
around it, which might lead an inattentive spectator to reverence this
establishment as a glorious Church; but corruption already preyed on its
vitals. The name prevailed, but the glory was departed. The profession
of Christianity had become general, but the power of it was nearly lost.
Ambition, pride, luxury, and all the legions of evils engendered by wealth
and power, lodged in her bosom. Heresies, contentions, schisms, rent
her garments and discovered her nakedness; whilst every hand grasp-
ing at pre-eminence, sought their own exaltation, instead of in honour

preferring one another, and in meekness instructing those who opposed themselves: the victors as well as the vanquished, afforded an humiliating spectacle of the absence of all divine principle and influence.

"The divided empire began to fall in pieces, and to be crushed by its own weight; whilst the feeble hands which grasped the trembling sceptre, scarcely defended the tottering throne on which they were seated. We are now sinking into Gothic barbarism, ecclesiastical usurpation, monkery triumphant, and the profession of christianity buried under fraud, follies, ceremonies, and all kinds of the most ridiculous and debasing superstitions." Haweis, vol. I. p. 301. Am. Edit. For much more to the same purpose, see Mosheim, Millot and Gibbons.

This was the state of the political catholic church, in that period, which Mr. Wylie selects for our imitation, in preference to the apostolic age, and the present state of the church in this or any protestant country. The period of history which I have stated, is from the council of Nice to that of Chalcedon, a period of 126 years, which he has held up as a period of the greatest perfection of the christian church, and this church dignified with the superb title of *Catholic* by Theodosius, who, in his own opinion, was guided by infallible *heavenly wisdom*. It has undergone no material change of principle since that period. It indeed progressed in ignorance and superstition, but not in the violence of persecution. If its *own infallible authority* was not called in question, it always admitted of more freedom of opinion than Theodosius and Justinian did. It always admitted of both the disciples of Augustine and Pelagius, to be in its communion, (viz. doctrinal Calvinists and Armenians.) The transfer of the infallibility from the emperor Phocas, to Boniface bishop of Rome, about the same time that Mahomet arose in the east, made no change of principle, nor did it prevent the struggle for power between kings and bishops. Theodosius, guided by *heavenly wisdom,* declared in a solemn decree, that the bishops of Rome were possessed of the infallible traditions which all must receive under the penalty of temporal and eternal vengeance. It was reasonable then, that those inspired bishops should enjoy and exercise the infallibility, and be the sole and final judges of truth on earth; they being the successors of St. Peter, and the vicars of Christ. If it was even now to be put to vote, I would prefer a learned clergyman to decide on religious truth, to such fortunate military adventurers as Constantine and Theodosius were, or as Napoleon now is. I am, however, so much of an infidel, as not to believe one word about the *infallibility* or *heavenly wisdom* claimed and exercised by these emperors and bishops. I have not faith enough to believe that Peter was ever at Rome. The scriptures say nothing of it; and he was an old man when he wrote his last epistle in Asia. Christ and his apostles gave testimony of their infallibility, by their holiness of life, and mighty and beneficent works, beyond the ordinary powers of nature. The author's standard emperors and bishops, by their general conduct, gave evidence that they were guided by another spirit.

I was astonished, indeed, on reading the Sons of Oil, to observe that he was so severe against the members of the catholic church of Theodosius in this state, as to assign the protection of them and their property from injury, as one of the reasons why he and those that think with him, could not obey (homologate) the civil government of the state. The author, and those who think and act as he does, ought, like honest men, to avow their creed, viz. that received and practised on, in what he represents as the purest time of the christian church; and declare to the world on what grounds they can, or do keep separate from the catholic church, or exclude papists from their communion; and what is still more extraordinary, endeavour to exclude them from breathing in the same air, or drinking in the same running stream with themselves. It cannot be for believing the infallibility of their church, nor in a purging fire, (purgatory) nor in the actual removal of the guilt of sin by baptism, nor the laying on of the hands of the bishops, nor for adoring the elements of the supper, nor worshipping and praying to the spirits of departed saints, or reverencing their supposed bones, nor indeed for almost any superstition that I know of, practised at this day in the Catholic church; surely not for the surplice, and endless ceremonies practised in their worship. All these were practised in his period of purity which he pompously holds forth as a perfect model for our imitation. Surely, to be consistent, the author ought to keep communion still with the church, dignified by the emperor Theodosius, with the honourable title of catholic. That emperor certainly set the most perfect example of ratifying and sanctioning the laws of the most high God, and the decrees of the church, and of that discretion so much recommended by the author.

He decided on the ordination and doctrine of the clergy, and purged the church fully, agreeably to the author's prescription, p. 24, &c. He, in the free exercise of this authority, appointed such bishops to princely thrones, as, in his discretion, he thought proper; and degraded from that pre-eminence more, perhaps, than a thousand, by one stroke of his pen. They might have deserved it, but they were not admitted to answer for themselves, agreeable to the Roman law, as the apostle Paul was, even in the reign of the monster Nero.

It is a received opinion, that the best things, when corrupted, become the worst. The persecuting laws of Theodosius, Justinian, &c. were more absurd and inconsistent than even the laws of the inhuman monsters Nero and Domitian. The laws of Moses did not permit any man to be condemned, but at the mouth of two witnesses. Theodosius, guided by heavenly wisdom, did not consider himself to be bound by such limits. He authorised the Catholics to kill the impious heretics at discretion. Charles II. and the parliament of England, followed this pious example; they cast two thousand gospel ministers out of the church in one day by the Bartholomew act, without hearing or trial, only because they would not prefer human authority to divine.[12] The same king and Scottish parliament acted in the same manner in Scotland, and with still greater severity.

Before presbytery or a political reformation was introduced in Scotland, the pious and justly revered martyrs, Mill, Hamilton, Wishart, and others, suffered martyrdom for the precious gospel of Christ; not for a political church establishment.[13] That church afterwards, under the instruction of the justly celebrated John Knox, who had been a preacher

12. Charles II (1630–1685) ruled as King of England from the Restoration of the monarchy in 1660; The Uniformity Act was passed in England on August 24, 1662 (St. Bartholomew's Day). It required that the Book of Common Prayer be used in all church services and that all ministers be ordained by bishops. Nearly two thousand ministers left the established church.

13. Walter Mylne (d. 1558), also Miln and Mill, was a Scottish priest influenced by the German reformers, and he was burned at St. Andrews as a heretic; Patrick Hamilton (c. 1504–1528), Scottish priest, became a disciple of Lutheranism, and was burned at St. Andrews as a heretic; and George Wishart (1513–1546), Scottish Protestant preacher, was a colleague of John Knox. He was convicted of heresy and burned at the stake at St. Andrews.

in the Episcopal church of England, during the reign of Edward VI.[14] to which he had retreated during the persecution in Scotland, taking the advice of the Saviour, when they were persecuted in one city, to flee to another, he, with the English divines, during the bloody persecution of Mary, fled to Frankford in Germany, and from thence to Geneva, where he became a worthy disciple of the celebrated John Calvin; from whence, returning to his native country, (Scotland) as soon as he could do it with safety, he, with admirable courage and perseverance, promoted the overturning of the religion of Constantine and Theodosius, and the substitution of the protestant, viz. the scriptural doctrine of the reformation in its stead, accompanied with the presbyterian form of church government, as nearly similar to what Calvin had introduced in Geneva, as was convenient; but not exclusive of moderate Episcopacy, such as appears to have taken place in the second century. Bishops who embraced the scriptural protestant doctrine, were continued in communion; and bishops, under the name of superintendants, to visit the parish clergy, were appointed to prescribed districts—they were responsible to the general assembly for their conduct, and removeable by it. This, however, did not succeed; the bishops, supported by the influence of the crown, though not constitutionally invested with the sovereignty over Christ's body, gradually prevailed, and overturned presbytery; but when the impositions of prelacy were increased by Charles I.[15] and archbishop Laud, the people revolted against it, and restored presbytery without the consent of the king. This dispute was silenced during the government of Cromwell,[16] who, though to this day called a usurper, always refused to usurp the authority of Christ over his own house. Charles II. had no such scruples. He restored prelacy on the ruins of presbytery, in a violent manner, and made many human sacrifices to the

---

14. Edward VI (1537–1553), son of Henry VIII and Jane Seymour, ruled as King of England from 1547 to 1553.

15. Charles I (1600–1649) reigned as King of England from 1625 until his execution during the English Civil War.

16. Oliver Cromwell (1599–1658): the leading Puritan figure during the English Civil War (1642–1651) between Royalists and Parliament. He served as Lord Protector of England from 1653 to 1658.

idol uniformity, which Constantine and Theodosius had set up. Under his reign, profligacy and every species of vice had full scope. After this, the inclination and the interest of the nation, in order to obtain internal peace, produced the re-establishment of presbytery in Scotland, and Episcopacy in England; and Ireland, where, to this day, eight tenths of the people are members of the Catholic church, as established agreeably to the heavenly wisdom of Theodosius and his successors, in the government of the church.

Time will not permit giving the history of all the political churches of Europe, but it would be easy to shew that those establishments checked the progress of the blessed reformation, and was at least the occasion of reconciling thousands, including many sovereigns, princes, and nobles, who, as their ancestors had supported the blessed reformation, back to the communion of the Catholic church. Finding they were only changing tyrants, they returned to their former masters. It must be known to every intelligent Protestant, that the blessed gospel was received and protected by the poor among the rocks of Piedmont, and the sterile islands of Scotland, after it was banished from the palaces and courts of emperors and princely bishops. The Lollards and Culdees in Britain kept up some knowledge of the word of life.[17] Wickliffe in England was the blessed instrument of reviving the church of Christ in that country, and throughout Europe. He not only preached the gospel as revealed in the scripture, but translated it and put it into the people's hands to judge for themselves. Lord Cabam,[18] and many other of his disciples in England, Germany, &c. expiated the guilt of heresy in the flames, agreeably to the laws of Theodosius. The church of Christ, banished to the

---

17. The Lollards were followers of Wycliffe and his teachings, in fourteenth- and fifteenth-century Britain. *Culdees* is Irish for "servants of God." They were loosely organized ancient communities of celibate men, chiefly inhabiting Ireland and Scotland. The last of the Irish communities disbanded in 1541 at Armagh. All Scottish communities converged on St. Andrews, where they disappeared in 1616.

18. Sir John Oldcastle (c. 1378–1417), known as Lord Cobham because he was married to the heiress of the Cobham family, espoused the teachings of John Wycliffe. He was condemned and hanged as a heretic on December 14, 1417. The gallows was set on fire while he was still hanging. He might therefore have been burned alive.

wilderness by emperors and princely bishops, was still, agreeably to his promise, preserved by the Waldenses, the Culdees, and the Wickliffites, and yielded a plentiful crop of martyrs to the flames. Their souls are represented (Rev. vi. 9.) as crying for vengeance on their persecutors.

Henry VIII. of England,[19] (of whom Sir W. Raleigh,[20] a competent judge, says, that if the record of all the other tyrants with which ever mankind had been cursed, were extinguished, his character would be a sufficient model for others,) quarrelled with the bishop of Rome, then the acknowledged head of the church of Christ on earth, about a question of divorce; he renounced the authority of the pope (bishop) of Rome, and declared himself pope, viz. head or supreme judge in all cases, civil or ecclesiastic, in England. And in the exercise of this authority, hanged or burned such as either acknowledged the pope's authority on the one hand, or denied his doctrine, as transubstantiation, &c. on the other. Governed by the *heavenly wisdom* by which Theodosius and his successors were guided, (which, however, I call wicked caprice) the religion of England, or at least the national creed, on this event, changed four times in twenty years. The clergy became perfect disciples in the change of oaths. Whoever would be king (head of the church) they would be vicar of Bray.[21] Oaths had become a form, and faith an article of traffic.

The choicest servants of God, in every age, have exhibited marks of imperfection; even the apostles, when not guided by divine inspiration, knew but in part, and were not already perfect. The primitive martyrs in the first and second centuries, laboured under great mistakes; so did those who suffered under bloody Mary in England, and in every other period. This appears to have been wisely ordered by divine providence, in a state of society in which all are depraved, and liable to frequent errors; in which he has made it our duty to depend on himself for reli-

19. Henry VIII (1491–1547), King of England from 1509 to 1547, removed the English Church from the pope's control.

20. Sir Walter Raleigh (c. 1552–1618), English statesman and adventurer, was a favorite of Queen Elizabeth I. He organized colonization expeditions to America and was ultimately convicted of treason and executed, under James I.

21. "The Vicar of Bray" is a folk ballad about the singing Vicar of Bray who changed his politics and religious convictions to suit what the times required.

gious instruction, as well as for the forgiveness of our offences, and not to depend on man, whose breath is in his nostrils, who goes astray from his birth, and drinketh up iniquity like water. To teach us this lesson, that the errors and mistakes of the eminent patriarchs, prophets, pious kings, apostles, martyrs and confessors, who enjoyed the smiles of heaven in an extraordinary degree, are not for examples but cautions. They are put on record for our learning. Yet, strange as it seems, it is nevertheless true, that erring men have not improved this practical lesson of instruction as they ought.

The Catholic church, in the third and fourth centuries, and to the present day, idolized the memories, the tombs, and even the bones of the martyrs of the first and second centuries, and substituted them in the place of the Saviour, by praying to them as intercessors with God. They copied their errors, and made additions to them, but not their virtues. In like manner, the rites, ceremonies, and forms, not introduced but from a principle of accommodation, practised by the godly bishops and other pious martyrs in bloody Mary's reign, was in the succeeding reign of Elizabeth,[22] copied after, as the testimony of the martyrs; and as error is always progressive, such additions were made to them by Laud and others, as would have excluded these martyrs from church communion, had they been living. The creeds and concordates, now in use in most of the political protestant churches, would exclude the reformers if they were now living. The solemn league and covenant would exclude all who did not with their hearts believe that Scotland, England, and Ireland were morally bound to be in a perpetual league, as separate and independent nations, and bound to support the royal prerogative, and the privileges of three distinct parliaments, as they stood in the year 1643. Those who suffered privations, tortures, and death, in the tyrannical reigns of the two last Stuarts, doubtless also laboured under mistakes. They were, however, deprived of their natural and unalienable right of worshipping almighty God agreeably to their own knowledge of his perfections and his will, by the sanctioning and ratifying power of the civil magistrate, agreeable to Mr. Wylie's system, and the public

---

22. Elizabeth I (1533–1603), daughter of Henry VIII and Anne Boleyn, reigned as Queen of England from 1558 to 1603.

conscience of Hobbes, then prevalent. If the Saviour was correct, in declaring to the Jews in his own day, (Mat. xxiii. 35) that all the guilt of *the righteous blood shed, from that of righteous Abel to the blood of Zacharias,* should be visited on that generation, the Rev. Mr. Wylie, and those who think with him, should carefully examine how far they make themselves heirs to the guilt of the blood of the martyrs, shed from the time of Constantine and the council of Nice, to the present day.

How far, or in how many things those who believe in the divinity of, and atonement made by him who was, by divine direction, called Jesus (viz. the Saviour from sin) may differ in other things, or even what degree of indistinctness their impressions may be of those very important principles, has employed the wisdom of ages, without success, to define; nor will it ever be defined with precision in this world. God, who knows all our motives of action, and the circumstances by which our actions are influenced, has reserved the power of this discrimination in his own hand, and has restrained men from usurping his authority. The obligation on all men to make the moral law of their nature, the rule of their conduct, can never be dispensed with, unless a change of the divine nature takes place, which, even to contemplate with approbation, is blasphemy. That law, as a condition of life, and the positive institution of the covenant of works having given place to the gospel, the plan and discovery of which, results solely from the free and sovereign will of God; by the same sovereign will all the conditions of enjoying gospel privileges are prescribed.

The conditions, as prescribed by the forerunners of the blessed Saviour who came to prepare his way are, John iii. 36. "He that believeth on the Son hath everlasting life, and he that believeth not the Son, shall not see life." And by Paul and Silas, to the keeper of the prison, "believe on the Lord Jesus Christ, and thou shalt be saved." But that believing, viz. faith if it is genuine, worketh by love, Gal. v. 6.—"love is the fulfilling of the law." They are only Christ's "friends, that do what he commands them." John xv. 14.—And faith without works is dead, James ii. 17. The Saviour's rule of moral conduct towards our neighbour, is, "whatsoever ye would that men should do unto you, do ye the same unto them." Mat. vii. 12. These are all the terms of christian communion, which I find prescribed by the Saviour and his apostles, to the New Testament church. Whosoever does not profess this faith, and endeavour to live agreeable to these rules, are not Christ's disciples, nor entitled to communion in his church; and to such as add to, or take away from them, he, in the conclusion of the New Testament, says, he will add to him the plagues written in that book, and take away his part out of the book of life. With such as reject this faith, or disobey these rules, they are to have no religious fellowship. Further than this, the church is not authorised to go by its glorious head.

Civil governments, appointed by the people in pursuit of their own happiness, are under a moral obligation to protect all men who lead quiet and peaceable lives, and punish such as do not; they are, in so doing, nursing fathers to the church, which few of them have ever been. Many of the heathen emperors persecuted it, but the imperial union of church and state, has far exceeded them in violence and cruelty, and in keeping the human mind in darkness.

The author, and others who think with him, complain much of our governments for granting liberty of conscience, toleration &c. There is no such thing in our laws. They made no religious establishment, of which toleration, as understood in national political churches, is the spurious brood. Jehovah, as the peculiar king of the Israelitish theocracy, tolerated so far as not to authorize the civil magistrates to punish much greater departures from the purity of the moral law, than any of the United States have. He tolerated polygamy, concubinage and divorces at discretion, the perpetual slavery of aliens and their posterity, and several other deviations from the moral law, which our laws prohibit and punish. Sadducees who denied the resurrection of the dead and the existence of angels and spirits, were not only tolerated to be in the communion of the church, but to be the priests of it. Such was the wisdom of God; but he gave them the moral law for their rule, as they should account to himself.

If these zealous enemies of that christian forbearance, agreeable to the spirit of the gospel, which they call toleration, would only with the spirit of meekness, without passion, peruse Rom. 14. throughout, they would perhaps think with me, that most of the regular protestant churches, might and ought still to be in one communion. None of them are perfect, but most of them, with the holy patriarch Job, "have the root of the matter in them." I have heard much of the importance and necessity of public testimony bearing. The histories and doctrines of the new testament, contain the testimony of Christ's church. To add to it is presumption.

I will conclude this paragraph with a few sentences from the apostle Paul, Rom. xiv. "Who art thou that judgest another man's servant? To his own master he standeth or falleth.—But why dost thou judge thy brother? or why dost thou set at nought thy brother? for we shall all stand before the judgment seat of Christ. Let us not therefore judge one another any more." If the same spirit which guided the apostle, had continued to guide the church, there never would have been political churches, nor persecution for difference of opinion. This would have passed to the judgment seat of Christ.

In page 40, the author says, "Most, if not all, of the state constitutions, contain *positive immorality*. Witness their recognition of such rights of conscience, as sanction every blasphemy, which a depraved heart may believe to be true. The recognition of such rights of conscience, is insulting to the Majesty of heaven." In the next page, he particularly denounces the constitution of Pennsylvania, for permitting the people to reserve from the powers of government, "The indefeasible right of worshipping Almighty God, whatever way a man's conscience may dictate; and declares, that this shall, *for ever,* remain inviolate."

The words *whatever way,* are not in that instrument; but I admit them. The constitution, in this instance only, reserved what they had no moral power to take away. The master has not the power of taking the right from his slave of worshipping God agreeable to his own knowledge of his perfections and his will. Worship offered in obedience to the master's knowledge and judgment of the will of God, that is, the master's conscience, would indeed be a mockery; it would be insulting to the all-seeing God, who knows our thoughts before we utter them. If the slave has this right, it must be unalienable. The representatives of Pennsylvania in convention, could have no greater claims on the obedience of their constituents, than masters have over their slaves. They could not oblige them to worship agreeable to their own reason and judgment, on an implicit faith. All acceptable worship is a reasonable service rendered in faith, agreeable to the discoveries of the will of God, as revealed to the worshippers. If he is ignorant, or ill-informed of it, his sin, if information is attainable, is but worship rendered agreeable to the judgment of another man, contrary to his own, is a presumptuous sin, nearly approaching to that which has no forgiveness.

The author, indeed, personifies conscience, as if it was an independent agent. He charges it with legitimating what God's law condemns; and acting paramount to the divine law, rendering virtuous and laudable the most damnable errors—the most horrid blasphemies, &c. Page 41.

It is necessary to enquire what this monster is. It is no person: it is an exercise of mind of every man possessed of reason. It is not even a faculty of mind. It is the exercise of memory, recollecting what the person has done; and of reason, comparing our conduct with the law; and of the judgment, drawing a conclusion. We may suppose Judas reasoned thus: He that betrayeth an innocent person to death, breaketh the law. I have betrayed an innocent person to death; therefore I have broken the law. Reason and judgment are exercised also before the action contemplated is committed, in comparing the proposed action with the law, and drawing the conclusion. This is called an antecedent exercise of conscience, and the other a subsequent exercise of it.

The apostle Paul treats of both, Rom. ii. 14, 15. "For when the Gentiles which know not the law, do by nature the things contained in the law, these, having not the law, are a law unto themselves: which shew the work of the law written in their hearts, their conscience also bearing witness, and their thoughts in the mean while accusing or else excusing one another." It is evident, from the context, that by *law* here is meant the written law revealed by the prophets; and that by *nature,* is meant the remains of the *law* of nature in man, by which their moral conduct is governed; which shews that the office of conscience is the same in all men, whether they have the written word or not. It *bears witness;* this is the exercise of memory, and a very important one. In this exercise, conscience may for a time be silenced or seared, but it cannot be extinguished. It haunts the slumbers, and even the pleasures, of the wicked, and will torment the finally impenitent through eternity.

Their thoughts (viz. their reason and judgment) *in the mean while accusing or else excusing one another,* viz. comparing their conduct with the law, and deciding favourably or unfavourably, agreeable to that rule. Conscience is not here represented as that rampant tyrant that *legitimates,* viz. makes laws to sanction every blasphemy, *paramount* to the divine law. It is the *recorder* of the actions, and the *accuser* or *excuser* of them, and is guided solely by the divine law, as far as that law is known. It is so far from being a law-making power, that it is a term solely relative to law. If there was no divine law, there could be no place or use for that exercise of the faculties of mind called conscience. It would have no rule nor object.

Many divines have called conscience God's *vicegerent* in the soul of man, and not improperly, for it is a faithful and diligent accuser of every known breach of the divine law; it will not give the sinner rest under the knowledge of guilt; and it is also a very comfortable approver of conduct, done agreeable to the divine law. The apostle (2 Cor. i. 12.) says, "Our rejoicing is this, the testimony of our conscience," &c. Heb. xiii. 18. "We trust we have a good conscience." The term conscience is more than thirty-six times used in the New Testament, but in no instance in the sense in which the author has used it, viz. as a law-making power, and not subject to the law of God, but itself a paramount law. Indeed I cannot reduce the use he makes of it to common sense. That many have exalted human reason above the revealed manifestations of God and his law, I well know; but that conscience, which is a relative term to law, and regulated by it, should be exalted above law, even to be law itself, seems a contradiction in terms. Deists substitute human reason and their knowledge of the law of nature, in the place of supernatural revelation; and thus, like the Jews of old, reject the counsel of God against themselves; but still they permit conscience to act in its proper place—to act agreeably to the law, the obligation of which they acknowledge. They cannot do otherwise; they may have their understanding blinded; they may, by the obstinate depravity of their will, refuse to receive instruction, and be destroyed for want of knowledge; but they cannot divest themselves of that exercise of the faculties of the mind, which is called conscience; and it will decide agreeable to the divine law impartially—agreeably to the knowledge thereof possessed by the understanding.

Here it is proper to premise, that the mind is a simple, undivided power of acting, or determining how it ought to act; that speaking of the faculties of the mind as distinct from each other, is only done for illustration, in the same manner as we are permitted to do of the divine perfections. God is one, undivided and indivisible; yet he permits us to speak of his divine perfections, in a manner suited to our capacities. The mind of man is so also, but in a very subordinate degree. Mind or spirit is indivisible, therefore immortal; and even in this respect it, though very faintly, resembles its Creator. He is infinite and independent of all creatures; angels, arch-angels, and the spirits or minds of men, are wholly dependent on him, not only for their existence, but for the continuance thereof, and their happy enjoyment of it: for it is in him they all live, and move, and have their being. It is in his hand the breath of man is, for he received it from his Creator, and none of his fellow men have a right to deprive him of the breath of life, which God freely gave, except in defence of his own life, or in obedience to a positive command of God, or to the laws of society, enacted agreeably to the moral law.

I was a member of the convention of Pennsylvania; and of the committee that prepared the constitution for public discussion. Knowing the mistakes that had been promoted, either through ignorance or artifice, or both, among pious well-meaning people; to prevent giving them offence, I endeavoured to have the term conscience suppressed, and the definition of it, viz. *That no man should be obliged to worship God contrary to his own knowledge and judgment of his will,* substituted for it; but failed. It was not easy to convince those with whom I acted, that people did not generally know the meaning of a term in such general use as *conscience*. It would have been much easier for Constantine or Theodosius to have made their own conscience the rule, than for a numerous convention to do it. They possessed above sixty different consciences, or judgments of their own, differing less or more from each other. They laid the constitution before the people before it was enacted; after this the convention was dissolved. The author's standard emperors had each but one conscience or judgment, and this was changeable; and they were possessed of absolute power, which enabled them to oblige the consciences of all their subjects to submit implicitly to their own conscience, in all its changes, or suffer for disobedience to it.

Mr. Wylie says, plausibly enough, that *the divine law is the rule;* so says the church of Rome. But what is that divine law? not the moral law, nor the precepts of the gospel, but such parts of the peculiar law of Moses, as he thinks proper to revive, after it has been eighteen hundred years abrogated, and even that only agreeably to the construction to be given to it by the civil magistrate, in the exercise of his *ratifying* and *sanctioning* power of the laws of the *most high God, equal to what he does with civil laws.* Hence, according to him, we must give up our own judgment and reason, (viz. conscience) implicitly to the conscience of *his* civil magistrate, and without any assurance of the infallibility of that magistrate. I will appeal to the author himself, if we are to give up our own judgment and our responsibility to God, if it is not better at once to join the Roman Catholic church, which is certified by Theodosius, to possess infallibility, and, as asserted from antiquity, the power of remitting our sins if we err; than to depend upon his own, or the deistical philosopher Hobbes' public conscience, who cannot forgive our offences.

That this is not a forced construction of his sentiments, is evident from his own words. He charges the constitution with sanctioning whatever a "depraved heart may believe to be true." I believe the hearts of all men are depraved, viz. have a corrupted nature, but that many increase their own depravity by habits of wickedness; but I ask the author whether he thinks that compelling them by civil penalties to profess or practice what they believe not to be true, or to be sinful, will remove that depravity, or increase it? He thinks it will remove it, or else he would not recommend the practice. I think directly the contrary, and have scripture and the experience of all ages on my side. Dealing deceitfully or in guile with the heart-searching God, and obeying man in preference to him, is, in scripture, branded as a sin of the deepest dye. The effects of this on the moral character of nations, might be shewn in numerous instances. It is sufficient to mention the well known rapid progress of profligacy, promoted by the laws of Constantine, to controul the consciences of men; and the extreme profligacy produced in England and Scotland, on the restoration of the house of Stuart. The conformity, enforced by the same means, in the preceding period in Scotland, had prepared an abundant nursery of hypocrites, who, on the change of the civil magistracy, became the most violent persecutors of what they, by compulsion, solemnly professed. The author ought to have known, however, that our laws provide for the punishment of vice and immorality; among which, blasphemy, viz. a profane use of the names of any of the persons of the trinity are expressly enumerated. The very section which he quotes, protects the worship of the Almighty God only, and not of

Baal or Molech, nor the idol of uniformity in religion, (prescribed and enforced by depraved man) which has been no less bloody; it has destroyed not only the bodies, but the souls of men.

In page 41, the author says, "But, supposing for a moment, that men had such a right, let us enquire how they came by it? Either they must have it by derivation from God, or hold it independently of him."

This supposition is contrived to be a foundation for a number of dilemmas, calculated to alarm the passions, but not to inform the judgment, accompanied with so many notes of astonishment, as seem to have affrighted himself; nor is it very singular, for men to be affrighted with monsters created by their own imagination. I will not, however, examine these sophisms in detail; but, to his supposition, I answer by denying the assertion on which it is founded, viz. that our constitution "gives a legal security and establishment to gross heresy and idolatry, under the notion of liberty of conscience."—p. 40. and that we maintain that "conscience can legitimate what God's law condemns."—p. 41.

I answer again, that the charges are wholly unfounded. The constitution gives no liberty of conscience. This was not in the power of the convention to give or to withhold. The members of the convention were of the same opinion with the Westminster divines, viz. "That God alone is Lord of the conscience, and hath left it free from the doctrines and commandments of men," and that "God, the supreme lord and king of all the world, hath ordained civil magistracy to be under him, and over the people, for his own glory and the public good." But they did not find it in any place in scripture, that ever God, the supreme lord of all the world, had transferred to the civil magistrate, his sovereignty over the conscience, viz. the reason and judgment of men in things for which they were only accountable to himself. If he had, there would have been lords of the conscience, as many as there were supreme civil magistrates. Christ instituted a gospel ministry for the edification of souls. Civil magistracy was introduced by the law of nature, for the happiness of society, as marriage and the subjection of children to their parents were; hence, the Westminster divines, and all approved commentators, derive the relation of magistrates and subjects, and their relative duties, from the fifth precept of the moral law, which is a compend of the law of nature. God positively instituted but one government among men, and that was temporary, suited to a peculiar dispensation; and in that government he left the conscience perfectly free from human restraints. Nothing was to be punished as a crime but by his express command; nor restrained even from deviations from the moral law, further than he explicitly prescribed. Christ and his apostles transferred no such power to magistrates; they taught obedience, agreeable to the law of nature, to such magistrates as God, in his providence, had set over them; and set the example by their own practice. The convention durst not usurp this authority, in imitation of Constantine, Theodosius, &c. In doing so, they would have rebelled against the sovereign Lord of all the world.

That they established gross heresy, blasphemy, &c. in the constitution, is therefore, false in fact. They did not dare to make any exclusive establishment of religion by their own authority; therefore, there was no place for qualified toleration, such as has arisen from the exclusive establishments in Europe. Mr. Wylie's denomination is as much established as any other, if they do not disturb the public peace, or defraud their neighbours or the government of their just dues. Why then should his eye be evil, because the government is good.

His dilemma, of a *right to obey the divine law, and a right not to obey it; a right to obey God, and a right not to obey him,* as given by the constitution, is a mere sophism. The constitution gives no rights respecting religion or obeying God; the convention had none to give, nor the power of withholding any; they were not constituted nor authorised by any law divine or human, to sit as judges on religious doctrines or rights; these were decided in the New Testament by the inspiration of the Holy Ghost, three hundred years before Constantine and the council of Nice sat in judgment on them, and perverted the apostolic decisions, and made additions to them. The Saviour and his apostles did not prescribe death or lesser punishments against such as disobeyed their infallible decisions, as the emperors and councils did against those who disobeyed their fallible, and, in many instances, corrupt decisions. Of consequence, Mr. Wylie is practically in unison with the emperors and councils, and not with Christ and his apostles.

To treat of *liberty* and *right* in a more abstract manner, is not necessary on this question, as it relates not to the government of Pennsylvania, but to the rights and liberties which the people retained in their own hands, and reserved from the power of the government, some of which are in their own nature unalienable; such as the right to which the author so violently objects; a right, which, as I have shewn, even a slave retains; and a right, for the retaining of which, all the martyrs of Jesus lost their lives, rather than part with it. Several of the reserved rights are of a political nature, for the security of civil liberty. Because the people reserve this unalienable right, the author pronounces the government *immoral, illegitimate,* &c. and denounces and excludes from church communion such as acknowledge, or as he expresses it, *homologates* its authority, or gives any *tessera* of obedience, even to its lawful commands, &c. This condition of christian or social communion is not derived from the New Testament. If the government had usurped that authority, for the want of which he denounces it, it would have been justly blamed by all who prefer the authority of Christ, to the authority of depraved man. But the author is so infatuated with the love of that characteristic mark of the man of sin, *persecution,* that he denounces all civil governments that have not that mark, and that do not exercise it agreeable to his opinion. Our governments are necessarily imperfect, being the work of imperfect men; but I sincerely bless God for it, that they have not usurped God's sovereignty over the conscience, and are not stained with having or exercising the dreadful power of persecuting for obeying God, rather than man. In this, the United States have set a laudable example to other nations, and the ministers of Christ are not entangled in the affairs of state.

If, in the constitution, instead of reserving *to every man the right of worshipping almighty God agreeably to the dictates of his own conscience,* it had been expressed, that *no man should be compelled to worship God agreeably to the dictates of the consciences of any other man or body of men,* it would have answered precisely the same purpose, and probably have been less liable to the cavils of those that are skilful to find fault. It has been impressed on the author's people, and he boldly, but very absurdly, asserts it, that the clause, as it stands, makes conscience a law-making power, paramount to the law of God. I have shewn already that conscience is not a law-making power, and that it exists only by its relation to the law of God; that this is its sole rule of acting, as far as it is known. The people of Pennsylvania have reserved, in this instance, no further right or liberty than that no other man's reason or judgment, (viz. conscience) shall have authority to interfere between their own conscience and the authority of God, to whom they are to be accountable at the last day. In fact, that they shall not be obliged to receive the divine law agreeable to the construction of such emperors and councils as the author, in unison with the church of Rome, sets forth as standard authorities. The constitution, thus understood, would be objected to by few who are well disposed to receive the gospel as it was revealed. This, however, would not satisfy the author, who considers the constructive and sanctioning power of the magistracy to be essential.

To simplify the subject still further, the question between the author and myself is not whether or not conscience should judge of and apply the law of God with respect to religion. It is presumed that all are agreed, that the worship of God should be a conscientious and reasonable service. Rom. xii. 1; 2 Tim. i. 3. "And that all true worshippers *serve God with their conscience*," as the apostle Paul did. But the question at issue is, whether we shall worship God with our own, or with another man's conscience. The apostle served God with his own conscience, so do all acceptable worshippers; this I advocate. The author says no, this is making conscience paramount to the law of God, &c. We must serve God with the consciences of emperors and councils, or of the civil magistrate, in the exercise of his ratifying and sanctioning power, at his discretion—[See Sons of Oil, p. 30.] I ask the author if ever the pope of Rome, Mahomet, or Hobbes asked more?

In p. 39, the author commences his attacks on the federal constitution, in a manner that discovers his ignorance of the nature and object of a federal government. He says this constitution "does not even recognise the existence of a God, the king of nations," &c. Did he seriously expect that a federal government must also have a federal religion, and a federal creed? None of the councils of Nice, Chalcedon, Constance, or Trent, have yet formed such a creed, nor prescribed such a religion as would apply to such a government.

Federal government is the result of the union of different sovereign states, not for internal purposes, but as a bond of union for general defence, and foreign relations. They are distinct from an alliance, which has only a particular object in view. The earliest account we have of confederation, was between Abraham and Aner, Eshcal and Mamre, neighbouring chiefs of the Amorites, viz. of the devoted nations. When Abraham removed from thence to the land of the Philistines, he entered into a similar covenant with the king of Geser, which Isaac renewed, to continue for three generations; they were also of the devoted nations. Religion surely was no article in their instrument of union. These chiefs possibly worshipped the true God, but they certainly had no part in the Abrahamic covenant. Of the Lycian confederation in Asia, or the Etruscan in Italy, we know but little. Of the Amphicton and Achian confederations in Greece, we are better informed; but there was no difference in religion, they were all worshippers of Jupiter, but each in his own way. The want of such confederation in Gaul, Spain, &c. gave facility to Caesar's conquests, and brought these nations under the Roman yoke. The Swiss confederation, being nearer our own times and circumstances, is more to our purpose. The cantons are eighteen in number, though they did not all confederate at one time, they were all of the Catholic religion, as it was handed down by Constantine and Theodosius, from the council of Nice. The blessed reformation was introduced by Zuinglius,[23] in the canton of Zurich, which, supported by other eminent reformers, was received in Berne and several other cantons. In short, several cantons are still Catholics, and others nearly equally divided. When Geneva, the seat of Calvin and Beza,[24] declared independence of their sovereign bishop, they put themselves under the protection of this confederation, which enjoyed the smiles of heaven in the continuance of peace and independence for the greatest length of time of any nation of Europe, and with the least expense. They have no federal religion or federal creed.

This famous confederation the colonies took for their model, as far as circumstances would admit. Their representatives, under the first confederation, were, from a jealousy of liberty, too limited in their powers; they had the power of peace and war—of raising armies and navies, but not of regulating commerce, nor raising money, except by requisitions on the state legislatures, to which they could not compel obedience. The

---

23. Ulrich Zwingli (1484–1531): Swiss Protestant reformer.
24. Theodore Beza (1519–1605): theologian and colleague of Calvin.

national character could not, in this way, be supported. The members were merely diplomatic characters, appointed, instructed, and liable to be recalled, by the state legislatures.

A revision of the confederation became necessary; by this the powers were so much enlarged as enabled them to carry their former powers into effect; the form was changed from one to two branches, and an executive magistrate chosen by the people for a short period; the representatives in both houses are also appointed by the states for a limited period; but congress still are representatives of sovereign states, who have the sole government of their internal concerns, both civil and religious. Congress has no more internal power than is necessary to carry the external powers, for the public defence and general welfare, into effect. No member can be voted for but by such voters as are qualified, agreeable to the laws of the respective states which he represents. How would the author himself contrive a religion or creed, to be sworn to by such a diplomatic corps, so as to correspond with the laws of the respective states? I am ashamed of this detail; every citizen does, or ought to know it—but the author says (p. 76) the members of their church are mostly aliens; for their information I have made this detail.

One qualification, however, is prescribed, in which all the states, notwithstanding the diversity of their laws and opinions, agree—that is, that all the members of the federal government shall swear, as they shall answer to God, to the faithful performance of their duty. This certainly excludes atheists. Several of them do so in the English form, using the bible in the oath; but many, probably most, with the hand lifted up to heaven. And each house of congress elect a minister of the gospel (of some protestant denomination) to open the business by prayer every morning, and to preach the gospel to them every Lord's day. This is certainly as great a testimony in favour of the "existence of God the king of nations," and their belief of the christian religion, as it is competent for such a diplomatic body, possessed of no internal power but for external purposes, to give. I leave it to the author himself to explain, how he came to assert that the federal government *did not acknowledge the being of a God, the king of nations.* I am sorry that this is not the only misrepresentation he has made of the government from which he receives protection.

CHAPTER III

Arguments from the law of Moses examined—Sufficiency of the scriptures vindicated—The reformed churches considered—Toleration and establishments—Some difficulties examined.

The author of the manuscript, after with propriety having strongly asserted the unchangeable perfection and perpetuity of the moral law, admits that the typical institutions, which were shadows of good things to come, as soon as the substance appeared, all fled away; but that the moral law, including the penalties of the Sinai covenant, existeth still, and adds: "*Indeed a law without a penalty, seems to me to be no law at all, but a mere directive thing.* Now the reason why the divine lawgiver ordered every open and manifest breach of the divine law to be punished, was because it was an open rebellion and sin against God."

Throughout the whole of the manuscript, he enforces the principle, that the execution of penalties by man, are punishment for sin against God. This is no new principle; it is the principle upon which all the persecutions by Constantine and his successors, of the Waldenses, Wickliffites, and other witnesses for the truths of the gospel under popery, was founded; and for this meritorious work, the executioners of those penalties were, in the later period, rewarded with the pardon of all the sins they had committed, and sometimes of what they would hereafter commit. On this principle Philip II. of Spain,[1] who knew of no better

---

1. Philip II (1527–1598), husband of Mary I of England, was refused coronation as

way of expressing his gratitude to God, for obtaining a great victory, than by applying to the holy court of inquisition, who were under his holiness the pope, God's vicegerents for punishing sin, to grant him an auto de fe, viz. a certain number of sinners to be burnt in the flames, for their sins against God. When this reputedly holy, and, at least, zealous prince, feasted his eyes with their torments, and one of them upbraided him with his cruelty, he answered, that if his own son was guilty of such sin against God, he would put him to death in the same manner. The sin was what they called heresy. This was acting up to the principles laid down by both the authors, viz. of the Sons of Oil and the manuscript.

Perhaps, however, they may object that this zealous prince and faithful son of the church, was mistaken in the application of the rule. This is granted. But have they any assurances, more than their own self-confidence, that they would not also be mistaken, in executing the same principle? Are they more infallible than the Pope? They plead scripture, and so did he, and acted on his opinion of the scripture, as laid down by the general councils of the church—so do they. This principle would also apply well to the Sadducees and mortal deists, who deny a future state of rewards and punishments—therefore sin ought to be punished in this world, lest it should escape altogether.

In maintaining the penalties of the Sinai covenant, to be a portion of the moral law, they both of them overthrow what they have advanced in favour of the perfection and immutability of that law. For the penalties of the Sinai covenant were not from the beginning, nor for twenty-five hundred years after mankind and the church had existed, and after crimes that deserved punishment were in the world. Therefore, on their own principles, it was imperfect all this time. A number of these penalties of death were for disobedience to such parts of the Sinai covenant as they acknowledge is abolished; such as making a compound of the holy oil, eating leavened bread at the passover, not keeping some of the solemn feasts, &c. consequently, their moral law has made another change, and is not immutable. The moral law not only reaches to overt acts, but to

King of England. He ruled Spain from 1556 to 1598. The Spanish Inquisition reached new heights during his reign.

the thoughts and intents of the heart; the Sinai covenant only reached the outward man; therefore the moral law of the authors is imperfect. It was never intended to be the moral law. To use the Saviour's words, "*It was not so from the beginning.*"

Christian nations have carried penalties much further than the peculiar law of Moses did; they punish for having more wives than one, or keeping a concubine besides their wives, and declare the children born by the additional wives or concubines, illegitimate; and they punish a married man, as for adultery, for cohabiting with a single woman. They punish with very high penalties, any man, whether citizen or stranger, for introducing a slave into the country, however honestly procured abroad. This was not only tolerated, but authorised, by the judicial laws. They protect such slaves as are in the country equal to the citizens; and, except in one state, punish the wilful killing of a slave with death. I apprehend, that even the author will agree with me, that these laws are agreeable to the moral law, and useful to enforce obedience to it; and perhaps that some of the penalties should be higher than they are. Now these, and other cases that might be named, are all different from, or contrary to, the law of Moses. Are these laws improper, or are they additions to the law of Moses? If they are additions, they are forbidden in that law, and on their own principles they ought to be abandoned. The peculiar law of Moses, including its penalties, therefore, is not the moral, perfect, and unchangeable law, equally obligatory on all men, in all times and circumstances.

The peculiar law of Israel, as I have said, was local and temporary, calculated for a special purpose, and particular situation and state of the world. If it had pleased God to select any portion of Sweden, Denmark, or Norway, instead of the very mild and temperate climate and very fertile soil of Palestine, for the theatre on which a peculiar law was to have been administered, it is not to be supposed that they would have been forbidden to kindle a fire, or seek provisions on the sabbath; otherwise they would have been in weekly danger of being chilled with cold and perishing with hunger, in those frozen regions, where, for a great part of the year, the sun only faintly glimmers on them but for a few hours in the day. Many other peculiarities and penalties might be mentioned, which could not have been supported in that country, without much more of a constant miracle than in Palestine, where its natural situation, warmth, and fertility, was exceedingly suitable for the purpose. The moral law was equally suited to mankind, in every situation and climate in the world; therefore the penalties and peculiarities of the Sinai covenant were not the moral law. This is evident, from their not existing in the time of the patriarchs, before or after the flood; and from their not being extended beyond the symbolically holy land, nor by the apostles of Christ to the christian church.

He admits "that the ceremonial and typical institutions, which were all shadows of good things to come, as soon as the things themselves appeared, the shadows did all flee away; but the reasons of the moral law, both of its precepts and penalties, do still exist."

That the reasons of the moral law, both of its precepts and its penalties, do still exist, is admitted. The precepts and penalties of the moral law must always be the same, because God is always the same. He will not hold the breaker of the precepts of this law guiltless at the final judgment; he will even in this world visit the iniquities of the fathers on the children; he no doubt has often done so; he no doubt did so in the destruction of the old world, and of Sodom, and also of the Canaanitish nations, with which he had borne long; he does so in the fall of empires; he has done so with the Asiatic and other churches; he has done so for a long time with the Jews; he has often, in his providence, done so with monstrously wicked men. But this is the prerogative of God, and not of man.

The moral law of nature makes it the duty of men to form civil societies, to provide for their own security; and when they have done so, he calls it his ordinance. The moral law of nature, written in the heart of man, and revealed to him, makes it both the duty and interest of civil government to enact laws agreeable to the moral law, and enforce obedience to it. This is necessary, for the peace of society, that the people may lead quiet and peaceable lives, in all godliness and honesty. But it is not their duty to interfere with God's authority over the reason and judgment of man, in those things, for which he holds them solely accountable to himself. No human penalties can punish pride, hypocrisy, or want of love to God and our neighbour.

In p. 5. he quotes 1 Tim. i. 9, 16, to prove the binding obligation of the law of Moses, shewing that the law is made to punish transgressors; and the apostle enumerates certain offences that ought to be restrained by penal laws; but because the catalogue is not full, he adds, if there be anything else contrary to *sound doctrine,* viz. the doctrine of the moral law, not the doctrine of the peculiar law of Israel; for God did not see meet, in that state of society, to authorise sinful judges to punish their fellow sinners, to the extent which the moral law requires. *Whoremongers,* the first in the catalogue, are much more restrained under our laws than under the judicial law; but they had the same moral law for the rule of their conduct towards God and their fellow men, that we have. But it prescribed no penalties for man to execute on man. The Sinai covenant restrained Israel for wise purposes, from changing or extending the penalties of it. Christians have power, from the law of their nature, to extend or change the penalties, agreeable to the moral law, according to circumstances. The moral reasons of punishment were restricted to the laws; they are not so to christians.

The learned Scott, on this text, says, "The moral law was holy, just, and good, resulting from the nature of God and man, and man's relation to him and each other. Even the ceremonial law had a relative goodness for the time, as typical of Christ's gospel, and the entire Mosaic dispensation was good, as separating Israel from other nations, affording them the means of grace, and introducing the christian economy; *but to enforce the Mosaic law on christians,* or to teach them to depend on their own obedience, for any part of their justification, was contrary to the real meaning of the law itself, and intention of the lawgiver."

The author admits that the typical part of the law of Moses vanished at the appearance of the substances. The apostle tells us of the whole law being a shadow of good things to come, and of a whole change of the old for the new covenant; that this happy change was not by their covenant, viz. the Sinai covenant.

What is the law of commandments which Christ abolished in his flesh? certainly not the moral law of the ten commandments; that can never be abolished. It certainly must be that law of commandments, which, like a middle wall of partition, kept Jew and Gentile separate, not only in their worship, but in their municipal laws, their eating, their clothing, and other common concerns of life; and this could be no other than the peculiar law of Israel, or old covenant, which the same apostle saith, elsewhere, was ready to vanish away. Having perfect confidence in the prophets and apostles, I do not suspect them of deceit—of saying a thing is vanished away, while it is only separated into two parts:—that instead of the Sinai covenant being abolished, it is divided into two Sinai covenants, the one of which is abolished, and the other remains in full force. If this had been the case, the prophets and apostles, being honest and inspired men, would have told us what was taken away, and what remained. I agree with the apostle Paul, that the whole of the Sinai covenant is abolished, and with Dr. Witsius, that the whole of it was a shadow of good things to come, viz. typical, and, as such, ceremonial. If it is not so, it is proper that these authors should distinctly tell us what remains. It is certain, that none of its penalties of death remain, because there are no courts to execute them. The priests and Levites, the sons of Aaron and Levi, were essential constituent judges of the court for life and death, and it was indispensable that those courts should sit where Jehovah gave his oracles in the sanctuary. There are now no priests and Levites, nor any local divine sanctuary; therefore, no such case can be decided and executed under that law. It will not do to say, that other judges may supply their place; for doing so, would be expressly contrary to that law, of which the priests and Levites only possessed the legal authority and records; and whoever usurped their station was liable to the penalty of death. Maintaining this is to give up the law. Has the Saviour and his apostles provided for this dilemma? They have not, in any other way than by abrogating the whole system, and turning the attention of men to the moral law, as explained and enforced by the prophets and apostles, divinely inspired. It is upon these the christian church is built.

But to return to the author's definition of the judicial law, viz. "That it was that body of laws given for the government of the Jews," &c. Now there was no law so closely connected with the civil government of the Jews, as the institution of the sabbatical years and grand jubilee. This was at the foundation of that republican institution, and secured republican equality, as originally instituted by Jehovah. It restored every man to his liberty, to his possession, and to his family. With this it does not appear that the priests and Levites had so much concern, as in the courts of justice, &c. yet it was the grand regulator of the liberty and property of the nation. It did not, however, belong to the external worship of God; it was a civil regulation, and, as such, belonged to the civil code. As far as appears, it might have been continued and put in execution without priests, Levites, or sacrifices. It was a law so important in the estimation of Jehovah, its author, that for the breach of it, he says, (Jer. xxxiv. 17.) "Behold I proclaim a liberty for you, saith the Lord, to the sword, to the pestilence, and to the famine; and I will make you to be removed into all the kingdoms of the earth."

That nation had been devoted to desolation and captivity long before, for the sins of Manasseh, by long continued breaches of the whole law, moral as well as peculiar. He made the streets of Jerusalem run with innocent blood; he did worse than the heathens or the Amorites, &c. Yet, on repentance, they got a respite; but for this one sin, in breaking through the fundamental regulations of the jubilee, they had no respite of the threatened execution of the sentence.

Why do not these authors charge our government with a total neglect of this institution, which lay at the foundation of the civil oeconomy of the Jews? There were some other statutes, perhaps not so important in their own nature, yet equally important from the authority of the divine legislator, such as the commands, *not to sow their fields with divers seeds—not to plough with an ox and an ass together—not to reap clean out, the corners of their fields, nor to return for sheaves they had left—not to glean or take all the fruit from off their vineyard—not to wear a garment of linen and woollen, and to wear fringes on their garments*—and several other commands of this nature, with which it appears that the priests had nothing to do, in their official character; therefore, they did not belong to the worship of God, which the priests superintended. The jubilee was a civil institution, of a high rank; the others were agricultural and domestic institutions; but all of them statutes of the Sinai covenant, and enjoined by Jehovah. Why are these forgotten or overlooked by both the authors? It could not be because they were ordained by inferior authority. They were certainly divine laws. Is it really the case that they have no regard for the Sinai covenant, further than they, in their own opinion, can apply it in favour of burning, stoning, hanging, fining and imprisoning. They give up the

ceremonial part, and all the judicial, except the penalties. It is indeed
not probable they will have this actually in their power, but it may con-
sole them, to believe, that they have a right to do it. It is their part to
examine whether this disposition is agreeable to the spirit of the gospel,
or the practice of the apostles and primitive christians. It is certain, that
such as have had the power, and have gone into the exercise of it in the
gospel day, have discovered a want of that spirit in numerous instances;
but they have been more consistent than the authors. The Pope revived
the grand jubilee, and it brought a prodigious concourse of people, and
influx of money to Rome, and other holy places; and if it did not restore
men to their estates, on going through the penance prescribed, it set
them free, in their own opinion, from the guilt of all their sins. The
authors do not offer this encouragement, nor claim infallibility.

As I have found in both the authors, something like a predisposi-
tion to mistake, I will explain two instances, wherein I may happen to
be misunderstood. The one is, that by denying the law of Moses to be
the moral law, I depreciate the character of the law of Moses. I do not
depreciate it, as a national code for a peculiar people, which it certainly
was. This is clearly stated in the books of Moses, from their first constitution, and in the whole history of their conduct, and God's dispensations
towards them, as a peculiar nation, until the ends of that peculiar national constitution were accomplished, and the peculiar constitution itself abolished; and those who objected to this abolition, long foretold by
the prophets, were cast out from being a people, and dispersed through
all nations of the earth, as monuments of the evil of rejecting God's
counsel against themselves. To them, in their national character, Moses,
with great propriety, appeals, Deut. iv. 9. "What nation is there so great,
that hath statutes and judgments, so righteous as all this law, which I set
before you this day?"

To those acquainted with the state of society in the period of the
world, the Mosaic law will appear incomparably superior to any other
national code then known in the world. The restraints on agriculture
and domestic usages, mentioned above, were probably calculated and
intended to counteract, and to be a standing testimony against superstition, that had, by its baleful contagion, enlisted ploughing and sowing,
food and raiment, in its train. All who have any knowledge of the miseries

brought on the human family—from the humane and civilized Hindoo in Asia, to the unpolished Hottentots in the south of Africa; and from thence to the savage Esquimaux in North America—know that more than half the miseries felt by them, is the result of superstition. To prevent the reign, and to stop the progress of this baneful offspring of ignorance, mistaken piety, timidity, and foolish curiosity, then making progress in the world, the law of Moses was well calculated, and exceedingly necessary. In its municipal laws, particularly with respect to justice between man and man, it was not only excellently adapted to the nature of the government, but highly worthy of imitation by every government, as far as circumstances admit.

The great excellence, however, consisted in the frequent introduction of the precious maxims of the moral law, of which an apostle has said, that *love is the fulfilling of the law.* This impression of the nature of the moral law, though more powerfully enforced by the Saviour and his disciples, was zealously inculcated by Moses, either as incorporated in the national law, or accompanying the delivery of it. In the nineteenth chapter of Leviticus, called in the context a repetition of sundry laws, I find about eight laws that are peculiar, and at least double that number that are moral, equally binding on all men, in all situations. Of these I will insert but two, viz. Lev. xix. 18. "Thou shalt not avenge nor bear any grudge against the children of this people; but thou shalt love thy neighbour as thyself. I am the Lord;" and that the term neighbour is here used in the same sense in which the Saviour explained it, in the New Testament, is evident from the following texts: Exod. xxii. 21. Lev. xix. 34. and many other texts in the books of Moses. I shall only quote Deut. x. 18. "The Lord loveth the stranger," &c. Every repetition of the fourth commandment is accompanied with expressions of love to the stranger, the servant, &c. This is the language of the moral law. The law of love, proceeding from that God, of whom an inspired apostle informs us, that "he so loved the world, that he gave his only begotten Son, that whosoever believeth in him should not perish, but have eternal life;" and of whom the same apostle tells us, in one of his epistles, that "God is love."

There was undoubtedly more of the law of love, viz. the moral law incorporated with, or accompanying the Israelitish theocracy, than the political constitution of any nation then in the world. The nations had not then the written word. But the Saviour himself has testified, that in that national constitution, prescribed by Moses, certain deviations from the perfection of the moral law were tolerated, out of indulgence to the hardness of the people's hearts, for whom it was made. From this, I conclude that though the moral law of love accompanied the delivery of it, and much of it was incorporated in it; yet considered as a peculiar national constitution, it was not the moral law, nor as a national law, obligatory on any but that nation, and on them only, while they continued to be a nation, and acted in that character within the territory to which the administration of this national constitution was limited. In short, I have the same opinion of it that the apostle Paul had. Heb. viii. 7. "If the first covenant had not been found fault with, no place would have been found for the second." Compare this with what the same apostle has said, corresponding with the prophet Jeremiah, with respect to the old covenant being abolished, to make way for the new covenant, viz. the gospel dispensation, accompanied with the perfect exposition and application of the moral law of love, not only of love to our neighbour, including the stranger, but of love to our enemies, whom we are bound to forgive, under the express stipulation, "that unless we forgive, we shall not be forgiven." This explanation, I presume, will afford a competent justification of all I have said respecting the Sinai covenant, or constitution of Israel, as a nation. I leave it to the author of the manuscript to justify himself, in his charges of defective morality against the New Testament, which out of sympathy to him, I have not thought proper to quote.

I have said that civil governments do not, and cannot punish sin, because none but the heart searching God is a competent judge of the demerit of sin. I believe that the prerogative of searching the heart, and of forgiving sin, he has not transferred to any vicegerent. I must admit, however, that Pope Leo, the tenth of that name, thought otherwise, and sold the pardon of sins, past, present, and to come, at a pretty cheap rate. A pragmatical fellow, however, named *Martin Luther*, interrupted the sale. I ask now if Leo X. who had the power to pardon all sins, had not also the power to inflict an adequate punishment for all sins? This, I presume, must be admitted, on the principle of analogy; and on this ground, after endeavours used to reclaim him, Luther was given to the devil, by the Pope.

If this is so, I ask, if hanging, burning, imprisoning, fining, and tortures, if they please, will, in the opinion of the authors, be an adequate punishment for the sins which the culprits have committed? If the punishment, to which they consign them, is an adequate punishment for their sin, it is well. If not, what does it amount to? Nothing, because a punishment of sin against God, if not necessary to protect society, only gratifies the bad passions of those that put themselves in God's stead.

Lest I should not be understood; by *sin*, I mean an act against the laws of God—a violation of the laws of religion, or, as it is otherwise defined, any want of conformity to, or transgression of, the law of God. By *crime*, I mean a transgression of the criminal laws of the state, proper to be brought before a court of criminal jurisdiction. In this sense it is used, not only in common law, but in scripture. Job. xxxi. 11. "This is a heinous *crime*, yea it is an iniquity to be punished by the judges." Ezek. vii. 23. "For the land is full of bloody *crimes*." Acts xxv. 16. "Have his accusers face to face, and he have license to answer for himself, concerning the *crime* laid against him," &c.

The term *crime* is probably sometimes applied improperly in common usage. It does not apply to what is called civil injuries, or wrongs between man and man; it does not apply to any thing that only subjects a person to the censures of the church. The church has no power to decide on crimes; their censures only extend to what in the New Testament is called offences. Rom. xvi. 17. "I beseech you to mark them which cause offences," &c. The terms *stumbling* and *offend*, used in the New Testament, (1 John ii. 10. and Mat. xiii. 41) are translated in the margin, and by commentators, *scandal*. By the Presbyterian church of Scotland, this term has been usually applied to such offences as were, by their discipline, subjected to church censure. On this subject the learned Durham,[2] one of the greatest ornaments of that church, wrote his celebrated treatise on *scandal*. Church judicatures have nothing to do with offences, considered as crimes, against the state; but as sins against God, or scandals to religion; they have no authority to punish crimes, but to bring offenders

---

2. James Durham (1622–1658), Scottish Presbyterian divine, *The Dying Man's Testament to the Church of Scotland, or A Treatise Concerning Scandal* (1659).

to repentance. A crime is not only a fault, but a *great fault;* it is not a private injury, which affects an individual only, but such as affects the public in general; therefore, belongs to what, in England, are called the pleas of the crown. A crime is a violation of public rights, such as *treason, murder,* and *robbery.* Conviction of crime renders the person infamous, and disqualifies him from public confidence. Every crime committed by a professor of religion, is also a scandal to religion, but every offence or scandal, which may offend our brethren, and subject the person to reproof or admonition, can only be figuratively called so; it does not render the person infamous, and ought not to be classed with such as do so; for it has a tendency to discourage offenders from submitting to church censures, when they cannot, in truth, confess themselves to be criminal, or infamous. This may be considered as a digression, but I trust not unuseful.

Under the peculiar constitution of Israel, as a nation, Jehovah was not only their God, in the same relation in which he stood to all the families of the earth, but he was also the immediate and peculiar king of Israel, as a nation. In that character, every offence committed against the peculiar laws of the national covenant, or constitution, was not only an offence, or crime against these laws, but a sin against Jehovah, their king. This national law did not forbid all offences against the moral law, nor authorise the courts to punish all the infractions of those laws, which were forbidden in the Jewish law; very many of them have no penalty annexed, to be executed by man. All transgressions of, or want of conformity to the moral law, even though not prohibited in the national law, were sins, for which sinners must account to God at the final judgment. In that solemn and general decision, there will be no respect of persons or nations—no difference between Jew and Gentile. Sins and the aggravations of them, will be weighed in an even balance, and all will be condemned who have not fled for refuge to the Mediator, according to the gospel.

If "a law without a penalty, to be executed by man, is no law at all, but a mere directive thing," as the author of the manuscript maintains, he may easily correct this mistake by looking into the Sinai covenant, which he maintains to be still binding on christians. In Exod. chap. xxi. xxii. and xxiii. which contain the principal precepts or rules for the courts of justice, and in that sense their judicial, or rather juridical laws; these were in the twenty-fourth chapter wrote in a book, and deposited with the priests and Levites, who were afterwards constituted the permanent and official judges of these courts. He will there find more than twenty cases forbidden or commanded, without any penalty annexed to be executed by man. He may, indeed, call these *mere directive things.* If so, let him look a little further. (Lev. chap. vii.) He will find many other statutes in that book which have no penalties annexed, that the judges are authorised to execute. In some cases of disobedience, it is said *they will be cut off from their people;* but where no authority was given to the judges, God reserved the execution in his own hand, of which he soon gave an example in the case of Nadab and Abihu, and afterwards in the case of Korah, &c. The issue lies between the author of the manuscript and Moses, who says they are laws. The author says they are *mere directive things.* I had always thought a law was a rule of action prescribed by competent authority, and that its obligation arose from the authority of the legislator; and that penalties were merely incidental, to enforce the execution of the law, but added nothing to its moral obligation; it appears Moses was of the same opinion. The law of the ten commandments prescribes no penalties to be executed by man; are those commandments, therefore, no laws, but mere directive things?

The author of the Sons of Oil not only introduces divine laws, as repealed and mitigated, on which I have already made remarks, but he adds, "Where the laws are silent or indefinite, with respect to particular crimes, and the punishment thereto annexed, great discretion and prudence will be necessary," &c.

I am no where in the Bible informed of the repeal of any law of God. The Saviour, who only had power to do so, repealed none. In the question of divorce, &c. he declared what the moral law of nature was from the beginning, and informed the people that Moses, in giving the peculiar law to Israel, had given this indulgence *for the hardness of their hearts.* He, in every instance, explained the moral law in its greatest purity, and applied it to the conscience. The delivery of a compend of this most perfect law preceded the national law to Israel; the one was a rule of conduct, as they should answer to God; the other a rule of conduct, as they should answer to the civil magistrate. The Saviour did not abridge, nor enlarge, the power of the magistrate; but he explained and applied the moral law to the conscience.

He not only sent the leper to the priest, to offer for his cleansing, according to the law of Moses, but a few days before he was crucified, he told his hearers, "The Scribes and Pharisees sit in Moses' seat; all, therefore, whatsoever they bid you observe, that observe and do; but do not after their works, for they say and do not."

Nothing can be more plain than this direction, to attend to the law, without regarding the character of the officer who administers it, if they are legally possessed of the office; and that the national law of Moses continued without repeal or mitigation till the great antitype had fulfilled all righteousness, including obedience to the symbolical law, and having, on the cross, fulfilled all its requirements, said "It is finished." This was the end and fulfilment of that law, not its repeal, like the repeal of the laws of short-sighted mortals.

Who, before the author, ever thought of a silent, or indefinite law of the *most high God?* I am at a loss to decide whether this sentence exhibits most of absurdity, prophaneness, blasphemy, or nonsense. To say that a law is silent, is nonsense. Silence is a negative; it is the reverse of law. The definition of law is, a rule of action, established by competent authority, and publicly known; against such only can a crime be committed. This definition is agreeable both to scripture and common sense; as sin in scripture is the transgression of a known law, so is crime with respect to municipal laws. How then can a crime possibly be committed against a silent, or unknown law?

The term indefinite is commonly used in two senses. The first is, *not determined; not limited; not settled.* The second is, *large beyond the comprehension of man, though not absolutely infinite, or without limits.* Such is the number of the stars, or of the sands on the sea shore. Does the author really ascribe this character to the laws of a just and a holy God? Does he assert that his laws, for the breach of which he authorises punishment, are in their own nature not settled or determined, or that they are incomprehensible and undefinable? He certainly does; and by so doing, depreciates the laws of God below the standard of the heathen oracles. They were dubious, indeed, but not indefinite; they required good guessing. The king of Lydia was informed by the oracle, which he consulted, that if he went to war with Persia, he would destroy a great nation; he wished, and therefore hoped and believed, that the oracle meant that he would destroy Persia; but the oracle, as explained by the event, meant that Persia would destroy Lydia. The responses of those oracles were, no doubt, the result of deep cunning, but the construction given to them was on the same principle on which the reverend author of the Sons of Oil and the author of the manuscript, construe the oracle of God. They form a system, founded on certain first principles, framed by their own imagination, contrary to which, they persuade themselves, it would be inconsistent for the divine character to act; and they practically say unto Jehovah, hitherto shalt thou come and no further; just as he set bounds to the overflowing of the ocean, and just as the Jews did in order to justify them in rejecting the counsel of God against themselves.

In the seventh chapter of John, we find no less than five self-created barriers that they had erected against their own happiness. In the first ten verses they object to Christ's doing miracles in secret, viz. in Galilee and such remote places, because if he was the Messiah, he ought to be known openly, not giving credit to the prophecy of his character, viz. that the Saviour would not cry nor lift up his voice, &c. Others concluded he could not be the Messiah, because he never had human learning. Others, more than half convinced that he was the Christ, yet it being a first principle or maxim with them, that when Christ came, no man would know from whence he was, but they both knew him, and from whence he was—therefore rejected him, notwithstanding the most incontestable proofs of his divine mission. A little further on, in the same chapter, he came out of Galilee, and not out of Bethlehem, therefore they shut their eyes against the clearest evidence. And a little further still, he was rejected by the rulers, because that those who approved of the Saviour had not studied the law of Moses, according to the rules then prescribed; they had not studied at the feet of Gamaliel, nor been dignified with a diploma. Nathaniel, the Israelite without guile, was entangled in the same manner, but did not, like the others, persist against reasonable demonstration; but he at first adhered to his maxim, that no good thing could come out of Nazareth. His candid mind yielded to evidence, and he rejected his own prepossessions.

Probably I would not have introduced these observations, had it not been, that when I was entangled with first principles, maxims and prepossessions, impressed by respectable authority, and received so much

at heart, that for some time I turned with a kind of alarm from examining their solidity. I was, in part, relieved from this bondage by the
divine blessing directing and assisting me in deliberately examining the
seventh chapter of John, and the case of Nathaniel. I was there convinced that we are very apt to make the snares, wherein we ourselves are
entangled, and have, of course, relinquished my former confidence in
maxims and first principles. Not that I have given up all first principles;
it is still a first principle with me, to receive, believe, and rest on scripture testimony in the most plain, simple, and obvious sense in which it
is revealed, unless it is so clearly figurative, that taking it literally would
be evidently absurd; and I am, from many years experience, the longer
the more convinced, that in this way only there is safety; that departing
from this rule has been the source of all the mysticism, enthusiasm,
superstition, idolatry, tyranny and persecution, by which the christian
religion has been dishonoured, and its genuine principles perverted. By
departing from this rule, even orthodox commentators have, in some
instances, gone wrong.

It is no uncommon thing, in church history, to find professors pro-
claiming *the law of God* as their exclusive rule, with regard to religion;
and this being a very simple proposition, enlisting and arming fire,
sword, tortures and lesser punishments, according to their discretion,
against others who not only make the same professions, but practice
more conformably to them. This might be demonstrated by facts, both
in earlier and later times. The church of Rome professes to rest solely
on the scriptures, but proves from scripture, as she believes, the right of
giving the true sense or interpretation of it, and the authority of tradition, to which all must conform under the penalty of death. The reformation took its rise from a free enquiry, by every man for himself; the
preachers (sometimes and not amiss, called the *apostles of the reformation*)
addressed every man's reason and judgment, in the same manner as
the gospel was offered by Christ and his apostles. In this way the gospel church was planted and spread abroad through the nations, and
continued in purity until the ministers of religion, in their councils, assumed a legislative authority in the church of Christ, towards the close
of the second century. From this time, the right of private judgment was
restrained, but so gradually, as to give little alarm; for it was *while man*

slept that the enemy sowed: but in proportion as this claim was extended, superstition, error, and corruption of every kind overspread the church, until the grand apostacy, foretold by the apostles, was consummated. When the clergy first assumed a legislative authority in the church of Christ, they exercised it with prudence, and professed to derive that authority from the scriptures, as the church of Rome still has done, and as Dr. Mosheim, treating of the second century, says, "The christian doctors had the good fortune to persuade the people, that the ministers of the christian church succeeded to the character, rights and privileges of the Jewish priesthood; and this persuasion was a new source, both of honour and profit to the sacred order. This notion was prosecuted with industry, some time after the reign of Adrian, when the second destruction of Jerusalem extinguished all hopes among the Jews of seeing their government restored to its former lustre, and their country arising out of its ruins. And accordingly, the bishops considered themselves as invested with a rank and character, similar to those of the *high priests* among the Jews, while the presbyters represented the dignity of the *priests,* and the deacons that of the Levites."

This is the first instance I find on record, of dividing the law of Moses into two codes, viz. ceremonial and judicial—The precepts for external worship of God prescribed in the Sinai covenant—and those for the peculiar civil government of the Jews. This last they gave up, but retained the former. But though they began with applying this rule only to the orders of the clergy, they soon extended it to the public worship, which they so loaded and disfigured with Jewish rites, that even Augustine, a bishop of eminent talents and rank, but not clear of the superstition of his time, says, "that the yoke under which the Jews formerly groaned, was more tolerable than that imposed upon christians in his time," viz. the fourth century; to what enormity it afterwards grew under this usurped legislative authority of the clergy, church history records.

It was not, however, till the clergy united with the civil magistrate, in the administration of Christ's legislative authority over his own house, that the judicial or civil part of the Sinai covenant was enlisted in the cause. The penalty of death and lesser punishments, were necessary to support this usurped authority, and consequently applied, not only to such heretics as perverted the truth of the gospel, but against such persons as testified in any manner against the legislative authority usurped from the church's head. Historians testify, that many did make efforts to stem the torrent of apostacy, without success.

After the doctrine of the reformation had been successfully addressed to the reason and judgment of individuals, so as to make a progress similar, in some good measure, to what the preaching of the gospel at first had done;—princes, under the profession of being protectors of the reformed churches, became its legislators, and the clergy generally supported them, and those who did not, were subjected to actual persecution; and thus, instead of union, divisions were promoted. Instances of those who held the truth of the christian religion, being persecuted by those who held the same fundamental truths, for not submitting to human and fallible authority in matters of worship, in a lesser or greater degree, are to be found in the histories of all the protestant national churches. The churches of Britain produced strong examples of this sort.

This application of the law of Moses to christians, both in the time of Constantine, and since the reformation, is wholly founded in mistake. I have before stated, that the Sinai covenant provided no legislative power to be exercised by man. Under that economy, the priests were the official repositories of the laws, and it was their duty to read them on stated occasions to the people; and when a king was permitted, it was his duty to take *a copy of that law before the priests and Levites, and to read in it all the days of his life,* but not to make additions to it. Consequently, though we find the prophets complain, *that the people were not obedient to his law—That they that handle the law knew him not—That they had not obeyed nor walked in his law—That they have forgotten the law of their God—That they have done violence to the law,* &c. they no where complain, that they did not make laws for reformation, or for punishing offences. Their sin, for which they were punished, was for the non-execution or transgression of the law of Moses. The prophet Malachi finishes the Old Testament system of prophecy, by saying, "Remember the law of Moses, my servant, which I commanded him in Horeb for all Israel, with the statutes and judgments"—and also by bringing into view the coming of the Messiah as near at hand. But neither he, nor any other of the prophets, calls their attention to the laws of their reforming kings, judges, or governors, because they could make no such laws, being merely entrusted with the execution of the law of Moses. But the prophets, from Moses inclusive, frequently introduce the Messiah as a lawgiver, to whom the typical law of Moses pointed, and who was to introduce a new covenant, or dispensation of it, on other principles.

It may be objected, that my arguments against political churches go against the abuse of the power, but not against the power itself. That all civil governments among men have been abused; yet, notwithstanding this, all governments are not to be rejected.

I answer, that all civil governments among men are founded on the moral law of nature, resulting from the will of God; that his reasonable and accountable creatures ought to pursue their own happiness; but the kingdom of Christ not being derived from this source, is founded solely on divine revelation—all its rules and authority are drawn from that divine source.

The moral law of nature obliges all men, in all stations of life, to pay respect in those stations to divine revelation, but does not authorise them to usurp any official authority that he has not transferred to them. Civil magistrates are not enumerated among the officers of Christ's kingdom, (which is not of this world,) prescribed in the New Testament; therefore they have no authority in or over it. Every attempt to exercise such authority, is usurpation on what is withheld from them. I may, however, with propriety be asked, if these political churches are not the church of Christ, where shall the church of Christ be found since the reformation?

I will answer, as near as I can recollect it, in the language of a much greater man on this subject than myself; I mean the very learned bishop Benjamin Hoadly, of the established church of England: "The church of Christ," says that great divine, "is to be found in the established church of England, and in other christian denominations, which she excludes from her communion, or who refuse to join in it; that all who believe in Christ and worship him according to his word, by whatever name they are called, are his church." I will apply this principle to all other political churches; I will apply it to the Javians and Vigilentians, who, in the fourth century, were excluded from the first political christian church. I believe they belonged to the church of Christ. I believe their persecutors, St. Ambrose, St. Jerome, &c. whose memories christians generally

revere, were also members of the church of Christ, though they persecuted his faithful witnesses. I believe that while the Waldenses, &c. were
persecuted, there were many of the church of Christ in the church of
Rome. I believe that the great Wickliffe of England, whose corpse was
raised and insulted after he was dead, and his disciples, John Huss, and
Jerome of Prague, who loved not their lives unto the death for the gospel
of Christ, and many others, who never had separated from the church of
Rome, were members of the church of Christ. I believe that Luther was
such before he disowned the Pope's authority, even when he obeyed that
church in attending the council; but after he was informed of the Pope's
bull of excommunication being issued against him, to be executed at a
given day, he was as much a member of the church of Christ, as he was
the day after he with solemnity burned the Pope's bull. I believe that
the ministry of Luther, and his coadjutors and disciples, was valid; and I
believe the same of Calvin and his disciples, notwithstanding that they
received their ordination, or, in the language of that church, consecration, from the church of Rome. Luther, however, deserves to be respectfully remembered for being the first who declared a separation from,
and disowned the authority of, that apostate church, of which he had
been a minister, and instituted a separate communion, in defiance of
anathemas of more than a thousand years standing, against schism, as
if it had been an unpardonable sin. We know the Waldenses, &c. were
under many mistakes, yet they were the church of Christ in the wilderness. They, as well as other witnesses, testified against the corruptions
of that church, but not against the church itself; they plead with their
mother. John Huss and Jerome of Prague were attending the council of
Constance, convened by the Pope and emperor, when they became martyrs. Luther narrowly escaped from his attendance at the diet of Worms,
whose summons he had obeyed, contrary to the advice of his friends.

The most important manifestation of the covenant of grace, after the
first discovery thereof to our first parents, in their fallen and ruined
state, seems to be the promise to Abraham. More special promises
were then made than had been theretofore, and more peculiar duties enjoined—he was to be a sojourner in a strange land, &c. External
promises were given him respecting the multitude and power to which
his seed should arrive, &c. but these were only typical of the spiritual

promises which contained the substance of the covenant of grace, by which he was constituted "the Father of all them that believe." Rom. iv. 16.—and from which all believers, of all nations, are accounted the children of faithful Abraham, to whom it was promised, that in him and in his seed, all the nations of the earth should be blessed—Gal. iii. 6–8. This is frequently called the covenant of circumcision, because this rite or sacrament was the sign and seal of it. It was not, however, applied or binding on Melchizedec, or any other believers of that day; but the household and seed of Abraham, not the promised seed only, viz. Isaac, but on all his seed. Though it is not founded on the law of Moses, yet it was incorporated in it. Levit. xii. 3. Therefore the Saviour says, John vii. 22. Moses therefore gave you circumcision (not because it is of Moses but of the fathers). Though this seal was continued in the law of Moses, yet the covenant, of which it was the seal, was totally distinct from the Sinai covenant. The apostle, reasoning on the stability and efficacy of the covenant with Abraham, concludes, Gal. iii. 17. "And this I say, that the covenant that was confirmed before of Christ, the law that was four hundred and thirty years after, cannot disannul it that it should make the promise of none effect." Thus the apostle puts the covenant with Abraham in direct contrast with the Sinai covenant. The first he says cannot be disannulled. This is admitting that the other is to be disannulled, of which he elsewhere says, it is *disannulled, vanished* and *abolished.* While this covenant was wholly abrogated, the Abrahamic covenant only underwent a change of the initiating rites. Baptism was substituted for circumcision, &c. The believing Jews were exceedingly opposed to this change, as well as the abolition of the law of Moses respecting meat and drink, &c. They did not claim the continuance of the passover, the sacrificial worship, the Aaronic priesthood, nor the penalties of the Sinai covenant. Their attachment to the law of Moses was strong; it was a divine law, given with the greatest solemnity, by the most high God.

It pleased God, out of condescension to their weakness, to tolerate the believing Jews to use such observances of the law of Moses, as were not wholly inconsistent with the gospel of Christ; not only so, but to give them an authoritative toleration for these observances. Acts xv. 19–29. But though they were thus officially tolerated in these things, the apostles never ceased to preach against them, as may be seen in all Paul's epistles. He combated error with instruction, the only means instituted by God for that purpose. He reproved and admonished, but did not exclude them from the communion of the church. This was not an error of little importance, for the Judaizing christian taught, that except they be circumcised they cannot be saved. Acts xv. 1. The apostle, on the other hand, taught, that if *they were circumcised* (viz. trusted in it) *Christ shall profit you nothing.* "For I testify again to every man that is circumcised, that he is a debtor to do the whole law." Gal. v. 23.

There is no doubt but the legal application of circumcision, for justification, was the most pernicious part of the error; but this was not peculiar to them. Christians to this day make a legal application of the moral law for justification before God; not only so, but even some christian sects turn the gospel into a new law, through obedience to which, they expect to be justified; but neither the moral law nor the gospel can be, therefore, abolished, because they are misunderstood or misused. The apostle did not require those that were called in circumcision to renounce it, but he constantly protested against continuing the practice. Titus, who was *with him, being a Greek, was compelled to be circumcised, and he took and circumcised Timothy,* (who was also a Greek by his father) *because of the Jews, who were in these quarters.* Acts xvi. iii. These instances discover indeed a high degree of toleration and sympathy towards weak and erring brethren. For these, and probably many others, who were thus compelled to be circumcised, out of accommodation to the prepossessions of the Jews, were Gentiles, therefore, out of the rule of permission granted by the apostles and elders, convened at Jerusalem. It is evident that this toleration was admitted after that decree was published. The apostle in so doing, was guided by the spirit of Christ. This is no doubt put on sacred record to shew the condescending patience of God. Our Saviour, who waits to be gracious to erring men, and bears long with their errors, and continued long with them the means of instruction, the appointed corrective of error before he casts them off.—He bore with the unbelieving Jews, and continued the means of instruction, not without its influence. His prayer for forgiveness was no doubt heard in behalf of many of his betrayers and murderers. Paul himself was a violent persecutor till some years after the Saviour's ascension; but when they became obdurate in rejecting the counsel of God against themselves, they were given up to that exemplary destruction which the Saviour, in the most affecting manner had foretold, and of which Moses, many centuries before, had prophesied; yet he continued to bear with the obstinate prepossessions of the believing Jews, who continued their attachment in favour of some parts of the law of Moses, because it was a divine law, and, as such, delivered to the fathers in whom they gloried. Without considering that all its objects were accomplished, and its requirements fulfilled, they gradually, but slowly indeed, relinquished this attachment, after their temple, their place and nation, as to them, were no more. It was not till the second great dispersion of the Jews, in the reign of the emperor Adrian, that the great body of the believing Jews coalesced fully with the christians from among the Gentiles, in the abolition of the middle wall of partition, which had, by divine authority, been abolished more than one hundred years before. A small remnant, who took to themselves the name of Nazarines, separated. Unfortunately, those who united with the Gentile churches, contributed to introduce the abolished hierarchy, and rites of the Jewish, into the christian church, as I have before stated.

I conclude this part of the subject with only remarking, that the apostle, in asserting, by divine authority, that by being circumcised, they became debtors to fulfil the whole law of Moses, strongly confirms what I have before stated from scripture, that the law of Moses, viz. the national law, or code of laws, consisting of many subordinate laws, which is always necessary to form a national system of laws, called by moderns a constitution of civil government, viz. that the nation must either submit to the whole, or to no part of it. This is evidently the declaration of the prophets and apostles, with respect to the old and new covenants, viz. the gospel dispensation of the covenant of grace, and the symbolical covenant with Israel, as a political and symbolical nation. That in this my opinion is correct, is evident, if the apostle is correct; and I wish no better authority.

The United States, notwithstanding the denunciations against their constitutions, by both the authors, precisely followed this divine example, when in pursuance of their own happiness, not consistent with the equal happiness, of their fellow men, they declared themselves an independent nation. They, by that very act declared all laws derived from the former government void. So many of them were revived, by special

acts of the state legislatures, as they thought proper; but none of them
by authority of the old government. This is denied by the author of the
manuscript. I am sorry for the confusion of his ideas on this question.
He has been an officer of the state government. He knows the laws; let
him examine them, particularly such as were enacted at the commencement of independence. They will answer for me. Let him read the revising act; till then there was no law in the states, but order was preserved
by committees throughout the states, acting on their moral discretion,
agreeable to the law of nature. In this manner they prepared the way for
a convention, with full power to give a constitutional establishment to a
state legislature. In this manner all the thirteen provinces became sovereign and independent states. These state legislatures agreed to articles of confederation, by which they transferred certain general powers
to a congress, composed of delegates from the respective states. A congress had been appointed before that time, by provincial committees,
or legislatures, acting in that character, for which the king dissolved the
legislatures. That congress, however, having no legal authority, could
do nothing but advise; but their advices were treated with great respect.
Thus being reduced to a state of nature, by the king declaring them out
of his protection and dissolving their legislatures, in pursuit of their
own happiness, they, agreeably to the moral law of nature, viz. the will
of God expressed in that law, formed civil society for the preservation
of order and protection; and being thus formed agreeable to the law of
nature, the only law which they then acknowledged, they proceeded to
institute civil, viz. political society; that is to say, to organize civil government. This proceeding being agreeable to the will of God, expressed in
the law of nature, is the ordinance of God, agreeable to the apostle Paul,
and being organized by man, is the ordinance of man, agreeable to the
apostle Peter, (See Rom. xiii. 1. and 1 Peter ii. 13.) therefore entitled
to obedience for conscience sake. A paragraph of the Rev. Mr. Wylie,
however, declares them to be immoral and illegitimate—that is to say,
bastard governments, whose authority ought not to be obeyed; and compares paying taxes to them, to compounding with a robber. As this will
be examined in another place, I will conclude here with observing, that
in all my acquaintance with the organization of civil governments, I
know of none that in every respect originated in a way so agreeable

to the law of our nature and reason. I know of none wherein the voice of the citizens, of all ranks, had so much weight, as in the forming of their constitutions, by which the people have transferred so few of their natural rights, or in which those they have retained, are so equally and so effectually secured.

As far as I have observed, the author of the manuscript does not go all lengths with the author of the Sons of Oil, in disowning the legal authority of the civil government; but they agree in censuring it very severely, on account of the protection it affords to the citizens in the exercise of their truly unalienable right of worshipping God agreeable to the discovery of his will to their own reason and judgment, as they are to be accountable to him in the day of judgment. This they, by a strange mistake of language, call *toleration*. Certainly they might have known, and it is strange that they did not know, that the term toleration, in religious matters, among christians, originated from political religious establishments, introduced with other conceptions of christianity, and too soon adopted, and too eagerly pursued after the reformation by protestant states, while they worshipped an idol of their own making, viz. uniformity, in obedience to rules of worship prescribed by human authority. They had formerly groaned under that power exercised by the Pope and councils of the priesthood, convened first by the authority of the emperors, and afterwards by the Pope, approved by the emperors. These, however, claimed to possess infallibility, and the immediate inspiration of the Holy Ghost, though they sometimes disputed whether this precious arcanum was vested in the Pope or in the council, or jointly in both. The emperor Phocas, however, having transferred it to Pope Boniface, and the councils having acknowledged the authority of the Pope to forgive sins, and to transfer the gift of the Holy Ghost to the subordinate clergy, and having acknowledged him to be the vicegerent of Christ on earth, the dispute, to all practical purposes, was settled. With those who believed the Pope to be the vicegerent of Christ on earth, as he had long before been as the successor of Peter, and the infallible judge of truth, it was perfectly consistent to worship and believe according to his dictates. But after the reformation had progressed through the influence of truth, addressed by the reformer to the reason and judgment of man, as the gospel had been by the apostles, princes,

as I have before stated, assumed the power of the Pope, as the judge
of truth, not to the whole church, but to their own subjects, and enforced their decisions with respect to doctrine and worship with civil
penalties, in the same manner as they did the municipal laws. Consequently, Europe produced at one period above twenty Popes, including
the free and sovereign cantons and cities, as well as the sovereign kings,
princes and dukes, who acted equal to the Pope of Rome in deciding
definitively on religious truth. But neglecting to assume infallibility, and
claim divine inspiration, such of their subjects as thought it their duty to
judge for themselves, in matters for which they were accountable to God
only, could not implicitly rely on such decisions, not supported, as the
Popes were believed to be by his votaries, by the immediate inspiration
of the Holy Ghost; these dissented from the political standard of truth,
or attempted to explain it, so as, in their judgment, to render it more
agreeable to the scriptures, which they believed were really given by
the inspiration of the Holy Ghost. For this, as I have stated before, they
were persecuted with greater or less severity in the dominions of these
diminutive Popes, until they gradually became convinced, that the
establishment of the worship of their idol of uniformity, could not be
supported; that it either made hypocrites, or excited their subjects to
oppose it; and, in short, that they were not God's vicegerents to judge of,
or punish sin against himself. Reluctant, however, to give up the hold
they had on the consciences of men, by their self-interest, they retained
the rewards of hypocrisy in their own hands. They made laws to *tolerate*
dissenters from the politically established religion, subject, however, to
certain disabilities and privations, while those who adhered to the established religion, not only enjoyed the clerical livings, but an extensive
preference of civil privileges. Can the Rev. Mr. Wylie, a native of Britain, where he received a liberal education, be ignorant of the toleration
act of William and Mary,[3] which gave no positive privilege to dissenters

---

3. Protestant dissenters were granted freedom of worship by the Toleration Act of
1689. William, Prince of Orange (1650–1702), married Mary (1662–1694), the daughter
of James II. They became King William III and Queen Mary II of England, in 1689, as a
result of the Glorious Revolution of 1688.

from the national religion, but only provided for exempting their majesties' protestant subjects, dissenting from the church of England, from the penalties of certain laws, commonly called the toleration act.

On the whole, religious establishments, by civil authority and toleration, are relative terms, as much as parent and child. Political establishments are the parents of political toleration. There is, however, this difference: An establishment may exist without toleration, and did so for many ages, till, by its baneful influence, darkness covered the earth, and gross darkness the people. It was the beast or dragon of the Revelations, which banished the woman into the wilderness, and made war with the remnant of her seed, and still continues the war, though with less power. I am the more astonished at the Rev. Mr. Wylie charging the United States with toleration, that I know it is not the opinion of all his brethren. The late Rev. Mr. King,[4] a member of the same Presbytery, being asked in my hearing, by some of his people, (who, from ignorance, objected to the constitution of Pennsylvania, as granting a toleration,) if that was the ground for objecting to the constitution, answered candidly, that it was not, because it gave no toleration; that having no religious establishment, there could be no toleration to depart from what did not exist; that his objection was, that it equally protected all religious denominations. This is admitted. It provides for the protection of all who lead a quiet and peaceable life in godliness and honesty. 1 Tim. ii. 2—"And who study, as much as in them lieth, to live peaceably with all men." Rom. xii. 18. Which the apostle, in these and other texts, has considered to be the great end of civil government to promote, and undoubtedly the principal object of its institution. That it may answer this purpose, the legislature of Pennsylvania has enacted laws for the suppression of vice and immorality, as already mentioned, and for punishing not only the grosser crimes, but all breaches of the peace, slander, &c. therefore it has provided laws for all the great purposes of civil government; and by the constitution, it has power to add, or more efficiently to enforce them. It has, by the constitution, and by the law of nature, power to provide

4. William King (d. 1798), itinerate Scottish Covenanter minister, visited societies in America from about 1792.

for its own security, by punishing those who slander the government itself, or excite opposition to its legal authority. No government on earth
can be more justifiable in doing so, than that of Pennsylvania. It has no
power to interfere with, or punish for, any thing that solely lies between
a man's reason and judgment, and his God, and of which God is the only
infallible judge. Though this doctrine may indeed be disagreeable to
the great and little Popes of Europe, because it tends to disrobe them of
their fancied godhead, and also disagreeable to both the authors, whose
arguments and manner of expression testify their opinion of their own
infallibility, in as high a tone as the Popes of Rome have formerly done,
but not so terrific, their denunciations against their neighbours, and the
government from which they receive protection, are not supported by
the flames of the inquisition, the gallows, the torturing boots and thumb
screws of Scotland, nor the fines and imprisonments of England. They
themselves are hitherto protected in promoting sedition and persecution, and charging their neighbours, and even the government, with
that blasphemy and atheism with which themselves alone are liable to be
charged; but I do not charge them with it, because I believe they did not
mean so. Of this God is the only competent and rightful judge.

The author of the manuscript, viz. *Observations on Toleration*, after oc-
cupying sixteen folio pages in advocating the perpetual obligation of
the national law of Israel, for fifteen pages further combats those whom
he calls *tolerants*—a new name, indeed, for a religious sect. I understand
it, however, to include not one particular sect, but all sects who are not
intolerants; who believe and teach that they have no authority to burn,
hang, fine or imprison other men for not believing as they do, in questions that they think belong to religion. People think differently about
the question, *Wherein does religion consist?* The Russians thought much of
it consisted in wearing very long coats and their beards unshaved, and
considered Peter the great as a persecutor,[5] because he made them cut
their coats short and shave their beards. This some may think ridiculous; but it is not more so than flying to caves and deserts, idolizing the
dead bones of supposed saints, considering holiness to consist in a single

---

5. Peter I (1672–1725): Czar of Russia from 1682 to 1725.

life, and bodily macerations, &c. which was in high repute among christians, not only in the fourth, but even so early as the third century, and
patronized by the greatest divines of that period. It was in the fourth
century, that a still more pernicious principle became a part of religion,
viz. *"That error in religion, when maintained and adhered to, after proper admonition, were punishable with death."* This is the principle for which both
the authors are zealous advocates, and they make their own judgment of
the scripture the rule. It was very necessary at that period, for there were
then a Javian, a Vigilentius, and many others, who testified against the
rapid progress of superstition, and having scripture and reason clearly
on their side, the then church not having recourse to these arms, the
only arms used by the apostles and primitive christians (2 Cor. x. 4.
Eph. vi. 13–16.) by the use of which the christian church was planted
and defended at the first, temporal punishments became a necessary
substitute for its defence. I believe, with the apostles, the reformers, and
the most celebrated modern divines, among whom I name the great Dr.
Owen, that scripture is always sufficient to overturn error. That divine
demonstrates, that those arms were always successful, until the church,
and afterwards church and state, usurped a legislative authority in the
church of Christ. That the spiritual armour would still have been so, if
other armour had not been resorted to.

It is an established principle in criminal laws, that they cannot be applied by implication, or by example, or by necessary consequence, agreeable to the author's rules of construction. This gives too great latitude
to judges. It made sad work in England, where the most virtuous men
went to the block for treason, in the tyrannical reigns of Henry VIII.
and of the Stuarts. They had judges to their mind, who judged from
necessary consequences in their opinion, and from examples. This, in
fact, makes the judges legislators. Criminal laws must be applied and
executed agreeable to the express letter and plain meaning of the law
in Israel; and where the case was doubtful, recourse was had to God,
as their peculiar king. This was done in several instances by Moses in
the wilderness, by Joshua, in the case of Achan, &c. In other cases, with
respect to which God, as king of Israel, did not think proper to entrust
man to execute his judgments for disobeying his laws, he reserved the
execution in his own hand, and applied it as he thought proper.

The reverend author of the Sons of Oil, however, considers these peculiar national laws as equally binding on all mankind at all times, or at least on all christians; and not only so, but that they authorize a discretionary power, and something which he calls *mitigated* and *silent* laws, of which I have spoken already, and of which, as they are not known to others, he is, no doubt, the repository. The author of the manuscript has expressly declared, as I have quoted before, that "the laws and examples of the Jewish church and nation, in the Old Testament, that are not repealed in the New, either by express precept, approven examples, or by necessary consequence, are still binding," as he afterwards states, on all christian nations. Thus the two authors are substantially agreed, though they differ in expression. The one claims the authority of *discretionary, mitigated* and *silent* laws, and the other a latitude of construction that would make them whatever his imagination would suggest. There would be just as many opinions of the application of examples, and of the various real or supposed necessary consequences, as there would be of imaginations and prepossessions. Neither the laws of God, nor any wise laws of man, ever subjected the lives, liberty, and property of men to such caprice, much less their consciences.

If the scripture foundation of the legislative authority, and infallibility of the church of Rome is unsound, where will the authors and other advocates of human legislatures, in and over protestant churches, find a scripture foundation to rest upon? Not on the law of Moses, because the operation and administration was intended for, and applied only to a peculiar people and precisely described territory, and the immediate superintendance of God, as before stated; and with relation to that peculiar people and territory, it waxed old and vanished away, agreeably to divine appointment. This is abundantly testified, both by the prophets and apostles. If this covenant and its laws were of general application, as plead by the authors, I demand proof of it, from the authority of the prophets and apostles. This they have not given, and cannot give. They make a general application of it on their own authority only, contrary to the testimony of the prophets and apostles themselves, on whose testimony, under Christ himself, the christian church is built.

The author of the manuscript says (p. 23) "I do not know that any allege, that civil or national establishments, of even the true religion, was necessary to the growth and increase of the church, but only to her preservation and security against her enemies. It is necessary to prevent the wild boar of the forest from making her a prey," &c. This principle the reverend author admits. All the abettors and supporters of human legislation, in and over the church of Christ, also admit it. In this they are completely in union with the church of Rome, who fully admit it. It is a common cause, in which they are equally interested; for though they seem on the greatest extremes, and oppose each other with the most ardent zeal, yet in this, and other fundamental principles, they harmonize. They cannot do otherwise. They agree substantially, though they differ in words, that the Mediator was deficient in wisdom to plan, or in power to procure such offices and officers as were necessary to the planting, the growth, or increase of his church, or that he had not power to employ kings or other human legislators to make laws for his church, or to send forth booted and spurred apostles to make proselytes of the Gentiles, with fire and sword, as was afterwards done, instead of humble fishermen, equipped with only spiritual armour, and authorised only to make converts, by means of the sincere milk of the word. I agree with both the authors, and even with the Pope, however much I am opposed to popery, that human legislative authority was not necessary to the planting, growth, or increase of the christian church in its infancy, nor for several centuries after, while the christians had to endure heathen persecution, and were accounted as the offscourings of all things, by the reputed wise, and by the mighty. I believe further, that it is not necessary for the preservation of the truth of the gospel.

A serious question, however, arises from the above. It is this: If civil establishments of religion, viz. a human legislative authority, in and over the church of Christ, was not necessary for its *growth* and *increase,* in its infant state, when all the powers of hell and earth were combined against it, how or when did it become necessary? Was it when the majority of the Roman empire, then called the world, had received it, and professed to be in its favour, and when the most despotic and powerful emperors found it to be their interest to embrace it? Again, if Christ and his apostles, authorised and directed by his spirit, really foresaw the necessity of such offices, such officers, and such laws in his church, how did it happen that they were so short-sighted or inattentive, as not to give warning of it, and provide rules suited to the occasion? It is necessary that these questions should be answered by those who advocate the change of Christ's kingdom, respecting which he gave his dying testimony, *that it was not of this world;* but who, contrary to this testimony, boldly declare that *it is of this world,* and subject to human authority, in matters of faith and worship. It becomes the advocates of civil or ecclesiastic government, or any human authority, assuming Christ's headship over his own house, whether they be advocates of the Roman or the protestant popes—I say it becomes them to inform us when, or by what authority, Christ's kingdom became a kingdom of this world. By what authority the church of Christ, which he has declared is one, (as his own body, which it is, was one,) became a church of England, a church of Scotland, a church of Switzerland, a church of Saxony, of Sweden, Denmark, and many others, without including the church of Rome, all regulated by laws less or more at variance with each other. Such a change could not be lawfully made by less than divine authority. It could not be lawfully made but by an authority superior to that of Christ or his apostles, to maintain which, is not only deism, but blasphemy; the very thought of which throws a doubt on the truth of divine revelation, on the truth of which all my hope of salvation depends. Whether it maintained that the body of Christ is not one, but many, viz. as many as there are political churches, prescribed by human authority, founded, as they say, on scripture, I appeal to the apostles of Christ, whom he authorised to plant and to prescribe the laws to his church, for which purpose he promised that the Holy Ghost would teach them all things; and to the fulfilling of which promise he gave testimony to the word of his grace, by enabling them to do signs, wonders, &c. Passing other testimonies to the unity of the body of Christ, I shall only instance 1 Cor. xii. 27. "Now ye are the body of Christ," &c. This is certainly not to be the body of twenty or thirty political churches; Christ's visible body is not so divided. Believers are members of his body, of which the apostle says, (Col. i. 18) "He is the head of his body the church." The church they advocate has many heads, who are very changeable in their laws.

But is the respectable author of the manuscript really serious, in admitting that civil or national establishments of religion were not necessary to the growth and increase of the church of Christ, but only to her preservation against her enemies, when she had come to *her growth*. I seriously ask the author, if the church had acquired her full growth and increase in the beginning of the fourth century, when she first became a kingdom of this world? Notwithstanding the vanity of the Romans in dignifying their empire with the name of the *world*, yet by far the greatest portion of the human race were not only without its limits, but, as since discovered, far beyond its knowledge. The regions of the north, whose numerous hordes overturned the Roman empire, and laid its glory in the dust, were then unexplored. The vast empire of China, called a world by itself, was then unknown. The very numerous savage nations of America, and the more lately discovered islands of the Southern and Pacific Oceans, containing a vast amount of the human race, had not heard the sound of the gospel. The dispersed tribes of Israel had not been converted, nor the fulness of the Gentiles brought in, agreeably to the divine promise. The church, therefore, was very far short of having completed her increase and growth at the period in question; consequently, the author, on his own principles, must admit that the church became a kingdom of this world too soon for his purpose. I believe it never will become so with the divine approbation; but that there is a set time in the councils of heaven when Christ's kingdom shall prevail throughout the world. This blessed time is yet to come. We know not the time how long. May the Lord hasten it in its time. There are signs of its approach, but I do not expect to see its accomplishment in my day, but I hope to die in the faith of its final and joyful accomplishment. He is faithful who has promised. Blessed be his name.

The reverend author has frequently appealed, in his book, to the reformers, martyrs, and approved commentators, without introducing the name of one of them, and without any quotations from their works. He has indeed made a quotation from the Larger Catechism, compiled by the Westminster Assembly on the question, "What are the sins forbidden in the second commandment?" In the answer they say, among other things, that "Tolerating a false religion is forbidden." To this I perfectly agree, because I believe, with the respectable author of the book called the "Hind let loose," which the Reformed Presbytery fifty years ago considered as a standard authority, that the term *toleration* is improper. It is the illegitimate production of political establishments, of what they are pleased to call the christian religion. The texts offered by the assembly, in answer to the demand of parliament for such proofs, called by one branch of the then civil government to answer such questions as would be propounded to them by the parliament who convened them, are all taken from the peculiar law of Israel as a nation, on which I have already given my opinion.

The author himself quotes the authority of the prophet Isaiah, xlix. 23. "Kings shall be thy nursing fathers," &c. This chapter, and others of that prophecy, look forward to the gospel day. It has its accomplishment in part in the United States. It had its first and most literal accomplishment, as all commentators agree, in the protection which the symbolical church and nation of the Jews received from the Persian kings and queen Esther. We know of no kings, since that period, but what were chargeable with *smiting* some of the most faithful witnesses for Christ. The government of the United States has provided against *smiting* any of the servants of Christ, and against pulling up the good wheat in order to root up the tares; but to leave all to the harvest, when the heart-searching Judge will make the discrimination, which no fallible man can do. The worship of God is completely protected by the government of the United States. The magistrates, indeed, have not turned preachers, to feed believers with the sincere milk of the word. It is believed this was not intended by the prophet, nor meant by the author. The prophecy is, therefore, in part fulfilled by the government of the United States, as a prelude to its more full accomplishment in the millennium, which I believe is certainly approaching; but not such as many expect, not a worldly kingdom.

The author, p. 24. quotes from the Larger Catechism the duties required in the second commandment, which are there described to be "the detesting, disapproving, opposing all false worship, and, according to every one's place and calling, removing all monuments of idolatry." Though I do not substitute the Westminster, nor any other human fallible authority, or creed of any church, for scripture, yet with the above I most heartily agree. I hereby declare that I detest, disapprove, and oppose all false worship, and, according to my place and calling, endeavour to remove all monuments of idolatry. As a proof of the truth of this, I offer my present endeavours to remove the idolatry of the *ratifying* and *sanctioning power of the laws of the most high God, by the civil magis-*

trate, as he does civil laws, and, consequently, of setting human authority above the divine, and other errors which this idolatry brings in its baleful train.

The author (p. 30) quotes Gillespie's Miscellaneous Questions.[6] "Is not," says he, "the mischief of a blind guide greater than if he acted treason, &c. and the loss of one soul by seduction, greater mischief than if he blew up a parliament—cut the throat of kings, or emperors; so precious is that invaluable jewel of a soul: and (says he) when the church of Christ sinketh in a state, let not that state think to swim. Religion and righteousness flourish or fade, stand or fall together. They who are false to God, will never prove faithful to men."

Mr. Gillespie, though neither a reformer nor a martyr, was a very respectable minister of the church of Scotland, during the distracting struggles between prelacy and presbytery, in the seventeenth century. If, as I believe, he wrote the above after 1660, when prelacy was restored on a change of the political head of the church, his warmth can be well accounted for. On that change, two thirds of the ministers of that church conformed to prelacy, thereby renouncing presbytery and the national and solemn league and covenant to which they had solemnly sworn. They turned out a disgrace, even to that church to which they had conformed, and violent persecutors of their former brethren, and patrons of dissoluteness; but they had been hypocrites before. For the proof of this, see *The causes of God's wrath,* which I have not now before me, and the *Solemn acknowledgment of sins and engagement to duties,* bound up with the Westminster Confession, both official records. You will scarcely any where find a more irreligious set of clergy described, than these had been while they were members of that church, during what many have thought to be the purest times of reformation. This is one to be added to many other proofs that the wrath or power of man in matters of religion, *worketh not the righteousness of God.* He in that instance in Scotland, as well as in every similar instance on record, *made foolish the wisdom of this world,* that he might thereby teach men *that their faith should not stand in the*

---

6. George Gillespie (1613–1648), Scottish Presbyterian theologian and member of the Westminster Assembly, *A Treatise of Miscellany Questions* (1648). Because Gillespie died in 1648, he cannot have written the quoted material after 1660.

wisdom of man. The apostle Paul's preaching, whereby he converted the Gentiles, *"was not in the words that man's wisdom toucheth."* The metaphysical wisdom of councils and emperors, never brought souls to Christ, nor did worldly wisdom, terrors or rewards, ever make a pure church of Christ. Mr. Gillespie, in the above quotation, is not speaking of political establishments or powers, but of *blind guides,* such as the Saviour described the Pharisees to have been. They are no doubt to be found in all christian sects, but they abound most in political churches, for obvious reasons. His observations of the importance of real religion to the happiness of a nation, are very just, agreeing with Proverbs xiii. 34. "Righteousness exalteth a nation, but sin is the reproach of any people." For this reason I am opposed to laws calculated to promote hypocricy, viz. prevarication with God and man. Against such the Saviour pronounces the most tremendous woes. Even Mahomet has sentenced such to the seven ovens in hell, the deepest and most wretched.[7] Civil government, using its power and influence to increase that guilt, is contributing to increase national guilt, and call down desolating judgments.

The reverend author has, p. 71, supposed us to object to his system, by saying, "The restraint and punishment of blasphemers and gross heresies, which you contend for, belonged to the Jewish theocracy, which was typical, and so ought not to be imitated."

The objection is not admitted, because it is not true. The law of Moses no where names or provides for punishing gross or other heresies. It provides against overt acts, which it expressly defines, committed by persons, and in situations which it explicitly describes; and where it prescribes punishment, it does not leave it to the opinion of the judges to decide whether the offence is *gross* or *small;* this is matter of opinion. The author ought not to have foisted this into the law of Moses. Did he forget that God, by Moses, had given a solemn charge not to add to it? The law of Pennsylvania defines and provides for the punishment of both blasphemy and prophaneness, not because it is forbidden in the peculiar law of Moses, but because it is contrary to the moral law, and a corruption of manners. The law may yet provide for punishing idolatry

---

7. Muhammad (c. 570–632): Arabian prophet and founder of Islam.

on the same principles, but surely the law of Moses did not authorise it but in the symbolically holy land, where priests and Levites set as judges; nor to execute it on any but the devoted nations and apostate Israelites, and in defined cases.

To support this system in his case, he introduces a long quotation from a publication of the Rev. John Brown, seceding minister of Haddington.[8] This pious and laborious divine, however, was neither one of the *reformers* nor *martyrs,* to which the author appealed. He lived down to our own day, many of his works are, and will be useful, but I do not see a sentence in the author's quotation from him, that supports his system. The quotation, in substance, is as follows:

"The typical magistrates of the Jewish nation *exercised* (intended *executed*) laws relative to murder, theft, unchastity, and other matters relative to the second table of the moral law. Ought, therefore, no magistrate now to do so? The laws respecting the second table pertained as much to the Jewish theocracy as the first. Must, therefore, the christian magistrate for fear of carrying the Jewish theocracy into effect, meddle with no morality at all? Must every thing that was once typical, be now under the gospel, excluded from regulating authority? Must all the laws, directing to elect men fearing God and hating covetousness, to be magistrates or directing men, to judge justly and impartially and prudently, and to punish murderers, thieves, robbers, &c. be discarded as typical? Must the ten commandments, and all the explications of them in the Old and New Testament, be discarded as published in a typical manner?" &c. &c. &c. I agree with the Rev. Mr. Brown, that they ought not; they all belong to the moral law, and their authority was not impaired by having been applied to typical purposes in the less perfect national law of Israel, nor do I know of any christian, or sect of christians, that thinks otherwise; nor do I know how the author came to introduce the quotation to support his cause. Surely he knows that Mr. Brown might, with propriety, be quoted, in opposition to the leading principles of his system. Why did he introduce the weight of that man's name, to prove

---

8. John Brown (1722–1787), minister of the Secession Church and noted biblical scholar, *Dictionary of the Holy Bible* (1769) and *Self-Interpreting Bible,* 2 vols. (1778).

what is nothing to his purpose? He knows that whatever particular opinions that divine might have had, he did not support the author's system, either in theory or practice. He never preached or practised disobedience to the moral authority *of the powers that be,* though he no doubt preached to reform them, as Paul did, who preached on righteousness, temperance, and judgment, before Felix, the Roman governor and representative of Nero, till he trembled; but he did not preach against the immorality of the government itself, but of those who administered it.

CHAPTER IV

Of subjection and allegiance to heathen princes—Law of Pennsylvania respecting murder vindicated—The occasion of making it—On the use of money and paying tribute—The government vindicated from the author's charge of robbery—His claims for aliens, and their swearing oaths—Taking deeds for land—Provision for amending the constitution, and not punishing heresy—The author's misrepresentation of the treaty with Tripoli examined—His misrepresentation of slavery in Pennsylvania refuted—The author demoralizes all the civil governments in the world.

The author says (p. 62) "But the saints accepted offices and places of trust under heathen princes; see the cases of Ezra, Nehemiah and Daniel, in the books called by their names."

This objection I undertake to support. His dilemmas, indeed, might pass unanswered; but as he has nothing better to give in support of his cause, I will give them a place. They are as follows: "If the saints accepted offices, &c. we may conclude, either, *first,* that the power was legitimate; or, *secondly,* that offices may be held under *illegitimate governments;* or, *thirdly,* that the saints sinned in accepting them." The illustration of these dilemmas I will pass over briefly. His supposition of the case of himself being a slave in Algiers, and being employed as president of a university, &c. as similar to the case of Daniel, in Babylon, is so absurd, that it would disgrace a school-boy. Captives made by the Barbary pirates, have their lives saved only for the sake of the ransom expected for their redemption, and are kept on hard fare, and at hard labour, to induce their friends to ransom them soon, and at high prices. Unless they conform to Mahometanism, they cannot be freed from their chains. The author, I presume, never read, even in romance, of a university in Algiers, much less of a christian slave being appointed the president of it, or to any other office. Imaginary cases may be introduced for illustration, but they ought to be imagined within the bounds of probability.

It is well known, that, according to the ancient customs of Asia, when a nation was taken captive, the people were not thereby made menial slaves, as in Algiers, but reduced to political slavery, and, for political reasons, removed from their native territory. But they were still subjects, in common with others, to the conqueror. To prevent the inducement which residing on the lands and in the cities of their fathers, would give them to revolt, they were removed to distant territories, to which they had no peculiar attachment. When the king of Assyria finally conquered the ten tribes, after they had revolted, he transplanted the inhabitants to the eastern parts of his vast empire, to a great distance from the land of their ancestors, and replaced them with captives from different nations of the east and north-cast—2 Kings xvii. 24 and when Sennacherib proposed to take Judah captive, from doing which he was only prevented by a miraculous interposition, he proposed to take them to a land flowing with milk and honey, like their own land—2 Kings xviii. 32. In both these cases they had before become tributary to the king of Assyria, and afterwards revolted. This was also the case with Judah, before Zedekiah was taken captive, and Jerusalem destroyed. The Jews, when captives in Babylon, were subjects, but not menial slaves. Except the removal to a distance from their own land, they were individually considered as free, and they remained a distinct people. Ezra has informed us, that they returned in their usual order, according to their families, not only with the priests and Levites, singers, &c. but the Nithinims, viz. those of the Canaanites who had agreed to do the necessary service of the sanctuary, and more than 7000 servants, male and female, that is, more than one seventh of the whole number, probably nearly equal to one slave to each family. It is well known that the judicial law not only tolerated but authorised the Israelites to procure and hold, in perpetuity, slaves from the nations around them; but not of their brethren, nor stolen. This political slavery in which the Jews were held in Babylon, is so different from the worse than menial slavery in Algiers, that I am astonished they should ever have been compared together. As well might the colonists before the revolution, be compared to slaves in Algiers.

I foresee, however, an objection may probably be taken from Dan. i. 34. where Nebuchadnezzar directs the master of eunuchs to select *certain of the children of Israel, and of the king's seed, and of the princes* in whom there was no blemish, to be instructed in the laws of Chaldea, &c. This was the accomplishment of the prophecy of Isaiah to Hezekiah—Isaiah xxxix. 7. and no more than Samuel the prophet forewarned Israel that their own kings would do, if they persisted in the desire of having a king, like the nations around them, viz. a despot—1 Sam. viii. 10–18. I admit, however, that according to our ideas of slavery, these young men were slaves, while, at the same time, they were nobles; but no man in his senses will compare this kind of slavery to the mercenary and barbarous slavery in Algiers. However, these young men being thus selected, is an indubitable proof that the rest enjoyed personal liberty, except as to returning to their own land.

In page 63, the author says, "Any office may be held, or service engaged in, upon the following conditions, viz.

1st. "That the duties be right in themselves." To this all agree.

2d. "That they be regulated by a just law." I answer, that is matter of opinion. He undoubtedly, agreeably to his principles, believes that a just law would authorise punishing me as an heretic. A just law, agreeably to my opinion, would let both his head and mine stay on us, and afford us both time to repent to the eleventh hour.

3d. "That there be no other oath of office required, but faithfully to execute official duties." This third rule affords a fair implication that the author would hold an office under the devil, or any of his servants, provided he got the salary, and the service to his mind. He will make no question of the right to bestow the office, if he gets the emolument. We have many others, at present, who act on the same principle. I wish to be informed, however, by the reverend author, how an office can be conferred by a person, who has no moral right to hold an office himself? This is a practical, and, therefore, an important question.

The author (p. 64, 65) states a case of being prisoner with the Indians, and, as their slave, assisting them in their lawful employment; but that connected with this they have a rule "that every morning and evening the officers shall take care that those under their respective charges shall pow wow, or worship the devil—Let an oath to support and maintain this little code, be made, by the community, an essential qualification for holding an office."

"Now, supposing these two men are called to accept offices, in their respective tribes, may they both comply with good consciences?"

I have not inserted this case of illustration with a view to answer it, otherwise than to shew its absurdity. It only goes to shew the weakness of the author's cause. Illustrations are not proofs of any thing; they are only introduced to explain or elucidate a case, but they can do this no further than the supposed case is similar to the real one, and founded on probability. In this case there is neither similarity nor probability. There is no similarity between the old organized governments of Babylon and Assyria, *who were of old like a pool of water,* and were the cradle of mankind, and of the arts, and were at all times civilized governments, and which eventually sunk by the excess of refinement and luxury, which always renders men effeminate; whose Magi or men famous for wisdom degenerated into self-seeking impostors, such as many of the christian clergy had done in the author's standard period, and who even exceeded the eastern magicians, in the number of their fabulous miracles and sainted impostors. The Indians never were, in this country, civilized; they have always been barbarous, and all attempts hitherto to civilize them have proved abortive. And yet, strange to tell, they understand the law of nature better, and practice more agreeably to it, with respect to the religion of their follow men, than the author. According to my information, received from those who have dwelt long among their various tribes, either as prisoners, public agents, or traders, they believe that men are accountable only to the *Great Spirit, the master of breath,* for their religion; they respect a really religious man, and have often reproved christian prisoners for not living agreeable to the principles of their religion. They sometimes savagely barbecue and eat a portion of their enemies taken in war, but they never have obliged either christians, or other tribes, to attend their pow wows; doing so is absolutely contrary to their rules, which prevent strangers from attending them. Hence it is that we know nothing certain about them, and are liable to be imposed on. One respectable person, who had long been their prisoner, informed me, that knowing of an unusual stir, and numerous meetings, made interest to be secretly admitted, but saw no pow wow, but only a man preaching morality from the law of nature, as far as he understood it, with relation to their dependance on the Great Spirit for their success in hunting, &c. He taught them that the ghosts of women and children murdered in war would hant them, &c.

Why should the author have recourse to the unlettered savages for the support of his cause; and, in so doing, slander even them so egregiously, as by implication to charge them with a conduct, of which they never were guilty, and which is contrary to all their established rules? With equal justice may he, as he has done, suppose the primitive christians, approved commentators, and the reformers, to have testified in favour of his system, which, with the apostles, they have uniformly testified against. In this case, as well as the case of Algiers, there is neither similarity nor probability. Therefore it is a mere sophism to deceive the misinformed, analogous to the so called *pious frauds* which prevailed in the fourth and fifth centuries.

After the author has at length gone on to prove how much better the government of Babylon was, with respect to holding offices under it, viz. holding them under a despotic government, than a government of compact and law, he says (p. 64) the despotic governments require no oath of allegiance, which the others do. He concludes the paragraph by asserting, "Daniel had not, therefore, to swear to support an immoral constitution, for there was none." In the next paragraph he says: "The office was either such as required allegiances to the constitution, or it did not. If the latter, it is the thing contended for, viz. that there was no immoral obligation connected with the office. If the former, he was *perjured*, not only by breaking it in several instances, but in taking it also, for he swore to a blank, *i.e.* to perform he knew not what; but there is no account of Daniel taking such obligation. Indeed it would have been inconsistent with the smiles of heaven, which he and others in office frequently enjoyed."

We have only the author's assertion, that the king of Babylon required no oath of allegiance, and that the government had no law but the will of the sovereign. This is not the case in the most despotic governments.

In these the sovereign is so much above the laws, that he changes them when he pleases. This was the case with the rescripts of the Roman emperors, when they were at the height of despotism, and, in the author's opinion, of perfection. He has indeed counted largely on the credulity of those for whom he wrote, when he asserted that the king of Babylon required no oath of allegiance, when he conferred a trust. How stands the fact?

After the same king of Babylon had carried Jehoiachin and other captives to Babylon, he made Zedekiah his deputy or governor over Judea, with the title of king. In conferring that trust he required an oath of allegiance. For breaking this oath Zedekiah forfeited the smiles of heaven, and procured its destructive frowns. The inspired writer says (2 Chron. xxxvi. 13.) speaking of the sins of Zedekiah, "And he also rebelled against king Nebuchadnezzar, who had made him swear by God." To the same purpose see Ezekiel, chap. xvii. from the 11th to the 18th verse, wherein Zedekiah is most severely reproved for breaking his oath of allegiance to the king of Babylon. v. 18. "Seeing he despised the oath by breaking the covenant, when lo, he had given his hand, and done all these things, he shall not escape. Therefore, thus saith the Lord God, as I live, surely mine oath, which he hath broken, even it will I recompense on his own head," &c. When we compare this with the pathetic, impressive, and prophetical exhortations of the weeping prophet Jeremiah to Zedekiah, to fulfil his allegiance to the king of Babylon, we will probably be convinced, that in taking that *oath,* and *giving his hand,* he had the smiles, *i.e.* the approbation of heaven; and that in breaking it, he had its high disapprobation. Of this oath we are only incidentally informed, through the breach of it, but it proves that the king of Babylon was in the habit of requiring such; that is to say, that it was the law of the kingdom to require an oath of allegiance when a public trust was conferred.

That oaths were required and given, as the highest assurance of confidence, in conferring trusts and pledging friendship, from the early ages of the world, is evident, from the history of the patriarchs in the books of Moses. It is authorised by the law of nature, the law of Moses, by the gospel, and by the highest possible imitable example, viz. the example of God Almighty; with this difference, that because he could swear by no greater, he swear by himself, and because he is infinitely the greatest, men and angels swear by him. To bind Zedekiah the more firmly to perform his oath, Nebuchadnezzar changed his name from Mettaniah, to what imports *the righteousness of God*. The Universal History, and others, inform us, in addition to what the Bible does, that oaths were in use and sacred among the Gentile nations from time immemorial. We know they were awfully so among the Greeks and Romans. The author himself will admit, that the term sacrament, which christians apply to baptism and the Lord's supper, as seals of the covenant of grace, is taken from the oath of fidelity given by the Roman officers and soldiers to that heathen and idolatrous government. That the Saviour, when he healed the centurion's servant, highly approved of his faith, but did not censure him for holding the military command under that oath, nor tell him to resign it. The centurion, who was directed by an angel to send for the apostle Peter to instruct him more perfectly, enjoyed the smiles of heaven while he was under an oath of allegiance, and while an emperor reigned, little, if at all, inferior in wickedness to Nero, viz. Caligula. The apostle's instructions are on record, but in none of them is he told to renounce his allegiance to the Roman government. This centurion enjoyed the smiles of heaven in an extraordinary measure before he received the divine mission of the apostle Peter, who taught him the blessed doctrine of Christ crucified, &c. but not a word about the immoral government to which he had sworn allegiance, nor a caution to renounce his allegiance; nor did the apostle Paul give any such advice to the centurion, who treated him courteously when he guarded him on his passage to Rome, and during his shipwreck on his way, to support his solemn and legal appeal to the supreme court of the empire, while the *monster* Nero was emperor.

The author (p. 63) has assigned another reason why Daniel did not take an oath to the king of Babylon. "The monarch was the legislator; his will was the law of the realm. Daniel v. 19. "Whom he would he slew, and whom he would he kept alive."

Has not the author, in this instance, proved too much. When Israel chose to be governed by a king, like the nations around them, viz. a despot, as all the kings in Asia had then become; God, as their king, severely reproved them for their choice, and by his prophet warned them of the result. I Sam. viii. 10–22. After this, we never hear of a king who thought proper to take a man's life, by applying for this purpose to the courts of justice instituted by the judicial law. Nebuchadnezzar was a mighty conqueror. History says he governed from India to the pillars of Hercules, *i.e.* the Straits of Gibraltar. When he took Jerusalem, which had most perfidiously rebelled, he slew the king's sons before his eyes, and whom besides he thought proper. This was agreeable even to the modern law of nations, as they, after rebelling contrary to the solemn oath of their king, and holding out during a long siege, contrary to the advice of Jeremiah the prophet, were taken without conditions. Was this worse than David did with the Ammonites? See 2 Sam. xii. 31. "And he (David) brought forth the people that were therein, and put them under saws, and under harrows of iron, and under axes of iron, and made them pass through the brick kiln; and thus did he unto all the cities of the children of Ammon." The children of Ammon never had taken an oath to David with the divine approbation, as Zedekiah had done to the king of Babylon. I vindicate neither of them. The scripture records the fact with respect to David, but makes no apology for his conduct in this instance. The Bible taken, even as a common history, is the most candid and impartial history that ever was wrote. In matters of fact, it has no favourites, and makes no apologies.

To come to the emperors to whom the author impliedly ascribes infallibility, as they were the first who pretended to give authority, by their civil sanction, to the law of the most high God, they had precisely the character given to the king of Babylon; *whom they would they slew, and whom they would they kept alive.* Constantine slew his own son Crispin, and afterwards his wife, a number of the nobles, his brother-in-law, after he had promised him protection, and his sister's son of twelve years old, without a form of trial, for which, at Rome, he acquired the name of the *second Nero.* He sometimes exposed prisoners, taken in war, to wild beasts for amusement, and shed as much blood in war, probably, as the king of Babylon, and grievously oppressed the empire. Theodosius, a better man I admit, than Constantine, in a passion massacred the inhabitants of Thessalonica, his own subjects, and committed other excesses. He shed much blood in war, but it was principally for the necessary defence of the empire, not in a struggle *for* empire, like Constantine. Yet the author acknowledges their authority, and compares them to good Josiah, &c. Was their murder and oppression the less criminal, because they were christians, and had usurped the authority of Christ over his own house?

In short, the prophet Jeremiah writes by divine direction to the captives in Babylon, and exhorts them (Jer. xxix. 4–7) to be good subjects, to marry, to plant, to build, to seek the peace of the city, and to pray unto the Lord for it, *for in the peace thereof you shall have peace.* Very similar this to the apostle Paul's directions in 1 Tim. ix. 1–3. "I exhort, therefore, that, first of all, supplications, prayers, intercessions, and giving of thanks, be made for all men: for kings, and for all that are in authority, that we lead a quiet and peaceable life, in all godliness and honesty." Here the testimony of an eminent prophet and apostle agrees in giving their united testimony, that allegiance expressed in every proper manner, to such powers as we receive protection from, and as God, in his providence, has set over us, is both our duty and interest. When they withdraw their protection, the allegiance ceases of course; yet this is not admitted by the author's political heads of the church of Christ on earth. They frequently have claimed allegiance where they have withdrawn protection from, and made war on such as would not worship the image they had set up, viz. human authority substituted in place of the divine.

An oath of allegiance, which God calls *mine oath,* and *my covenant,* was exacted from Zedekiah, on being appointed governor, with the title of king, of the small territory of Judea, afterwards but a small portion of the province on that side of the river Euphrates. Of this oath and covenant of allegiance to the king of Babylon, God highly approves, and by his prophets exhorts, in the most pathetic manner, to the faithful fulfilling of it, and denounces and executes desolating judgments for the breach of it, and commands the captives to be good subjects, not only in their outward practice, but in their prayers to God, for the welfare of the government to whom they were captives; and they enjoyed the smiles of heaven in doing so.

Daniel was appointed to, and accepted of the of the office of chief governor of the extensive and powerful province of Babylon, including the seat of empire, and of chief justice of the empire, implied by "sitting in the king's gate," viz. the supreme seat of judgment. Yet the author assures us, on his own authority only, that he took no oath of allegiance, or that if he did, he was perjured, and could not enjoy the smiles of heaven. Now we are assured he did enjoy the smiles of heaven, that the king of Babylon was in the habit of requiring such an oath, on conferring a trust, that God approved of giving it, and punished the breach of it, and smiled on those who took and fulfilled it. By what authority then can the author say, that the king of Babylon did not require an oath of allegiance from Daniel, or that if he gave it, he was perjured, and could not enjoy the smiles of heaven?

How opposite to Jeremiah the prophet is the author. Jer. 27. from the first to the last verse, God asserts his sovereign right to dispose of all nations of the earth, and dispose of them to whom he will, and declares that he has given into the hand of Nebuchadnezzar all the kings and their dominion and property, before named, to serve him, and his son, and his son's son, until the time of his land, viz. of the fall of the Babylonish empire come.

In the 12th verse the prophet applies particularly to Zedekiah and the Jews, saying, "Bring your neck under the king of Babylon, and serve him and his people, and live." "Why will you die, thou and thy people, by the sword, by the famine, &c.—Therefore, hearken thou not unto the words of the prophets, who speak unto you, saying, Ye shall not serve the king of Babylon, they prophecy a lie unto you."

In the above, the smiles of heaven are connected with submitting to the authority of the king of Babylon, of which we know by the case of Zedekiah, that taking an oath of allegiance was one instance of obedience required and approved of by God, and the breach of it called rebellion by the authority of God Almighty. The author, however, in his superior wisdom, has chosen his lot with the false prophets, and may be addressed in the words of the prophet Ezek. chap. xxviii. 3. "Behold thou art wiser than Daniel," &c. The above applies equally to the cases of Zerubbabel, Ezra, Nehemiah, Mordecai, three of them successively governors of Judea, and the fourth prime minister of Persia, and to all similar cases. God, by the prophet, expressly gave the dominion to Babylon for three generations, and after this gave it to Cyrus, king of Persia, without express limitation of duration, but with a prophetic intimation that it should pass to the Greeks, to whose authority, in the person of Alexander, it was transferred.

All authors, whether divine, moral, or political, whose works I have had an opportunity of perusing, except the author's, agree in maintaining that allegiance and protection are inseparably relative terms, and that their relation is founded in moral honesty, viz. the moral law of nature. The author not only reverses this universally established doctrine in theory, but in practice; he and those for whose benefit he professes to write, have, and still continue to receive protection from the government of Pennsylvania, which has been distinguished for hospitality to strangers, agreeably to the directions of the apostle, ever since it became a colony. This principle was carefully introduced by Mr. Penn, its original founder, and not less carefully cultivated by the state government.[1] Of this the reverend author, and those who adhere to his system, are standing witnesses. But what is the return made for this protection? It is not allegiance. It is not even quiet and inoffensive acquiescence. It is *perversion, slander,* and *sedition.* This, indeed, is a high charge, which ought not to be made on light grounds. If I do so, the candid reader will condemn me; therefore I am responsible for the charge.

I pass over his insidious, but trifling objections to the oaths administered to jurors, &c. &c. (p. 54) as unworthy of notice or reply, but cannot pass over his note on the criminal code of Pennsylvania, p. 55.

"In no case does the violation of the divine law appear more flagrant, than in the law of Pennsylvania, respecting murder. God expressly commands, in the most pointed manner, Gen. ix. 6. 'Whoso sheddeth man's blood, by man shall his blood be shed.' And, Numb. xxxv. 31. 'Moreover, ye shall take no satisfaction for the life of a murderer, which is guilty of death; but he shall be surely put to death.' Verse 23. 'And the land cannot be cleansed of the blood that is shed therein, but by the blood of him that shed it.'

"The divine law distinguishes between manslaughter and murder; but not between murder of the first degree, and murder of the second. How flatly contradictory to the law of God, is the law of Pennsylvania, which declares, that, after April 22, 1794, 'No crime whatsoever (except murder of the first degree) shall be punished with death, in the state of

---

1. William Penn (1644–1718): Quaker founder of Pennsylvania.

Pennsylvania.' See Read's Digest, page 288. How could a juror, who was a Bible believer, act in this case?"

I am very sorry that I cannot avoid saying, that the author, in the above paragraph, has indulged in asserting an absolute and palpable falsehood.

He says the divine law, probably meaning that the peculiar law of Moses distinguishes between murder and manslaughter. I say, and say it with confidence, *that it does not.* It neither mentions nor distinguishes between manslaughter and the most innocent accidental homicides; between a man being "killed by the axe slipping off the helve," (Deut. xix. 5) nor the case where the "man lies not in wait, but God delivers him into his hand; then I will appoint thee a place whither he shall flee. But if a man come presumptuously upon his neighbour, to slay him with guile; thou shalt take him from mine altar, that he may die"—Exod. xxi. 13, 14. "But if he thrust him of hatred, or hurl at him by laying of wait, that he die; or in enmity smite him with his hand, that he die: he that smote him shall surely be put to death; for he is a murderer: the revenger of blood shall slay the murderer, when he meeteth him. But if he thrust him suddenly without enmity, or have cast upon him any thing without laying of wait; or with any stone, wherewith a man may die, seeing him not, and cast it upon him, that he die, and was not his enemy, neither sought his harm; then the congregation shall judge between the slayer and the revenger of blood according to these judgments"—Numbers xxxv. 22–24. "But if any man hate his neighbour, and lie in wait for him, and smite him mortally, that he die, and fleeth into one of those cities, then the elders of his city shall send and fetch him hence," &c.

On these extracts from the law of Moses, I observe, that they do not fully correspond with that given to the sons of Noah. They very materially restrain the power of the avenger of blood, both by the institution of the cities of refuge, and courts of justice. The penalties for the breach of the moral law being no part of the law itself, but incidentally becoming necessary, because of transgression, to enforce obedience to it; they are chargeable according to circumstances, and the will of the legislature.

I have before observed, that the law respecting the punishment of murder given to the sons of Noah, was the best that the then state of society would admit. That all penalties being positive and changeable institutions, agreeable to the will of the legislature, a different and improved criminal code was given by Moses. And by the same rule, every nation taking the moral law, applicable for their own circumstances, for their guide, have a right to enact such penalties as are necessary to protect their people *in living quiet and peaceable lives in godliness and honesty,* agreeable to the prayer which the apostle directed to be offered up by the churches.

The legislature of Pennsylvania very properly exercised this right, and accommodated her criminal code agreeably to circumstances, and the state of society. But was their decision contrary to the moral law? No, it was not. Was it contrary to the judicial law of Moses? No, it was not. It was an improvement of it, and no doubt such as it would have been, if circumstances had been equal. But why did not the author state the law of Pennsylvania as any honest man would have done? He quoted the introductory or heading line, repealing other criminal laws, and gave it out for the law itself respecting murder, and falsified the law of Moses to give plausible currency to his seditious slander of the law of Pennsylvania.

No crime, except murder in the first degree, shall be punished with death. All murder which shall be perpetrated by means of poison, or by laying in wait, or by any kind of witful, deliberate, and premeditated killing, or which shall be committed in the perpetration, or attempt to perpetrate, arson, rape, or burglary, shall be deemed murder in the first degree.

The above is the law of Pennsylvania for punishing murder, of which he has not inserted one word. He has only inserted a negative introductory line, which applies more particularly to other crimes formerly punished by death, than to murder, for it made no change in the punishment of murder, nor abatement of it. The definition of murder to be punished with death, includes the definition of the law of Moses, with the addition of poisoning, and without the exception in favour of the master who killed his servant. The law of Moses, in every instance, shews the greatest detestation of shedding human blood, but distributes the punishments, as it pleased divine wisdom to entrust to fallible judges in that state of society. For the same reason, two witnesses were indispensably necessary, under that law, to convict a murderer. In the present state of society, Pennsylvania, and all the other states (except one) make no exception in favour of the master who wilfully and deliberately kills his slave, and all of them are convicted on the testimony of one positive witness; hence the law of Pennsylvania is more severe against murder than the judicial law. It is similar to the law of England, and both in a degree copied from the law of Moses, adapted to change of circumstances. Murder is defined by the law of England to be "a person of sound memory and discretion, unlawfully killing any reasonable creature, in being, and under the king's peace, with malice aforethought, either express or implied." Torture was not admitted in the judicial law, but it was introduced among christians in the dark ages, and applied to several real or supposed crimes, especially against heresy, under the notion of punishing sin.

Murder, in the English law, is called *felonious homicide.* In the judicial law all manslaying, short of murder, is considered as one kind of homicide, and equally punished with death, if caught by the avenger; or, if he escapes, with banishment to the city of refuge, except the master who slew his servant, for whom the punishment, in the most aggravated cases, was a fine. The Roman civil laws, however, which generally prevailed among christian nations, and the common law of England, distinguish homicides into different classes, such as *justifiable, excusable,* and *felonious;* and those are again subdivided and punished according to their different degrees of criminality. But whoever kills a man, however innocently or justifiably, must stand his trial as a murderer, and bear the burthen of proof to vindicate himself. This, no doubt, for good reasons, was not the case with the judicial law. In prosecutions under it, the burthen of proof lay on the prosecutors, who must produce two positive witnesses to prove the fact.

The English law, &c. also distinguish felonious homicides into different classes, viz. treason, murder, and manslaughter. The last they define to be the unlawful killing of another, without malice, either express or implied, but in a sudden passion, or in some unlawful act, without any known malice aforethought, or premeditated intention. Such would, under the judicial law, have been entitled to their refuge, and protected from the avenger, equally with more innocent homicides. This embraces most of the cases of homicides that take place in unpremeditated quarrels, frays, &c. and unfortunately it has been applied to the case of duels. Men of sobriety and reflection, both in England and this country, have long lamented, that through the aversion of juries to take men's lives, murderers frequently escaped with only the punishment of manslaughter, viz. a slight touch on the hand with a hot iron, which, from habit, has come to be attended with little or no disgrace. Forfeiture of estate is mentioned, but seldom executed, even in England, and cannot in this country, where that kind of royal robbery of families is constitutionally forbid, even in cases of treason. All whipping, cropping, burning the hand, &c. which disguises or maims the body of a man, is also forbidden by our laws. This rendered it necessary to enact some other punishment for manslaughter, that it might not escape, and also that murder, in doubtful cases, might not escape altogether, under the name of manslaughter. They did not, for this purpose, abate the punishment of murder, nor qualify the definition of it, but to render it more detestable, called it by the opprobrious name of "*murder in the first degree;*" and on the same principle, to render manslaughter, in the higher grades of it, more detestable, they called it "*murder in the second degree.*" And instead of a slight burn on the hand, at the discretion of the executioner, who might easily be bribed, the delinquent must be condemned to a period of imprisonment and hard labour, for a term, not exceeding fourteen years—no trifling punishment. When the criminal code was revised, the judges were authorised to offer this in preference of death, to some who were liable for crimes committed under the former law to death; some of them refused the exchange.

Here it is observable, that the author has palmed a line, repealing other criminal laws, on his readers, for the law of Pennsylvania, providing for the punishment of murder. And to aid him in his deception, took advantage of its being entered as an introduction to that law, not to repeal it, as he insinuates, but to prepare the way for giving it more explicit force. He artfully conceals the definition of murder, and, to give the deception the greater force, he profanely quotes the texts of scripture before mentioned, to countenance, if not an assertion, at least a disingenuous implication, that Pennsylvania does not punish murder with death, equal to what is required by the law of God, but takes satisfaction for murder, which they do not do.

I am justified in saying, that though the author has, in numerous instances, discovered want of candour, or that he wrote without due information, or understanding the subject, this is a case that admits of no apology; in no case does the author's want of candour appear more flagrant, than in this instance. How flatly contrary to the law of God is his perversion of truth and candour, in order to deceive others, and disturb the public peace.

If any should think the above too severe, I ask, *Is there not a cause?* There is cause sufficient in the statement of the case, which is aggravated by the effects it has had.

But it is not in this instance alone that the author seditiously slanders the government and people of the United States. This is done in a lesser or greater degree in every one of his seven reasons why he cannot homologate our governments. Besides the case last noticed, every instance in which he calls them immoral and illegitimate, *i.e.* bastard governments, is a slander. None had ever any claim on us but Great Britain, by which we were indeed considered as illegitimate or bastard governments, while deemed by them in a state of rebellion. But since that question was decided in favour of the United States, Britain herself, and all other nations, have, and do, acknowledge and treat with them as legitimate moral governments; and at a time when all the governments of Europe have been charging each other with immorality, &c. the United States escape clear from any such charge, except from the author.

In page 69, he supposes us to object—"But you make use of the money which receives its currency from their sanction; and you support them by paying tribute, &c. Why not swear allegiance, hold offices," &c.

To this he answers, "We make use of the money, to be sure, but when we give an equivalent for it, by industry or otherwise, it is our own property; and, another man's *stamping his name* upon our coats, is no reason why we should throw them away."

What contemptible sophistry! What analogy is there between one individual stamping his name on another man's coat, to claim a currency to it, and the giving currency to money? This is one of the highest sovereign acts of government. It is authorised by law, and, in monarchies, stamped with the image and superscription of the sovereign. In republics it is stamped as authorised according to law, otherwise it is not money. The laws of the United States have authorised a particular coinage of their own, and adopted by law some foreign coins, to which they have affixed a legal value, and for which it shall pass. Both are money by the sovereign authority, and not like an unauthorised individual stamping his name on another man's coat.

He adds: "It must be granted, also, that we do support them, by paying tribute, &c. So do we the robber, unto whom we give a part, to save the remainder. But will it, therefore, follow, that I may legally swear allegiance to him, or become one of his officers in the business of robbery and plunder!"

Another wonderful illustration, by which the American governments *are designated robbers.* Did ever the American government rob any man? No. The very insinuation of this is a seditious slander. The author knew that the sedition law was repealed before he wrote his book, but the same authority can renew it again.[2] Robbers, if ever they are so generous as not to take all, give no equivalent for what they take. For what small tribute the author pays in this state, which goes wholly to making roads and bridges, or for court houses, courts, &c. the protection and accommodation of which the author and all aliens enjoy, as fully and freely as citizens do, is a full and ample equivalent, which they accept of, and enjoy. They pay no direct tax for the expense of the civil government of the state—this is paid out of another fund, which arose from the state doing more than her share during the distressing period of the war with Britain; of this, the hard earnings of the citizens, in other times, the author, &c. enjoy their proportion, without any equivalent, and they pay none to support the federal government. In England, from which we have copied much of our jurisprudence, allegiance is divided into two kinds, namely, the natural allegiance of natives, which they consider as perpetual, and the local and temporary allegiance, which is incidental to aliens. We have required hitherto only this last, for we have as yet made no law against expatriation, either of native or alien, but freely protect aliens without their giving allegiance. I have already shewn that all approved commentators on the Bible, or on civil and common law, and all moral and political writers, consider it a first principle or established moral maxim,

2. Sedition Acts passed by Congress in 1798 made it a crime to criticize the government or the president. They had expired or been repealed by 1802.

that protection necessarily draws allegiance—that they are morally connected together—that they cannot be separated. This being the case, I
recommend to the author to examine the questions over again, on more
correct moral principles. In so doing, he will find he has been mistaken;
that the state has not robbed them; that it has received nothing but for
an ample equivalent; that it did not seize their persons to bring them
within their power, nor *put them in fear, nor take from them, in this situation,
money or goods.* This is the legal technical definition of robbery. He will
find also, from his own statement, that those whose cause he advocates,
intruded themselves within our territory, enjoyed protection to their
persons and property, and to their industry in acquiring property—And
by his advice refuse allegiance, the only moral return for those very valuable benefits; but instead thereof spurn at the hand that received them
when they were strangers, and fed and protected them without receiving
the equivalent, which the law of nature, and nature's God requires. If he
does this impartially, he will certainly be convinced that he has cast the
charge of robbery on the wrong side—that by the decision of the moral
law, himself, and those whom he advocates, are the *robbers,* in receiving
protection without an equivalent, and not the *government,* from whom
they have experienced protection and forbearance, but no violence. He
certainly would be convinced of the fallaciousness and indecency of his
next illustration in the same page:

"Should a robber meet me on the high way, and, upon finding that I
had no money, put his bayonet to my breast; and should it appear evidently, that he intended to kill me, unless I would solemnly engage to
take, or send him, a certain sum of money, in a given time, say fifty dollars, ought I not to comply?"

This, as an abstract question, has been decided differently by casuists,
but what has it to do with the United States? Did they act the part of robbers in such a manner as he describes? The insinuation is a slander, too
absurd and too ridiculous to require further notice.

His fifteenth supposed objection is: "But you are mostly aliens, and
have no business with our governmental affairs." This is an objection of
his own framing. No country in the world has received aliens with more
freedom, nor admitted them to the participation of all their privileges
with more liberality. But we will hear his own reply to it.

"Admitting that we were all aliens, what does this prove? 'The earth is the Lord's, and the fulness thereof.'—Ps. xxiv. 1. We are moral subjects of the Lord of the whole earth. While we maintain true and faithful allegiance to him, and conscientiously obey his laws, we have a right to live in any part of his dominions, where, in his providence, he may please to cast our lots. We ought not to infringe upon any of the rights of others, &c.——We meddle not with your governmental affairs, farther than their morality or immorality is concerned. We have a right to give our opinion. We do so, and the reasons on which it is founded."

How are we to understand the author? Does he profess to come with a divine mission? Let him then shew the proofs of his apostleship. He contradicts the most explicit language of the apostles of Christ, and of the law of Moses, which he professes to substitute for the moral law, as has been already shewn. That he patronizes a practice, and practices himself, totally repugnant to the practices of the patriarchs, the prophets, Christ and his apostles, the primitive christians, the witnesses during the dark ages, the martyrs and reformers, has been heretofore shewn. He ought to work greater miracles than any of these have done, before he succeeds in overturning their doctrines, and condemning their practice. The moral law being addressed to every individual (or, to use the author's words, "every man necessarily possesses it") and the gospel, both in its promises and precepts, as well as the instructive examples it records—these are addressed to the people of the United States, as well as others, and they have received from God the same powers of reason and judgment as other men, and are equally accountable to him for the exercise of it.

Though the earth, with dominion over the creatures, be given in a general grant to the human family, yet that it is not so given to be held in common but to be distributed according to certain established rules, is evident from scripture, reason, and the history of nations. This distribution is of two kinds—national and individual. The property of all the individuals which compose the nation, is the property of the government of the nation, so far as is necessary to provide for its protection against the claims or invasion of other nations, robbers or intruders; but it is distributed and appropriated to individuals, in such proportions, and subject to such rules, as the laws of each nation prescribe. This is essentially necessary to civil society, agriculture, &c. No alien nor foreigner has any right to intrude himself, or interfere with the property and enjoyments of the nation or individuals, further or otherwise than the law of the nation authorises.

There is one exception to this rule. If by providential distress through shipwreck, or any other unavoidable cause, strangers are left on our territory, we must treat them with hospitality, and protect them until they have an opportunity to return to their own country. This is a moral duty, binding individuals as well as nations; any thing further depends on moral discretion. In the positive institution of government given to Israel, they are enjoined to be kind to the stranger—but it was provided that strangers, under that law, could never hold land in fee simple. The land was entailed to the Israelites and their families in an unalienable perpetuity; it could not even be mortgaged but for a very short period; therefore, under that law, strangers could never hold real property, nor were they assured of liberty. In the very prosperous times of Israel, numerous strangers resorted to them; king David had numbered them, for what purpose we are not informed, but Solomon made them slaves to the public soon after his father's death. When he began to build the temple, he put fourscore thousand of them to be hewers in the mountains, and threescore and ten thousand to be bearers of burthens, and three thousand six hundred to be overseers to set the people to work—2 Chron. ii. 17, 18. The gospel teaches not to be neglectful to entertain strangers; but no law obliges states to encourage aliens voluntarily to settle among them. This depends on the discretion of the civil society. If they followed the example of Solomon, they would employ them in public works.

The author, indeed, claims a right to live in any part of his (God's) dominions, where in his providence he may please to order his lot. This he claims from his conscientious faithfulness to Christ Jesus. Paul was as confident as the author, while he was under the influence of an erring conscience. But how did providence order their lot so as to claim independent rights? Were they cast on our shores by shipwreck, or were they specially commissioned by God? If in either these ways, they can shew the proofs of it. But if they came voluntarily, to better their worldly condition, they derive no more claim from providential protection in this case, than the man who enjoys providential protection in the act of robbing or stealing. Most nations hold their lands by prescriptive possession, from times unknown or uncertain. The United States alone hold theirs by fair moral purchase. What the inhabitants had not formerly purchased from the proprietor of Pennsylvania, the legislature purchased from him during the revolution, for 130,000*l.* which was honestly paid, as well as the Indian rights, which they afterwards purchased. The United States purchased from Britain, by treaty, in lieu of the expenses and depredations of the war, to which near $3,000,000 were added by an after treaty. Their claim to a pre-emption of the Indiana territory, the proceeds of which they appropriated to pay the debts of the war, which it is never likely to amount to—it has not yet amounted to sufficient to pay the expenses accrued by purchasing the actual rights from Indians, and annuities engaged to them, and the surveying, protection, &c. The New-Orleans, &c. was purchased, in order to get a peaceable outlet to the ocean, for $15,000,000, and the rights of the inhabitants secured. In short, no nation can shew such a fair moral right of property to the territory they possess. They hold none by conquest; they did not even avail themselves of the right of conquest from the Indians, though they were twice subdued; but purchased from them at a fair price, only when they chose to sell, and add an annuity to make it their interest to continue at peace. Yet the author, &c. who he says are aliens, invalidate our title. I would not have distinguished aliens, if he had not introduced them with a superior claim, independent of the government.

No nation ever had, or can have, a clearer moral title to their territory, than the United States. The foundation of civil government is laid on the law of nature, and all approved commentators agree that the fifth commandment contains an abstract of all relative duties among men, as all other relations flow from the relation of parents and children, or partake in a certain degree of its nature. Nations, like families, have their rules and rights. It is my moral duty to receive into my family, and relieve a stranger in distress. But if he sows sedition in my family, and says I have no moral right to govern it—that, therefore, even my lawful commands ought not to be obeyed; that by enforcing them for the support of the family, I act the part of a robber with my bayonet at his breast, &c. I certainly have a right, and it is my duty, to refuse to continue to support him in my family. This is just the case with civil government, with respect to seditious and slanderous aliens, and they have the further right, for the peace of the citizens, to punish them.

If our government has no moral right to govern, it has no moral right to hold or dispose of land, to coin money, take legal testimony, or make decisions in law; nor the citizens who hold land under warrants or patents from the government, to hold them, nor to transfer them to others, nor others to hold it under such transfer—testimony taken or decisions made under immoral authority and laws, cannot be valid. The author and his aliens, however, appear to have made or found a new moral law, suited to their own convenience, to justify them in taking all the benefits of government, and refusing the corresponding relative duties enjoined by divine authority. If the government is immoral, all its official acts are so likewise; not only its grants of land, judicial decisions, &c. but even its protection of the aliens must also be immoral.

The author (p. 69) in his ninth supposed objection—for he makes the objections, which he means to answer himself, to his own mind—says, "You swear oaths administered by them, and hold deeds of land, &c. whose validity rests entirely upon their sanction."

Not to follow the author through his metaphysical refinements about oaths and deeds, I will inform him, that a deed gives no title in law, further than it is founded on an original grant from the government, and finally confirmed by its patent. Is it possible that the author has wrote with so little information, as not to know that a deed is a conveyance, from one citizen to another, of his own right to the thing conveyed; but that a patent, is the transfer from the government itself, and that unless founded on this, as directed by law, all deeds are a nullity; and that so are all testimonies taken on oath otherwise, or by other authority, than the government authorises. An oath, not taken as the law directs, is no lawful testimony. A man may commit perjury, for which he is accountable to God, but not to a municipal court, which did not require or authorize such testimony; but if proved, it will prevent the person thus perjured in the sight of God, from being admitted as a witness thereafter in any court, because it affects his moral character. Therefore, infallible in his judgment, and immense in his knowledge, as the author represents himself to be, every deed for land which he or his friends purchase, depends for its validity on the moral authority of the government under which it is held. If it has no moral right to grant it, they have no moral right to hold the grant; and that what they receive as money, in this or any other country, is money, no further than the government has made it so. That counterfeiting it would subject him to the penalty of death, but not to the more severe penalty of treason, as in Britain, from whence he came. This being the doctrine of the moral law, that an oath, without acknowledging the authority of the magistrate, is no testimony, and of the municipal law of all civilized nations, and the law between civilized nations and the citizens of each, and consequently the law of God, agreeably to his former decisions.

I will here take a concise notice of his fourteenth objection, likewise, I presume, of his own making, namely—"But the constitution makes provision for its own amendment," &c. He answers, "The representatives must take an oath to support the constitution.——This oath we have formally shewn to be immoral," &c.

What! is it really immoral to give the security of an oath to act agreeable to the law of nature, which the author has assured us every man possesses, and which obliges all men, and all governments, to pursue their own happiness? Is it immoral to support the social compact, until it is by common consent revised? Is it immoral to engage to support the government, while it protects you? If so, he should have recourse to such a government as that of the Medes and Persians formerly was, who affecting to be gods, and infallible, could not revise their own most iniquitous decrees, not even to save Daniel from the lions, or the Jews from massacre. In this instance he objects to one of the best principles of the government, and the most agreeable to the moral law of nature. In page 71 he has objected to the voice of the majority deciding on governmental affairs, without informing us to whose decision we shall have recourse, in such cases. We know, from what is before noticed, that he prefers the decision of a despot, such as Nebuchadnezzar was (p. 64) to the decision of a republican government. With these principles, he ought not to have sought an asylum in a republican government, whose principles, agreeable to the advice of the apostle, is, "if it be possible, to live peaceably with all men."

I have passed over some of the author's objections to the governments of the United States, thinking them so evidently unfounded, as not to require notice; but understanding they had weight with some, I will give them a brief review.

In page 49, he says, "The good people of the United States of America, concentered by representation in the senatorial council and chief magistrate, disclaimed the religion of Jesus, and cast away the cords of the Lord's anointed, in the ratification of the treaty of peace and friendship with the Bey of Tripoli!

"The American plenipotentiary availed himself of it, as an important circumstance in the article of negociation, that the American government was not predicated upon the christian religion; and, consequently, a government that the bey might safely treat with. Take it in the words of the treaty itself. 'The government of the United States of America, is not, in any sense, founded on the christian religion. It has, in itself, no character of enmity against the laws and religion of Mussulmen.' And, what is further worthy of notice, by the sixth article of the federal constitution, this treaty is made the supreme law of the land! Must it not be dishonouring to Christ," &c.

The constitution does not say *this treaty* alone; as, by way of eminence, it says, "*all treaties* that are made, or that shall be made hereafter, shall be the supreme law," &c. What he has quoted as the treaty, is no article of it. It stipulates nothing to be performed on either side, nor any engagement of any kind; therefore the senate did not ratify it. They only ratified, or could ratify, the treaty or mutual engagements. If these were agreeable to the instructions given to the minister, the senate was morally bound to ratify it; and they were morally bound to redeem our captives from the most cruel slavery and death, with as little delay as possible. The words quoted by the author are inserted by the negociator as the preamble to the treaty, at his own discretion. It is not easy to believe, that the author was so badly informed as not to know that the formal preamble, or introduction, to a treaty or law, is no obligatory part or article of the treaty or law itself. If he was so, any attorney or member of a legislature could have informed him. He maintains the solemn league and covenant to be binding on this country, but surely he will not say that the introductory preamble to it, descriptive only of the character of the parties contemplated to be engaged in it, and not at all of the then colonies, is an article of the covenant, and binding on this country. The words quoted by the author are in like manner descriptive of the character of the United States, given by the negociator, who had himself suffered long and cruel slavery in Algiers, where he saw the exit of many of his fellow captives. He well knew the long rooted and deadly enmity that still subsisted between the Barbary powers and the christians, on or near the Mediterranean coast, viz. since the inhuman persecution, robbery and expulsion of the Moors from Spain, Portugal, &c. and their barbarous treatment from the inquisition. At that period, the king of Spain reigning over a great proportion of Italy also, was the most formidable power in Europe; but Spain has ever since rapidly declined in population and power. The Barbary powers have sometimes made a short truce with them, but no treaty of peace. They are all popish powers, and it is from these the character of christian governments are taken by the Barbary powers; to avoid this prejudice, well known to the negociator, he stated this character.

The articles of the treaty were ratified, our captives ransomed, and the treaty faithfully fulfilled on our part; but the negociator was recalled, and not since employed. On the first breach of the treaty by Tripoli, the United States renounced it and went to war, which produced the release of other captives, and another treaty, to which no such preamble was annexed. This is a plain statement of facts. It remains with the candid reader to judge if this was "disclaiming the religion of Jesus, and casting away the cords of the Lord's anointed," by the United States, in their representative character. If it does, what does the author's setting the crown of Christ's kingdom, which is not of this world, on the head of a mortal man, viz. a prince of this world, with the same power exclusively to ratify and sanction the laws of the *most high God,* as he has with respect to civil laws, amount to? The government of the United States recalled their ambassador, and did not employ him again, though he had suffered and done much in their service; and they, in making a new treaty, renounced the supposed offensive introduction. Candour would have thought this a sufficient atonement for error, if it was one; but the author passes this unnoticed. So much for matter of fact. I will now give my own opinion.

If the Saviour is correct in testifying that *his kingdom was not of this world,* and practicing accordingly during the whole course of his ministry, and the apostles guided immediately by the Holy Ghost in supporting that testimony, both by their practice and doctrine, I cannot find wherein the honest old seaman has greatly erred. Wherein does the mighty error consist? It is according to the author, in saying that the "American government was not predicated upon the christian religion, and consequently a government that the bey might safely treat with."—Or that "the government of the United States is not, in any sense, founded on the christian religion. It has in itself no character of enmity against the laws and religion of Mussulmen."

Honest old captain O'Brien,[3] the negociator, might have been wrong, in point of expedience, in speaking at all on this subject; but supposing it was necessary that he should speak as the patriarchs in Egypt did, in telling they had a younger brother, at which their good father Jacob was grieved, what should he have said? Suppose he had answered more to the author's mind, viz. that the government of the United States was predicated on the christian religion, and possessed enmity to the government of Mussulmen, &c. In so doing he would have told a lie, and scandalized the christian religion. Whoever says that any civil government is predicated on the christian religion, in so far contradicts the dying testimony of the divine Jesus, declaring that his kingdom was not of this world. Civil governments being founded on the moral law of nature, can lawfully possess no enmity against other governments founded on the same law.

We are not well got over one objection, not only to the defects of our government, but to its moral existence, till we meet with another. Page 49—"The major part of the states recognize the principle of slavery, some partially, and others without yet taking any steps towards its abolition.

"Strange it is, indeed, that in a land of such boasted liberty, such horrid inhumanity should be tolerated! It is contrary to the declaration of independence, and most of the state constitutions.——Is it not strangely inconsistent, that the constitution, the paramount law of the land, should

---

3. Richard O'Brien (1758–1824), American naval officer, negotiated a treaty, in 1796, between the United States and Tripoli.

declare all men to be free, and the laws, pretended to be constitutional, doom a certain portion of them to hopeless bondage, and subject them to the wanton barbarity of savage and inhuman masters, who, in many instances, treat their brutes with more tenderness?——Indeed, it is too shocking to find advocates among any, but those whose conscience is seared with a hot iron.——But, supposing the Scripture silent on the subject, it is even impolitical and dangerous. What interest has the man, whom I unjustly detain, to work for me, seeing he receives scarcely any other compensation for his labour, than a hungry belly and hard blows? By what tie is he bound to spare my life, seeing I rob him of that which is dearer than life itself?——Of this barbarous traffic, the judicatories of our church have given their pointed disapprobation, and all approving of, or engaging in it, are excluded her communion."

Strange, astonishingly strange, indeed, to hear an author, who is the avowed champion for the moral obligation of the judicial law, declaim against slavery in such terms. That law, the perpetual and universal obligation of which he advocates, as binding on all nations, at least on all christian nations, even to putting them to death for the breach of it, says, "Both thy bondmen and thy handmaids, which thou shalt have, shall be of the heathens that are round about you; and of them shall you buy bondmen and handmaids. Moreover, of the strangers that sojourn among you, of them shall ye buy, and of their families that are with you, which they beget in your land, and they shall be your possession: and ye shall take them as an inheritance for your children after you, to inherit them for a possession. They shall be your bondmen forever."

The above, if the law of Moses is, agreeably to the system of the author, to be divided into judicial and ceremonial, cannot belong to the ceremonial part. It was a civil regulation, and unalterable. It could not be changed while that system continued. The master probably might set his bond servants, *i.e.* slaves, or their children, free, if he pleased; but the government could not interpose to set them free, nor to protect them from violence and oppression, nor avenge even their murder on their master. They were the inheritance of *their children forever.* They were not, however, to be of their brethren, but of the heathen around them, and of the strangers, viz. aliens that sojourn among them. Of those Solomon took 153,600 for servants to be carriers of burthens and hewers of timber for the temple and his other buildings. Now this law is neither repealed nor mitigated in the New Testament, otherwise than by the whole peculiar law of Moses being abolished. It is not only not repealed, but servants, viz. slaves, are strictly enjoined "to be obedient to their own masters, not only to the good and gentle, but even to the froward. Let as many servants as are under the yoke count their own masters worthy of all honour, that the name of God and his doctrine be not blasphemed. And they that have believing masters, let them not despise them."—1 Tim. vi. 12. Paul the apostle, sending Onesimus back to his master, reduced this doctrine to practice. In writing to the Corinthians, he tells those under the yoke of slavery, *art thou called, being a servant, care not for it,* &c.

The author says—"Of this barbarous traffic the judicatories of our church have given their pointed disapprobation; and all approving of, or engaging in it, are excluded her communion."

How strangely inconsistent is the Rev. Mr. Wylie. By what authority have the judicatories of his church excluded slave-holders, and all approvers of it, from their communion? If this has any relation to the kingdom of heaven, they have virtually excluded Job, Abraham, and all the patriarchs, acting under the moral law of nature, aided by occasional revelations from heaven. They have likewise excluded Moses, and all who obeyed the law given by him, and also the apostles and the primitive church; but what is still more extraordinary, they have virtually excluded Constantine and the council of Nice, and the other orthodox emperors, and his standard ecumenical councils. They have, in fact, added a condition of holding communion with God, in his ordinances, which Christ and his apostles never enjoined. May they not as well institute a new ordinance, or sacrament? Surely it requires the same divine authority to institute an indispensable condition of holding communion with God, in an ordinance, that it does to institute an ordinance itself.

The United States, formerly British colonies, never enacted laws to promote "this barbarous traffic." They had not by charter, nor did they claim, the right of regulating commerce. Queen Elizabeth was deceived when, with hesitation and reluctance, she permitted capt. Hawkins to import them into the British colonies. She was assured it would better their condition. The colonies had no power to prevent it. Good governor

Oglethrope did every thing he could to prevent it in Georgia, but without effect.[4] In Pennsylvania, the legislature not having it in its power to controul the British commercial laws, laid ten pounds of a tax on every original indenture or sale of a slave in that state. This was evaded by taking them to other colonies to sign the indentures. This was considered as a heavy grievance by the province, but unavoidable.

I arrived in Pennsylvania in August, 1763, and was not inattentive to the state of the country, particularly with regard to slavery; and though I was then but a lad, I considered both the moral and political effects of slavery on a country; nor was I wholly unacquainted with the history of slavery in the earlier periods of the world. My parents had taught me to read my Bible, and I had read some ancient history. I had then the world before me, and Providence my guide, where to choose my place of rest. The Carolinas at that time appeared the most inviting, and from there I had the most encouraging offers, and, I believe, the most sincere invitations. My aversion to slavery determined me to decline these advantageous proposals, and to hold my own plough, hoe my own corn, and reap my own grain in Pennsylvania, rather than raise a family in a place where slavery prevailed. I determined to have no slaves, and I never have had any. I contributed, as far as I believed it to be my duty, in both private and public life, to promote the abolition of slavery. This will be testified by all those acquainted with me. But I never thought of consigning the patriarchs, who had slaves in abundance, nor the apostles, who acknowledged the relation of master and slave, and prescribed their relative duties, to the devil.

No nation in the world ever made such exertions to abolish slavery, as the United States has done. In the general convention which proposed the federal constitution, a vote was carried, by a large majority, to vest in congress the power of preventing the importation of foreigners. So great was the aversion to slavery, that slave is not named in that instrument. Some states declared their dissent from the union, if that vote was carried into effect. A separation of the union, threatened the

4. James Edward Oglethorpe (1696–1785): English philanthropist and founder of the colony of Georgia.

dissolution of the whole. This produced a bargain. The vote was rescinded on condition that the importation of foreigners should not,
for twenty years, be prevented, or taxed higher than ten dollars each.
I voted in congress myself against levying this impost, because it must
have been laid equally on all foreigners. The constitution did not recognize slaves; and because the state made laws in the mean time to prevent
the trade.

Pennsylvania, and other states, had long before this time, viz. as soon
as they had it in their power, made laws to prevent the importation of
slaves. That state went still further; she enacted a law for the internal
abolition of slavery. When this law was passed, the event of the war was
doubtful, and much of the territory laid waste by the enemy, or his savage allies.

This was the most important exertion for the suppression of slavery, it
is believed, that ever had been made by any nation in the world. It would
be tedious to relate the difficulties which the legislature had to combat,
in passing that law. They arose from opposite questions, viz. *self-interest*
and *religion*. Self-interest said it was robbery. Religion founded on mistake, viz. on the same ground taken by the author, said it was contrary
to the law of the most high God, and, to support this assertion, applied
the text from the law of Moses before quoted, the examples of the patriarchs, &c. which had so much influence, as at the next election to turn
out many, I believe most of the members who voted for the abolition law;
several of whom were never elected again. Those, however, who were
elected in their place, had so much understanding as to know, that they
had no authority to make men, once free, return to slavery, viz. to enact
an ex post facto law. They did not attempt to repeal the abolition law,
notwithstanding the numerous petitions for that purpose; but believing
that too short a time had been given to record slaves, they extended the
time to the distant counties, which, by indulging those (who, agreeably
to the author's opinion, obstinately adhered to the law of Moses, as if
it had been the law of Pennsylvania, refused to submit to the abolition
law) with an opportunity to change their minds, and record their slaves.
This prevented the freedom of many slaves.

But the author mentions a certain "portion of them being *doomed
to hopeless bondage.*" I deny the charge; at least, as far as it relates to

Pennsylvania, it is an infamous slander. No law of the state has doomed any man, or class of men, to hopeless bondage. There were, indeed, slaves in Pennsylvania, under the English government. Those being already by law the property of their owners, the legislature could not interfere more than they could do with real estates. Such interference would have been an *ex post facto* law—a law made after the act was done. The principle is abhorrent both to the laws of God and man. Preparatory to the abolition law, the importation of slaves had been prohibited, and after it all are born equally free. This could not have been done under the Jewish law, and it is certainly all that human laws could do, and more, it is believed, than ever has been done by any other nation. This state legislature redeemed thousands now living, and many thousands yet unborn, from hopeless slavery, but never doomed any one to it. By the Jewish law, these were to be the property of their masters and their posterity *for ever.* The owners of slaves from other states cannot retain them in Pennsylvania, and the law cannot be repealed; doing so would be *ex post facto.*

There cannot now be a slave in this state but what is upwards of thirty years of age. The Society of Friends (Quakers) who, with their peculiar system of church discipline, have incorporated municipal regulations for their own sect; had set their slaves free before the declaration of independence. Many were of the same opinion. I was informed, that early in the last century, the Presbyterians took up the question in Synod, but the majority were of opinion that it belonged to the civil laws to provide the remedy. That as keeping of slaves was not made a term of communion by the apostles, they had no authority to make it so. Many of them, however, discouraged slavery. Hence it was that Pennsylvania contained fewer slaves than any of the adjoining states; but on account of the scarcity of hands during the war, a trade had commenced of introducing them from Maryland, &c. which was happily stopped by the abolition law. Several attempts were made to purchase the remaining slaves, at the expense of the public. The last that was, or perhaps will be made, was about ten years since, when a bill for that purpose passed the numerous branch, but was postponed by the other till their number would be taken, which was ordered. When this was done, it appeared that there were but a few hundred of them in the state, and many of these old and frail, who were of no more use to their masters, who enjoyed their labour in their best days, and with whom they lived better than they would do in a poorhouse, at the public expense. Very many of the younger slaves had procured their freedom by bargain; in doing which they were encouraged, and some of them assisted, by the Abolition Society. It was, therefore, judged inexpedient to tax the citizens, in many cases, to enrich the masters at the expense of their neighbours who had never held slaves. How many slaves has the author's society set free, or assisted in purchasing their freedom, as the Quakers did?

If, however, the author's assertion be true, "that they are subjected to the *wanton barbarity of savage and inhuman masters, who, in many instances, treat their brutes better,*" it is lamentable. But he ought to have produced instances of it. Those who persevered for twenty years in England, in opposing the barbarous slave trade, did not rest their plea in general charges. They stated and proved numerous facts. I have resided near half a century in this country, eighteen years of it in Maryland, and in the parts of Pennsylvania adjoining, where slaves were the most numerous of any part I have known in Pennsylvania; and before I had a house of my own, I resided in some families, and very pious families too, who held a number of slaves, and was very intimate in others; and I was myself then opposed to slavery, as I have been ever since; but I did not, like the author, oppose it with slander and declamation, but with such views as I had of expediency, and of the moral law, and the gospel. I was, however, powerfully combatted with the judicial law, the examples of the patriarchs, and of the ancient civilized nations; nor was the curse on Canaan forgotten. These peoples consciences were not *seared as with a hot iron,* as the author asserts; they were all professors, and, several of them at least, distinguished for piety. They paid a religious attention to the apostle's directions for the treatment of slaves. None of the slave-holders, with whom I have ever had the opportunity of being acquainted, "*give them scarcely any other compensation for their labour, than a hungry belly and hard blows,*" as the author asserts. I declare I never saw a slave receive one hard blow from his master, nor any complain of a hungry belly. The masters that keep them hungry must be fools for their own interest. A hungry belly will perform little labour. They were generally well fed, and comfortably clothed.

Slaves in the southern states, on account of their number, probably fare worse; yet I am assured, from undoubted authority, that they are sufficiently fed, and that since independence, their condition has been greatly ameliorated with respect to the lash of the overseer, which was chiefly connected with the raising tobacco, and which is now happily, in a degree, superceded by the more agreeable labour of raising cotton; which being done chiefly by task, affords much leisure to industrious slaves to work for themselves, on land allotted to them. They raise sweet potatoes and other truck, with which they feed hogs, poultry, &c. with the last of which they frequently supply their masters, at a price. In speaking of hungry bellies, as the reward of labour, the author must have had some other country in his eye. He no doubt might have seen it in Britain, which is frequently dependent on the United States for bread. His thoughts, indeed, might have been occupied with the cruelty practiced on slaves in the British sugar islands, where, it has been a result of calculation, that it was more profit to work a slave to death in two or three years, and purchase others, than to permit them to propagate, and to which, before the slave trade was at last happily abolished, they imported 57,000 new slaves in two years.

He says the major part of the states recognize the principle of slavery. I am at a loss to know where he found that recognition. It is not in their constitutions he admits, and I do not recollect to observe it in any of their laws, except those of South Carolina, which has, on that subject, adopted the Jewish law so far as not to consider the most wilful and barbarous killing of a slave, by his master, to be murder. Virginia, in several counties of which slaves are the majority, as well as Pennsylvania, early interdicted the introduction of slaves, either by land or water. Slavery was hung like a mill-stone about the neck of the colonies by the British naval and commercial laws; they were obtained and held by contract under those laws, and the state legislatures have no authority to impair the obligation of contracts. If they had they would be tyrants, and, according to the author's favourite phrase, immoral, or illegitimate governments. They would at least be despotic ones.

I was not in the legislature which, with so much difficulty, and in such doubtful times, nobly passed the abolition law, not indeed equally perfect as their wishes or their first attempt, but so perfect as to give a notable example to other states—but I was in it when much was done to ameliorate their condition, to prevent their being sent out of the state, or their families separated to a distance. Their laws in this, and, it is believed, in all other states but one, protect their persons equal to free-men. In eight out of the thirteen old states, provision is made for the final abolition of slavery. In the Ohio state it never existed, and in all the Indiana territory, contemplated to be eight states, of which one is now a state, and three are organized territories, provision is made against the introduction of slaves. Over the cession of North Carolina, viz. the state of Tennessee—the cession from Georgia, viz. Mississippi territory, obtained on contract, and New-Orleans and Louisiana obtained by treaty, congress had no such power, but has prevented their increase by importation. The author is, therefore, certainly mistaken, in asserting that the majority of the states recognize the principles of slavery, when it is certain that no states, recorded in history, ever made such exer-tions to extirpate that evil entailed on them by the British government; and while that government had taken the lead in the slave trade, and made an interference in it by other nations, for more than a century past a cause of war, and procured by treaty the right of supplying the colonies of other nations with slaves from Africa, we do not hear of the Reformed Presbytery in Britain testifying against it. I believe it is not even noticed in their judicial testimony. But the reverend author, who, with some other brethren, have instituted a presbytery under that name in this country, makes holding slaves a term of christian communion, which the apostles did not do, nor their own brethren in Britain.

The author certainly could have been but a few years in the country when he wrote the above base character of it. I presume he himself met with that hospitality that belongs to the American character. I am sure he has met with protection and a free press. He had not certainly so good an opportunity to know the treatment received by slaves, almost immediately after his landing, as I have had in near half a century, with an extensive opportunity of observing and conversing on the subject with people of all ranks and situations of life. My testimony and his be-ing opposite, one of us must be wrong. Mine being of the negative kind, is not conclusive; his being affirmative, ought to be supported by facts applicable at least to the majority of the states. A few solitary facts will not establish a national character—but he has given none. Instances may be found in all countries, of even parents treating their children barbarously; but that does not establish a national character.

The apostle taught servants to be obedient to their own masters, not only to the good and gentle, but to the froward; and says, "art thou called, being a servant, care not for it;" and practically confirms this doctrine by sending Onesimus back to his own master.

But the doctrine of the author is, that they ought not to work for their master, nor to *spare his life*—that the master robs him of what is dearer than life itself. He calls on the philosopher to execrate, and the philanthropist to shed a tear over this state of things.

Could he do more to contradict the apostle Paul, or to promote the insurrection of slaves against their masters, and to repeat the shocking scenes of St. Domingo in the United States?[5] That the enjoyment of liberty is to be preferred to the risk of life, when there is a rational probability of securing liberty by that risk, has been verified by the conduct of the United States; but that life should be risked or lost for liberty, without any prospect of securing it, is contrary to the opinion and practice of the generality of mankind, and to the doctrine of the gospel. On the author's principles, it is the duty of slaves to assassinate their masters, and to take away their own lives also, in preference to living in slavery. This is not the opinion of Moses and the patriarchs, nor of the apostles of Christ.

There were no slaves in the ark. The sons of Noah had equal rights. We know not how slavery was introduced among them; but we know that by noticing those belonging to Abraham, who, little more than four hundred years after, had 318 born in his house, trained for war, which, allowing the usual proportion of women, children, old men, &c. unfit for war, will amount to near about 2000 slaves in his possession. Going a little further, we find his two grandsons, Esau and Jacob—the first coming to meet the other with 400 (no doubt trained servants)

---

5. "Shocking scenes of St. Domingo" refers to the slave insurrections on the island of Hispaniola in response to the principles of the French Revolution. Haiti proclaimed independence from France in 1804.

and Jacob making a present to him of as many slaves as conducted five droves of different kinds of cattle, along with the cattle themselves. We afterwards find that the patriarch Job had very many slaves. His 500 yoke of oxen would require as many men to work them, besides such as attended to his other very numerous flocks, and a very great household. We cannot, therefore, estimate his slaves at less than 6000; they might have been many more. We cannot, however, consider these to be all as miserable as the author represents them to be. We are little acquainted with that state of society, but have reason to believe, that to get into the servitude of a good master, was a privilege. There were some, whose service Job would not accept of. Of such he says, "they dug up mallows by the bushes, and juniper roots for their meat; whose fathers I would have disdained to have set with the dogs (probably shepherds) of my flocks." I conclude from this, that to be servants to such as could protect and provide for their sustenance, was probably in those ages a privilege. Throughout the Bible, servants were slaves, except the hired servant of the law of Moses.

I admit, however, that there is something in the slavery of the Africans more disagreeable in its consequences, and more unjustifiable in its origin, than the ancient slavery; but I do not admit that they are treated with equal cruelty as the slaves of Greece or Rome, or of the Jews. That slavery in the United States is also a mighty political evil, is admitted. We did not need to be informed of this by the reverend author; but we wish he would inform us how to get clear of it, without worse consequences.

I have stated before, that what of the moral law is incorporated in the judicial law, is binding on all men. Of this kind is Exod. xxiii. 1. "Thou shalt not raise a false report; put not thine hand with the wicked, to be an unrighteous witness;" and seditions and revilings are ranked among the works of the flesh in the New Testament. If the author had examined the subject maturely, before he wrote, and searched the authentic records, his mistake might be set to the account of weakness; but if he did neither of these, it arose from a worse principle.

With respect to the abolition of internal slavery in the southern states, it is a difficult question, over which congress has no controul. Mr. Jefferson, the late president of the United States, when governor of Virginia, before our independence was acknowledged, proposed a plan for the gradual abolition of slavery in the United States; but the horrid consequences of the abolition of slavery in the great island of St. Domingo (sufficient to make the ears of those who hear of it to tingle) teach a serious lesson of caution. The slaves there first extirpated their former masters, then butchered the people of different shades of colour; and now, after near twenty years have elapsed, are butchering each other in support of contending chiefs. Christianity, as far as it prevailed in the world, promoted the amelioration of slavery. When the Roman empire became christian, some salutary laws were made in their favour; but none, by even the emperors to whom the author indirectly ascribes infallibility, to abolish slavery. The crusades, and a mistaken opinion that the end of the world was at hand, made way for the freedom of many slaves, but it was not finally abolished in the west of christendom, till the sixteenth century, when queen Elizabeth, as landlord, abolished it in the royal domains. In almost every instance it was abolished by the masters voluntarily, or for a valuable consideration, and not by governmental acts. It still prevails in the east of christian Europe (in Russia, Poland, and some parts of Germany) where the common people, *i.e.* slaves, there called *serffs,* are transferred with the soil, like the trees that grow on it. No christian states have exerted their legislative authority in this cause, in so short a time, to so great an extent, as the people of the United States. But for this, instead of praise, they receive slander from the author. The liberal policy of Pennsylvania, in abolishing slavery, and ameliorating the condition of such as could only be set free by their masters, and the disinterested conduct of the Quaker masters, at a great expense to them, has been treated with high approbation by European writers; but the author has not found ground for approbation on this, nor any other acts of the people, or the governments. They have, in his opinion, no authority to give or enforce even a command lawful in itself, viz. to free a slave.

Yet I must admit, that though he has declared the American government to be immoral and illegitimate, he gives them some commendation.

He says, (p. 51) "But, as we have stated our objections to the civil constitutions of these states, candour requires us to declare, at the same time, that we consider the American government, with all its evils, the best now existing in the christian world." I only observe here, that I know of but one world of the human family, of which Adam was the primeval progenitor, and the first federal representative; and, with the apostle Paul and the author, I know of but one moral law of nature, common to, and possessed by, the whole family of mankind.

But the author goes on to say—"And, if we know the sentiments of our own souls upon this subject, desire nothing more than its reformation, happiness, and prosperity."

From the above, taken in connexion with the rest of his system, he practically disowns all the civil governments that are, or ever were in the world. He disowns, demoralizes, and bastardizes all the American governments so far, as to assert, that they can give no lawful command; that in levying taxes, for necessary uses, they act the part of robbers; and, at the same time solemnly declares, that, with all their evils, they are the best in the christian world. Consequently, all the civil governments of the christian world are more immoral and more illegitimate, *i.e.* greater bastards, than the United States. He also considers the government of the Roman empire as immoral and illegitimate, and will not allow us to believe that the apostle Paul meant what he said, when, in explicit language, he enjoined the church to obey the powers *that be;* to pay them tribute as a debt morally due; to honour the few who administered the government, and to pray for them, and all in authority under them; and when he appealed to them and availed himself of the privileges of their laws—Nor the apostle Peter, in his general directions to the christian churches, when he enjoins them to "submit to every ordinance of men, for the Lord's sake: whether it be to the king as supreme; or unto governors, or unto them that are sent by them." Consequently he disowns all the governments of the Gentile nations; they all had, one time or other, their *monsters,* like Nero, who, however, did not reign five years well, as he did; nor were degraded and condemned to death for their crimes, as he was.

One government, indeed, was immediately instituted by God, of which he became the immediate king or supreme magistrate. In this government, certain offences against the moral law were subjected to the decision of those who acted as civil judges under Jehovah, as the immediate sovereign of that theocracy, or immediate government of God. But other offences against the moral law were tolerated, so far as to be withheld from the cognizance or punishment of the civil courts. Of these slavery was one, and for this the author demoralizes the governments of the United States in a higher tone of crimination than almost any thing else. The Jews were not authorised to punish any idolatry but such as was expressly defined, and committed by persons expressly described, and within a territory expressly limited by divine authority. For not going beyond the limits prescribed by Jehovah to that government, of which he condescended to be the immediate sovereign, the author demoralizes the governments of the United States. Other instances might be mentioned, but the above is sufficient to demonstrate that the author, to be consistent, could not have acknowledged, or, to use his own words, *homologated* the peculiar government of Israel. Nor could he have acknowledged the government of Constantine, Theodosius, &c. They indeed punished for many things; for doing which they had no authority from the law of God; but they also patronized certain kinds of idolatry, such as relicks, pilgrimages, and tradition, which they set above, or, at least made equal to, the laws of the most high God; and they were themselves the high priests of Jupiter, viz. of the heathen idolatrous religion, while at the same time they had usurped the headship of, and sovereignty over, the church of Christ. Certainly, on the author's principles, he could not *homologate* such a government, or do any thing that would amount to a tessera of obedience to it. Consequently, as far as known, there never has been a civil government in the world, which the author, on his declared principles, could have acknowledged as a moral or legitimate government, or even whose lawful commands ought to have been obeyed. I will conclude with a quotation from a learned and judicious commentator, Scott.

Exod. xxi. 2—"In these ways, slavery had been, or would soon be, introduced among them; even that of their brethren as well as strangers: and God did not see good in *the judicial law* totally to prohibit this, and several other things which are not agreeable to the perfect demands of the *moral* law, which is the standard of every action, whether right or wrong in itself. In the government of nations, legislators must judge how far it is practicable, expedient, or conductive to the grand ends of magistracy, to require *all* that is right, and forbid *all* that is wrong, *under penal sanctions:* and in this respect, Israel was like other nations. Indeed, the moral and judicial law were enacted by the same Lawgiver, and coincided, as far as infinite wisdom saw it to be conducive to the grand ends in view: but as they were intended for such distinct purposes, they must in many things vary. The *moral* law commanded every thing spiritually good in its utmost perfection, and tolerated nothing wrong in the smallest degree: but the sentence of it is reserved 'to that day, when God shall judge the *secrets* of men by Jesus Christ.' The *judicial* law commanded nothing morally bad, and forbade nothing morally good; but as sentence according to it would be pronounced by the civil magistrate, it did not insist on the same perfection: and, besides that, it enjoined nothing concerning the state of the heart, except as the intentions could be judged of by words and actions; it had also respect to the situation, character, and peculiar circumstances of the nation to be governed; and supposed the existence of some evils which could not be eradicated without a constant miracle; and provided against their effects.—This distinction, carefully attended to, will account for many things *seemingly tolerated* in the Mosaic law, which are condemned in the New Testament; and not only there, but in the moral law of 'loving our neighbour as ourselves.'—They are not sanctioned, but *merely suffered,* because of the hardness of the people's hearts, or on some account to prevent worse consequences. Slavery was almost universal in the world: and though like wars, it always proceeded of evil, and was generally evil in itself; yet the wisdom of God deemed it better to regulate, than to prohibit it: yet we should not judge of the practice itself by these *judicial regulations,* but *by the law of love."*

CHAPTER V

Of persecution—The author's glosses on Romans xiii. 1–7, and Mat. xxii. 21, examined and refuted, by extracts from the venerable divines of Westminster, approved by the Assembly of the church of Scotland—The testimonies of the Presbyterian clergy of England and Scotland, against Cromwell's usurpation, and of Luther, Calvin, and other approved commentators—Martyrdom a test of sincerity, not of truth—The Protestant martyrs under Popery against the author—Thoughts on creeds—Opinions of the Reformers—Objection, that the apostles' doctrine was not applicable to that period, refuted.

The reverend author's thirteenth supposed objection (p. 74) is, that we say, "Your principles lead to persecution, and are cruel and unmerciful." This objection I admit in all its force. I admit also his reply to it, which is—"*The church of Christ never persecuted. If our principles lead to it we are certainly wrong.*" In this I perfectly agree with him; but with his following arguments to evade the force of his own concession, I do not agree. There is no principle of persecution in the religion of Jesus, the blessed Saviour of the chief of sinners; who waiteth long and is kind; who waiteth even to the eleventh, *i.e.* to the last hour, on careless and negligent sinners; and who brought the thief on the cross to repentance at the last hour, as he has done many sinners since; and who himself declared that he did not come to destroy men's lives, but to save them; and who, on his last parting, gave a solemn charge to his apostles—"And he said unto them, go ye into all the world, and preach the gospel to every creature. He that believeth and is baptized, shall be saved; but he that believeth not, shall be damned." This solemn, gracious, and awful commission is given to the ministers of the gospel, who are thereby constituted—2 Cor. v. 20. Ambassadors of Christ to pray and beseech men to be reconciled to God. There is not a word here of persecution, but of teaching or beseeching men to be reconciled to God. There is not here, nor any place else, a commission given by the Saviour to ecumenical councils or emperors to *ratify* or *sanction* his laws, in order to given them validity; nor is there any commission given them as officers of his kingdom, which he has, in the most solemn manner declared, is not of this world. There is no commission given to convert sinners by the sword, or other physical force.

The author is fond of dilemmas, and ingenious in stating them; but having admitted that *the church of Christ does not persecute,* his detailed arguments immediately following in favour of persecution, may be safely passed without further notice, except one observation, viz. that by the *church of Christ,* I mean, the church or spiritual kingdom instituted by Christ and his apostles, with express provision that they should not add to his laws, under the penalty of having the plagues written in God's book added to them—Rev. xxii. 18. The author treats on quite a different subject, viz. on what he calls a church of Christ, instituted by a Roman emperor, in connexion with a number of bishops, who laid the foundation of what is since called Popery, or the church of Rome, which has ever since been built on that foundation. The laws, in all political churches, as such, do not originate from the *ratifying* and *sanctioning power of Christ or his apostles,* but of the civil magistrate; and are subject to all the changes of the opinions of human legislatures, and all the varieties that are to be found even in the various protestant national churches.

His sixth objection (p. 58) is founded on Romans, chap. 13; and his seventh (p. 66) on Mat. xxii. 21, viz. the Saviour's answer to the question of paying tribute to Caesar. I admit the solidity of these objections to his system. The author has in p. 67, and elsewhere, appealed to approved commentators, and to such I shall now appeal.

The Westminster assembly, was composed of about one hundred divines, selected for their orthodoxy, learning, and talents, many of whom were eminent commentators, joined also with four able divines from the church of Scotland, and thirty lay assessors, many of them such as Seldon, Hales, Whitelock, Pym, &c. very eminent for learning, talents, and virtue, and three lay assessors from Scotland.[1] These he will not deny to be approved commentators, and I claim no other authority for them. Confession of Faith, chap. xxiii. sec. 3—"It is the duty of people to pray for magistrates, to honour their persons, to pay them tribute and other dues, to obey their lawful commands, and to be subject to their authority, for conscience sake. Infidelity and difference in religion doth not make void the magistrate's just and legal authority, nor free the people from their due obedience to him: from which ecclesiastic persons are not exempted," &c. The 127th question of the Larger Catechism, viz. What is the honour that inferiors owe to their superiors? The answer is quite agreeable to the above. This venerable assembly of divines, and learned noblemen and gentlemen, give this doctrine as a comment on Rom. xiii. 5–7. and on Mat. xxii. 21, and other similar texts; and with this fully corresponds the Directory for worship.

We find by Neal's History of the Puritans,[2] that there was much dispute and division in both the assembly and parliament, about the form of church government and discipline; but they were unanimous in approving the doctrines of the Confession of Faith and the Catechisms—the Directory for worship passed with equal unanimity, and they were all approved and enforced by church and state in Scotland. Here is a mighty cloud of witnesses indeed. No less than one hundred divines, and more than thirty noblemen and gentlemen of England, all selected for their eminence in learning and piety, by parliament, and that parliament itself. Add to this all the puritan divines who suffered for non-conformity during the tyranny of the Stuarts, of which there were two thousand

1. John Selden (1584–1654) was an English jurist and member of the Westminster Assembly; John Hales (1584–1656), English scholar—a fellow of Eton College—and theologian, offended both Archbishop Laud and Oliver Cromwell. In 1659 his collected works were published as *The Golden Remains of the Ever-Memorable Mr. John Hales of Eton College;* Bulstrode Whitelock (1605–1675) served as an English diplomat, member of Parliament, and lay member of the Westminster Assembly; and John Pym (1584–1648), English statesman and lay member of the Westminster Assembly, strongly supported the supremacy of parliament and opposed the arbitrary actions of James I and Charles I. He was buried in Westminster Abbey.

2. Daniel Neal (1678–1743), English clergyman and historian, *The History of the Puritans, or Protestant Non-conformists,* 4 vols. (1732).

ministers ejected from the established church, and their congregations in one day, in a summary manner, by act of parliament. Among those divines are found the names of Manton, Calomy, Case, Baxter, T. Goodwin, Owen, Allen, Flavel, Henry, and many others, who, being dead, yet speak, to the edification of the christians in the protestant churches.[3] These, though differing in other things, after the example and agreeable to the doctrine taught by Christ and his apostles, taught obedience to the lawful commands of an oppressive and tyrannical government, and monstrously wicked kings, such as Charles II. and James II.[4] They taught also, both by their doctrine and example, to suffer in preference to obeying unlawful commands. It was in their day, and in opposition to them, that the learned deistical philosopher, Hobbes, taught the doctrine of the public conscience, *i.e.* the conscience of the supreme civil magistrate being the criterion of truth and error, sin and duty—whose principles, with some variation, the Rev. Mr. Wylie has copied into his system, the refuting of which employed the learned protestants of different denominations, for half a century.

Such are the witnesses in favour of the objections to the author's system, produced in England. Scotland, however, affords a mighty addition. No less than the testimony of the whole Presbyterian church of Scotland, in general assembly met, in their representative capacity. After submitting the question, the presbytery, who, as well as the parliament of that nation, approved of the Confession, Catechisms and Directory,

---

3. Thomas Manton (1620–1677): English Presbyterian divine and scribe to the Westminster Assembly; Edmund Calamy (c. 1635–1685), English Presbyterian minister, Rector of Morton, and member of the Westminster Assembly, underwent ejection from his parish as a Nonconformist by the Uniformity Act of 1662; Thomas Case (1598–1682), English Rector of St. Giles-in-the-Fields and member of the Westminster Assembly, was ejected from his parish by the Uniformity Act of 1662; Richard Baxter (1615–1691), English Puritan minister and theologian, was ejected by the Uniformity Act of 1662; Thomas Goodwin (1600–1680): English Independent minister and member of the Westminster Assembly; Thomas Allen (1608–1673), English Nonconformist divine, was a fugitive in New England from 1638 to 1651, and served as minister at Norwich, England, until experiencing ejection by the Uniformity Act of 1662; and John Flavel (1630–1691), English Presbyterian minister, underwent ejection from his Dartmouth parish by the Uniformity Act of 1662.

4. James II (1633–1701): son of Charles I, King of England, 1685–1688.

without any exception or additional explanation on such parts as are founded on Rom. xiii. Mat. xxii. 21, &c. The above is human, and, therefore, fallible testimony, but of pious and learned men, and many of them great sufferers for what they, on the strictest examination, believed to be truth. It can scarcely be outweighed by any uninspired testimony.

But as the author (p. 24) says, "an approved example is equal to a precept; but precepts are not wanting"—see Deut. xiii. 16, &c. "Were it needful, we might quote also the authority of most of the reformed churches of Europe, as also of the most eminent martyrs." In p. 73, in answer to the objection arising from the Confession of Faith, now under consideration, he says, "The sense in which the General Assembly, as also the current of the reformers and martyrs of the seventeenth century, understood this passage, is fully stated in our testimony, as also in the letter from Stirling, by the Rev. John M'Millan, jun.[5] They distinguished between reformed and enlightened lands, and those that were unreformed and unenlightened."

Is the author really sincere in his boasts of a cloud of witnesses, of reformers, martyrs, and reformed churches, &c.? If so, why does he not produce instances? Is he really serious, in asserting, that the Westminster Assembly made such a distinction? That they taught such a public doctrine on the authority of Christ and his apostles, as equally applies to all nations and all individuals, like the moral law of nature, on which it is founded, and another doctrine for particular cases, couched in the same words? The Confession, however, makes no such distinction, nor is it founded in scripture. That it is founded in their testimony, is admitted, and it is no doubt founded in the letter to which he alludes, and which I have not seen; but this only shows what ingenuity even pious men will sometimes resort to, to vindicate a favourite mistake. This is, however, a strong example of mysticism.

In the Directory for public worship, ratified and enforced in both nations in 1645, while the king and his parliament were at war about their respective claims of prerogative; while the parliament resisted what

5. John Macmillan (1752–1819), Scottish Reformed Presbyterian minister, was the grandson of John Macmillan (1670–1753), the founder of the Reformed Presbyterian Church.

they deemed the king's unconstitutional, *i.e.* unlawful commands, they
at the same time acknowledged what they believed to be his constitutional or legal authority, and directed all the ministers, in their prayers
before sermon, to pray for all in authority, especially for the king's
majesty—and for the conversion of the queen, &c. and in several treaties for settling the distractions of the government they treated with,
and addressed him as their lawful king, and continued to do so till after
the assembly at Westminster was dissolved, and the parliament purged
by the army, by expelling all the Presbyterians, and leaving few members but officers of the army. Just after parliament had voted the king's
proposals at Hampton court to be satisfactory, the remaining members,
with Cromwell at their head, usurped the whole governmental authority.
In pursuance of this, they disowned the king's authority, brought him to
trial before a court, not known to the laws, and put him to death. This
proceeding was solemnly protested against by the whole body of the
Presbyterian clergy in England, and the commissioners of the church
of Scotland, in language expressive of sincere loyalty. Among these are
many of the names of the most respectable members of the Westminster
assembly. They declare that, "though parliament took up arms in their
own defence, and of the Protestant religion, and of the fundamental
laws of the country, yet this cannot be plead in favour of usurping authority over the king." And again, "Moreover, though parliament took
up arms in defence of the laws, *it was never their intention to do violence to
the person of the king, or divest him of his royal authority.*" Again, "you cannot
but know, that the word of God commands obedience to magistrates;
and that, consonant to scripture, this hath been the judgment of Protestant divines, at home and abroad, with whom we concur."

The commissioners of the church of Scotland solemnly protest against
casting off his authority, and proceeding to try and put him to death, as
absolutely inconsistent with the solemn league and covenant. The aforesaid memorial of fifty-seven eminent London ministers, tells the nation,
"you have engaged by oath to preserve his majesty's person."

The same ministers, and indeed the whole body of the Presbyterians,
acted conformably to this, after the restoration. They acknowledged the
legal authority of Charles II. and James II., they obeyed their lawful
commands, but suffered severe persecution, in preference to obeying
such as were contrary to the moral law, *i.e.* such as interfered with the

authority of God, over the reason and judgment of his reasonable creatures, in such cases for which they are solely accountable to himself.
They did the same in Scotland, except that a much greater proportion
of the Presbyterian clergy conformed, and became generally the disgrace of even Episcopacy. In England, the few that conformed, such
as the learned doctors Lightfoot, Reynolds, Williams, Tuckney, &c. did
honour to that church, as they had done to the Westminster assembly,
of which they had been eminent members.[6] They were not there, however, in favour of exclusive establishments, *i.e.* of persecution; nor when
they conformed, did they become persecutors, as the conformists in
Scotland did. The non-conformists in Scotland were most cruelly persecuted; many of them left the country; a few of those who remained,
took up arms in their own defence, when they were, while attending the
gospel ordinances, shot down like wild beasts of the field, or otherwise
murdered. They disowned the authority of the king, who had withdrawn
his protection from them, and refused to pray for him. In this, however,
they had no judicial concurrence of that church, but a few presbyterian
ministers concurred in, or openly patronised, this conduct; it never,
therefore, became the act of that national church. It was fully justifiable,
however, on the principle of self-defence, if success had been probable;
but that not being the case, there was no ground to expect miracles.
This is the only exception to their conduct. Those who fled from the
storm till it would blow over, like Athanasius, acted on the Saviour's
advice. "When they persecute you in one city, flee you to another." The
nation a few years rejected the Stuarts from being kings.

In this distracted state of that church and nation, those who disowned the civil authority, as well as those who fled from its violence,
were admitted to communion with the Protestant churches of the
Netherlands; but after the persecution ceased, and the Presbyterian
religion was restored, and politically reestablished in Scotland, these
churches refused communion with such as disowned the civil authority

6. John Lightfoot (1602–1675), English Hebraist and Presbyterian biblical scholar, was
a member of the Westminster Assembly and complied with the Uniformity Act of 1662;
Edward Reynolds (1599–1676), English Puritan, Bishop of Norwich, and member of the
Westminster Assembly; and Anthony Tuckney (1599–1670), English Puritan and member of the Westminster Assembly, experienced ejection by the Uniformity Act of 1662.

in Scotland. In short, they were not acknowledged by any of the political Protestant churches in Europe.

The author, having confidently appealed to the current of the reformers and martyrs of the 17th century, as quoted above, has occasioned this review of that period, in which it appears that the Westminster assembly and parliament, and the general assembly and parliament of Scotland, were consistent; that they did not say one thing and mean another. I appear only as an advocate for their consistency, while I think, perhaps through the circumstances of the times, they carried their loyalty too far. After the death of Cromwell, when the parliament was restored, and the Presbyterians the decided majority, they brought the perjured, unprincipled, and extremely dissipated Charles the second to the throne, without any legal restraints on his absolute power, while he had no claim but from his royal blood, or hereditary right; he had not been in possession, except in Scotland; they were under no obligation of oath or covenant to receive him as their king in England. In 1688 they had learned better. When James, the brother of Charles II. with all his royal blood, had abdicated the throne, passing over many other nearer royal stems, they fixed on a remote branch, not for the amount of the royal blood in his veins, but from political causes. This was not inconsistent with the principles laid down in the Confession of Faith, viz. that "infidelity, or difference of religion, does not make void the magistrate's just and legal authority, nor free the people from their obedience to him." He whom they chose was a Protestant, but of a different denomination.

He appeals to the martyrs of that century—on which I observe, that martyrdom is a proof of sincerity, but not of truth. If this principle is given up, the Manichees,[7] and other heretics in the fourth and fifth centuries, who opposed or perverted the truth of the christian religion, and the Donatists and Novations who suffered martyrdom for not submitting to the established order,[8] could appeal to a very numerous

---

7. Manichaeism was a dualist religion founded in Persia in the third century, and although often considered a Christian heresy, it was really a religion in its own right.

8. The Donatists, a fourth-century sect, were declared to be heretical because they refused to accept the spiritual authority of priests and bishops, who denied their Christian faith, during the Diocletian persecution of A.D. 303–305. The Novatians condemned

catalogue of martyrs; and, in later times, the church of Rome can produce fifty thousand martyrs in Japan, Abyssinia, China, and elsewhere.
The Arians and Socinians have also the testimony of martyrs in their
favour. They were, no doubt, erroneous; some of these sects were so in a
high degree—therefore we do not take their testimony, for which they
suffered, as a test of truth; but it would be uncharitable not to admit it
as a test of their sincerity. The thousands of martyrs under the baleful
union of church and state, during its unabated reign, laboured under
errors and mistakes; but the testimony for which they greatly suffered,
was the gospel of Christ. The godly bishops and others, who suffered under the union of church and state in queen Mary's reign, acknowledged
the king's headship over the church of England, though even Cranmer
himself had lamented the imperfection of their reformation; but this
was not what they sealed with their blood—it was the truth of the gospel
of Christ, with respect to which bishop Latimer said, *that though he was
too old to argue for Christ, he was not too old to die for him.* Yet unfortunately,
on the re-establishment of the protestant religion in the reign of queen
Elizabeth, on this principle, the papish rites were as the testimony of the
martyrs re-established in the nation. Here was the snare arising from
pinning their faith on the martyrs. The earliest idolatry in the christian church was idolizing the memories of the martyrs, and afterwards
their relics or bones. In Naples, St. Janesarius is worshipped to this day,
and the like is done in other superstitious churches. Let none substitute
their confidence in martyrs, instead of the gospel of Christ in the scriptures of truth, which is the only sure foundation and pillar, and ground
of truth—resting on any other foundation is idolatry.

There were, indeed, numerous martyrs in the seventeenth century. In
France, Piedmont, and other popish countries belonging to *Babylon the
great, the mother of harlots—drunken with the blood of the saints;* and there was
also the blood of martyrs shed, and other grievous oppressions inflicted,
both on the spiritual and temporal interests of christians, by the little

---

apostasy, refused to accept the sacrament of penance, and refused to accept back into the
church those who had lapsed during the persecutions. They were followers of Novatianus
(c. A.D. 200–258).

Babylons, viz. the antichristian, political, protestant establishments in Britain and elsewhere, who, after the example of the author's standard authority of emperors and councils, usurped Christ's legislative authority over his body, the church; but he has not told us to which of these martyrs he appeals. I am still more at a loss to know what reformers he means. I know of no reformation which took place in the seventeenth century. There were, indeed, many great and pious divines who endeavoured to promote reformation, but without success. In Britain there was a successful struggle to overturn the prelatical hierarchy, and the superstitions accompanying it; but the prevailing party in church and state substituted another tyranny in its place. Those, since called independents, consisting of such learned and godly divines as Goodwin, Burroughs, Nye, Simpson,[9] &c. who had contributed largely to prepare the Confession of Faith and Catechisms, first opposed the political establishment, and then plead an exemption from the civil penalties of it, so far as to enjoy the right of ordination, &c. It was refused. They plead for toleration; it was refused. These men, who had been among the ornaments of the assembly, dissented from necessity. The army petitioned *that no civil restraints should be laid on tender consciences.* They said they had shed their blood to pull down the tyranny of the bishops, united with the state, but not to erect another in its place. Their petitions were treated with silence. They had arms in their hands; they turned out the majority of the parliament; the members of the assembly of divines had gradually withdrawn the Presbyterians to livings under the establishments; the Independents to their voluntary, unprotected, and unendowed congregations—hence called *Congregationalists.* When the army seized the government, they protected these congregations, as friends to the liberty where with Christ had made his church free; and they also protected the Presbyterians in their livings, as holding the same faith—when the government of the army was over-

9. Jeremiah Burroughes (1599–1646): English Congregational minister and member of the Westminster Assembly; Philip Nye (1596–1672): English Independent divine and member of the Westminster Assembly; and Sidrach Simpson (c. 1600–1655): English Independent divine and member of the Westminster Assembly.

turned, after the death of Cromwell. The parliament was restored, in which the Presbyterians were the majority; they called Charles II. to the throne, without limitations or conditions. After the election of a new parliament, the hierarchy, with all its tyranny and superstitions, with several additions, besides that of personal resentment and revenge, were restored, and the Presbyterians and Independents suffered equal severity of persecution during the two succeeding reigns.

This was the greatest struggle for reformation during that century; but it is evident that only a very partial reformation was attempted. The bishops tyrannized over the lower clergy and the people, as they had done in the reign of Constantine, and supported the despotic power of the kings. Against this double tyranny, both doctrinal and political puritans joined to overturn the tyrants; the doctrinal partizans were gratified by the removal of bishops and a number of popish rites—but they only changed the tyranny into other hands; though they reformed many abuses, they still retained the fundamental principle of Popery, viz. the power of making laws over Christ's house. They indeed declared the scriptures to be the perfect rule of faith and practice, but prescribed the exclusive sense in which christians should receive it, under civil penalties. That the Westminster parliament and assembly, and the assembly and parliament of Scotland, agreed upon and ratified a system of doctrines much more agreeable to the scriptures than any, or all the creeds established and enforced by the author's standard councils or emperors, or all the canonical councils from the first, viz. that of Nice, ratified by Constantine, to the last, viz. that of Trent, ratified by the emperor and other sovereign princes, is admitted. The council of Trent ratified all the decrees of the former canonical councils, including those recommended by the author, and, as all the others had done, made additions and explanations to them. The doctrinal puritans were not to blame for the result.

To prevent mistakes, I approve of the doctrines contained in the Westminster Confession, as the doctrine of the reformers, and agreeable to the word of God; and I take it as the exposition of my own faith, as far as I ought to do any human composition or compilation, but not on the authority of the assemblies and parliaments which ratified and enforced them by civil penalties. God forbid, that I should subject my conscience to the dictates of the consciences of other men, who cannot answer for me at the judgment seat of Christ, or that I should receive any substitute for the scripture. The expediency of creeds and confessions, as a bond of union among christian denominations, does not result from any divine command of Christ, nor from any example of the christian church, in its purest state. What is called the apostle's creed, it is now admitted, was not known till about the fourth century, when creeds, and what has been very improperly called pious frauds, became fashionable. However, it contains such a plain and simple summary of apostolic doctrines, that both Popish and protestant churches respect it, without difference of opinion, except with respect to *the descent of Christ into hell, or the state of the dead.* It is taken wholly from the evangelists. The metaphysical Nicene creed, instead of promoting union, laid the foundation of endless division and bloody persecutions; and every one of the author's standard councils did the same. Even the council of Trent laid the foundation of new controversies in the church of Rome—several of the Popish nations never received it.

God having addressed both law and gospel to every man's understanding and reason, as he shall answer for himself, and abide the pains of *everlasting fire in hell, where the worm dieth not, and the fire is not quenched,* as the penalty of rejecting or misimproving them; or else, on improving them, to enjoy inconceivable happiness in heaven to all eternity: and also having indued every man with that exercise of his memory, understanding, judgment, and reason, which we call *conscience,* which, by comparing the conduct and opinions with the divine laws, gives peace by its approbation; or, by condemning, turns even the softest bed into a bed of thorns, and the apparently most eligible situation into a kind of hell, which disturbs the slumbers, embitters the most pleasing enjoyments, and renders the approach of death tremendously awful. Considering this, I have often wondered how it entered into the heart of vain, ignorant, and sinful men, to add to the rewards and punishments of divine appointment, with respect to those things for which we are solely accountable to God; especially when it has been confirmed by near 1500 years experience, that civil punishments of the most excruciating kinds, or rewards the most flattering, never could convert a soul to Christ, not having the divine appointment for that purpose. That it was by the terrors of the

Lord, and the constraining love of Christ, that the apostles persuaded men to be reconciled to God, is the scripture account.

In the present divided state of the church, in order that christians, in holding communion with God, and with each other, should know each other's opinions, in matters of such religious controversy, as prevail in the present day, it is necessary that terms of communion should be agreed on. This necessity does not arise from the nature of the christian religion, of which the scriptures are both the foundation and the rule, but from the distracted and divided state of the church. It was not so from the beginning, nor will it be so when the happy time comes, *when the knowledge of the Lord shall cover the earth as the waters cover the sea; and when Jew and Gentile shall be as one stick in his hand; and when the rust, acquired through long ages of apostacy, ignorance, and distraction, shall be purged away.* But let the framers of these tests of orthodoxy take care that they do not exclude such christians from church communion, as the apostles, under the immediate influence of the Holy Ghost, admitted. Doing so, is not feeding Christ's sheep or weak lambs, but smiting and banishing them from his sheepfold.

The author must have laboured under some mistake, in appealing to the reformers of the seventeenth century; that was not the age of reformation. It is the opinion of all the divines, whose works I have perused on that subject, that during that century the protestant churches were degenerating, and some of them drawing nearer to the church of Rome; while, at the same time, the church of Rome was slowly and silently becoming more enlightened, and purging off her dross. To this purpose, see the evangelical Mr. Trail's Vindication of the Protestant Doctrine, &c.[10] Certainly in no period since the reformation, were so many princes, nobles, and other protestant professors, reconciled to the church of Rome, as in the seventeenth century. During the sixteenth century, before the political establishment of the reformed churches, the learned Mosheim says, "the church of Rome lost much of her

---

10. Robert Trail (1642–1716), English Presbyterian divine, *A Vindication of the Protestant Doctrine Concerning Justification, and of its Preachers and Professors, from the Unjust Charge of Antinomianism* (1692).

ancient splendour and majesty as soon as Luther, and the other lumi-
naries of the reformation, had exhibited to the view of the European
nations the christian religion, and restored it at least to a *considerable part
of its native purity,* and delivered it from *many of the superstitions,* under
which it had lain so long disguised."

Here the historian admits, that the reformation was not perfect; that
purity was only restored *in a considerable degree;* and that the church was
delivered only from *many,* not from *all* the superstitions under which
she lay disguised. This indeed was a fair and a blessed beginning of reformation, but alas! its progress was stopped too soon; princes stepped
into the throne of Christ, and made laws for his house; and they made
it the temporal interest of the clergy to acquiesce with this usurped authority. Thus church and state combined to stop the progress of reformation, and said unto it, *hitherto shalt thou come, and no further.* Hence it
came to pass, that, instead of a reformed church of Christ in Europe, we
have a church of England, of Scotland, Holland, Sweden, Denmark, &c.
each of them modelled by the authority, and agreeable to the policy or
caprice of the respective civil governments. Hence arose a number of
little Babylons, separated indeed by various shades of difference from the
great Babylon, but, like her, in a greater or lesser degree, stained with
the blood of the saints, and trading in the souls, *i.e.* the minds or consciences of men, and agreeing with her in the foundation on which she
has erected her throne, viz. on a human legislative authority in Christ's
spiritual kingdom, paramount to the laws of Christ himself.

But to return to the objections founded on Rom. xiii. 1–7, and Mat.
xxii. 21. on which I have given above the opinion of the Westminster
divines, and of the divines of the church of Scotland; to these I will add
the opinions of some of the reformers, among which Luther and Calvin
stood on high ground.

On the freedom from the law of Moses, that great reformer, and eminently evangelical divine, Martin Luther, on Galatians iii. 19. shews at
large, from the design and circumstances of giving that law, that it was
to endure but for a short time, and on the well known allegory of the
bond woman and the free—chap. iv. 21, &c. he shews the difference
between the Jerusalem that then was, and was in bondage with her children, viz. the Jewish church, and the Jerusalem that is above, viz. the

gospel church, which is the mother of all true believers. He agrees with the school doctors in the abolishment of the judicial and ceremonial law—but condemns the different senses they assign to scripture, and particularly their maintaining obedience even to the moral law, as a condition of acceptance with God, and that the unbelieving Jews erred in this respect, as much as in teaching obedience to the law of Moses, as a condition of justification with God.

After proving this at large, he says: "There is also another abolishment of the law, which is outward, to wit, that the politic laws of Moses do nothing belong unto us." That is to say, the parts of this law which belong to the civil administration of the Jewish government, have no relation to christians.

On chap. v. 3.—"He that is circumcised, is also bound to keep the whole law. For he that receiveth Moses in one point, must of necessity receive him in all. And it helpeth nothing to say, that circumcision is necessary, but not the rest of the laws: for by the same reason that thou art bound to keep circumcision, thou art also bound to keep the whole.— Some would bind us, even at this day, to certain of Moses' laws that please them best, as the false apostles would have done at that time. But this is in no wise to be suffered: for, if we give Moses leave to rule over us in any thing, we are bound to obey him in all things. Wherefore we will not be burthened with any law of Moses. We grant that he is to be read among us as a prophet and a witness bearer of Christ: and moreover, that out of him we may take good examples of good laws and holy life. But we will not suffer him in any wise to have dominion over the conscience."

As to this great reformer's opinions, with respect to obedience to the lawful commands of such governments, as God, in his providence, had set over them, I have not access to his writings on that subject, but we know well his practice and his instructions to the persecuted churches; his letters to those who received his doctrine, and who were subjects to the Popish persecuting duke of Brunswick,[11] who charged the reformers

---

11. This could be one of several dukes of Brunswick, perhaps Henry the Younger (1489–1568), Duke of Brunswick-Wolfenbüttel, who tried to restore Roman Catholicism to his realm after it had been lost to the Lutherans.

as inimical to his government, because they withdrew from his religion, exhorting them to loyalty and sufferings, least, by doing otherwise, they should bring reproach on the doctrine of the reformation, is well known, and perfectly corresponds with the instructions of the apostles to the churches. It is well known that the learned Melancthon,[12] the intimate colleague of Luther, who wrote a common-place book or system, (received at that period as a standard authority) it is understood, maintained the same doctrine. Indeed all the Lutheran divines did the same.

The great reformer Calvin, long looked up to as the great vindicator of the reformation, and teacher of the reformed churches, and whom Melancthon, an elder reformer, then called his divine by way of eminence, wrote his institution of the christian religion, dedicated to the persecuting king of France, and principally for the persecuted churches in France, of which he had been minister; this work he revised several times till his death, and it became the common-place book of divinity for all the reformed churches, till it was opposed by the Arminians. From that time till now, those who continue to preach the doctrines of the reformation are still called Calvinists. This learned work is in many hands, and from it the following extracts are taken:

"But whereas. I promised to speak with what laws a christian civil state ought to be ordered. There is no cause why any man should look for a long discourse of the best kind of laws, which should be infinite, and pertained not to this present purpose and place: yet, in a few words, and as it were, by the way, I will touch what laws it may use godlily before God, and be rightly governed by them among men, which self thing I had rather have passed over in silence, if I did not understand that some do herein perilously err. For there be some that deny that a common weal is well ordered, which neglecting the civil laws of Moses, is governed by the common laws of nations. How dangerous and troublesome this sentence is, let other men consider; it shall be enough for me to have shewed that it is false and foolish. Neither in the mean time, let any man be cumbered with this doubt, that judicials and ceremonials also pertain

---

12. Philipp Melanchthon (1497–1560): German reformer, colleague of Martin Luther, and author of the Augsburg Confession.

to the moral laws. For although the old writers which have taught this division, were not ignorant that these two latter parts had their use about manners, yet because they might be changed and abrogate, the morals remaining safe they did not call them morals. They called that first part peculiarly by that name, without which cannot stand the true holiness of manners, and the unchangeable rule of living rightly.

Sec. 15. "Therefore the moral law (that I may begin thereat) since it is contained in two chief points, of which the one commandeth simply to worship God with pure faith and godliness, and the other to embrace men with unfeigned love, is the true and eternal rule of righteousness prescribed to the men of all ages and times that will be willing to frame their life to the will of God. For this is his eternal and unchangeable will——The judicial law given to them for an order of civil state, gave certain rules of equity and righteousness, by which they might behave themselves harmlessly and quietly together.——As, therefore, the ceremonies might he abrogate, godliness remaining safe and undestroyed: so these judicial ordinances also being taken away, the perpetual duties and commandments of charity may continue. If this be true, verily there is liberty left to every nation to make such laws as they shall foresee to be profitable for them.——Now since it is certain that the law of God, which we call moral, is nothing else but a testimony of the natural law, and of that conscience which is engraven of God in the minds of men, the whole rule of this equity whereof we now speak is set forth therein. Therefore it alone also must be both the mark and rule and end of all laws. Whatsoever laws shall be framed after that rule, directed to that mark, and limited in that end, there is no cause why we should disallow them, howsoever they otherwise differ from the Jewish law, or one from another."

The great and learned reformer here goes on to shew, at considerable length, that the same penalties, for the same crimes, would not equally apply to all nations, nor to the same nation at all times; that the same severity that is requisite for the protection of society among a stubborn people, prone to disorder, would be unnecessary to a people peaceably disposed; and that the same penalties that often became necessary in the time of war, attended with murder and rapine, are seldom necessary in settled times of peace; that, therefore, nations have a right, and it is their duty, to change their penal laws according to circumstances; but all of them ought to have the same end in view, to punish what is condemned by the eternal and unchangeable law of God. I will give the conclusion in his own words.

"For, that which some say, that the law of God given by Moses is dishonoured, when it being abrogate, new are preferred above it, is most vain. For neither are other preferred above it, when they are more allowed, not in simple comparison, but in respect of the estate of the times, place, and nation: neither is that abrogate which was never made for us. For the Lord gave not the law by the hand of Moses, which should be published into all nations, and flourish every where: but when he had received the nation of the Jews into his faith, defence, and protection, he willed to be a lawmaker peculiarly to them." The author elsewhere calls the moral law of the ten commandments "a taste or instruction of the law of nature."

We are well informed that not only Zuinglius, the reformer of Switzerland; Hulrick Campbell, the reformer of the Grisson country,[13] and all their eminent associates, but the persecuted reformers of the French churches, maintained the same principles on this question. The celebrated John Welsh, of Scotland, when at Rochelle, with the persecuted protestants, when called on to answer before the persecuting Louis XIII. for the doctrine he taught, answered, that he taught that he (Louis) was lawful king of France, and not subject to any foreign jurisdiction, *i.e.* not subject to the Pope. Thus testifying in favour of the legitimate authority of that Popish persecuting king; but at the same time bearing testimony against the authority of the Pope. The persecuted reformers in Savoy, Italy, Austria, Hungary and Poland, supported the same testimony.

That pious and learned divine, professor of divinity and eminent preacher, David Dickson,[14] who taught divinity to the other eminent Presbyterian divines in Scotland, and did honour to that church in the seventeenth century, in his *Truth's Victory over Error,* containing the doc-

---

13. Ulrich Campbell (c. 1510–1582), Swiss reformer and pastor at Coire and Süs in the Canton of Grissons, or Graubünden.

14. David Dickson (c. 1583–1663), *Truth's Victory Over Error* (1726).

trine which he taught his students, fully supports the doctrine of the Confession of Faith on these texts—and so also did his associates and students; so also did the learned Pool,[15] and other eminent commentators in England, of that century. I am, therefore, at a loss to know to which of the reformers of the sixteenth or seventeenth century, or to what learned divines and protestant churches he can turn for support.

But to demonstrate that the doctrine of the reformed churches on this subject has been one at all periods, I will examine some of the learned and approved commentators of the last century, through more than half of which many of us have lived.

The venerable Henry, on Mat. xxii. 21—"They say unto him Caesar's; then saith he unto them, render, therefore, unto Caesar the things that are Caesar's, and unto God the things that are God's." "His convicting them of hypocricy might have served for an answer; such captious questions deserve a reproof, not a reply; but our Lord Jesus gave a full answer to their question, and introduced it by an argument sufficient to support it, so as to lay down a rule for his church in this matter, and yet to avoid giving offence and to break the snare. He forced them, ere they were aware, to confess Caesar's authority over them—v. 19, 20. In dealing with those that are exceptions, it is good to give our reasons, and, if possible, reasons of confessed cogency, before we give our resolutions.—The coining of money has always been looked upon as a branch of the royal prerogative, a flower of the crown, a royalty belonging to sovereign princes, and the admitting that as good and lawful money of the country, is an implicit submission to these powers.——Christ asks them, *Whose image is this?* and they owned it to be Caesar's, and thereby convicted those of falsehood who said, we were never in bondage to any, and confirmed what they afterwards said, *we have no king but Caesar.*——From thence he inferred the lawfulness of paying tribute to Caesar. v. 11. Render, therefore, to Caesar the things that are Caesar's, not give it him, as they expressed it (v. 17) but *render* it, return or restore

---

15. Matthew Poole (1624–1679), English dissenting minister, *Synopsis Criticorum aliorumque Sacrae Scripturae Interpretum,* 5 vols. (1667–1676); *The Nullity of the Romish Faith, or A Blow at the Root of the Romish Church* (1679).

it; if Caesar fills the purses, let Caesar command them; it is too late to dispute paying tribute to Caesar, for you are become a province of the empire, and when once a relation is admitted, the duty of it must be performed.——His disciples were instructed, and a standing rule left to the church."

The learned and evangelical Scott, an approved English commentator at the close of the eighteenth century, as Henry was at the beginning of it, on Mat. xxii. 15, 22, says, "But Jesus gave them to understand that he was fully aware of their insidious designs; yet, he chose to answer the question, because he intended to graft on it important instruction. Having, therefore, obtained the coin in which the tribute was paid, and drawn them to acknowledge that it was stamped with Caesar's image and name, he tacitly inferred that Caesar was the civil ruler to whom God had subjected them: and, therefore, as they derived protection and the benefits of magistracy from him (of which the currency of the coin was evidence) they were not only allowed, but required, to render to him both tribute and civil honour and obedience. At the same time they must render to God that honour, worship, love, and service which his commandments claimed, and which were justly due to him, and not disobey him out of regard to any earthly sovereign."

I subjoin some extracts from Henry on Rom. xiii. 1, 5. "We are taught how to carry ourselves towards magistrates, and those that are in authority over us, called here high powers, intimating their authority; they are powers; and in their dignity, they are the higher powers; including not only the king as supreme, but all inferior magistrates under him; and yet it is expressed, not by the persons that are in that power, but the place and power itself in which they are. However, the persons themselves may be wicked, and of those vile persons which the citizens of Zion contemneth, (Psal. xv. 4.) yet the power which they have must be submitted to and obeyed.——The duty enjoined, *Let every soul be subject.* Every soul, *i.e.* every person, one as well as another, not excluding the clergy, who call themselves spiritual persons, however the church of Rome doth exempt them from subjection to the civil powers. Every soul: not that our consciences are to be subjected to the will of men; it is God's prerogative to make laws immediately to bind the conscience, and we must render to

God the things that are God's; but it intimates that our subjection must be free and voluntary, sincere and hearty.

"This subjection of soul, here required, includes inward honour (1 Pet. ii. 17.) and outward reverence and respect, both in speaking to them and speaking of them; obedience to their commands in things lawful and honest, and in other things a patient submission to the penalty without resistance; a conformity in every thing to the place and duty of subjects, bringing our minds to the relation and condition, and the inferiority and subordination of it."

The author, after shewing the expediency of such directions to christians in the Roman empire, says, "The apostle, for obviating that reproach, and the clearing of Christianity from it, shews that obedience to civil magistrates is one of the laws of Christ, whose religion helps to make people good subjects, and it is very unjust to charge upon christianity that faction and rebellion, which its principles and rules are so directly contrary to." After describing the objects of the institution of civil magistracy, and the necessity of it, he says, "This is the intention of magistracy, and, therefore, we must, for conscience sake, be subject to it, as a constitution designed for the public good, to which all private interests must give way. But pity it is that ever this gracious intention should be perverted, and that those that bear the sword, while they countenance and connive at sin, should be a terror to those that do well. But so it is, *when the vilest men are exalted*—and yet, even then, the blessing and benefit of a common protection, and a face of government and order, is such, as that it is our duty in that case, rather to submit to persecution for well doing, and to take it patiently, than by irregular and disorderly practices, to attempt redress. Never did sovereign prince pervert the ends of government as Nero did, and yet to him Paul appealed, and under him had the protection of the law and the inferior magistrates more than once. Better a bad government than none at all.——Thou hast the benefit and advantage of government, and, therefore, must do what thou canst to preserve it, and nothing to disturb it. Protection draws allegiance. If we have protection from the government, we are in subjection to it; by upholding the government we keep up our own hedge. This subjection is likewise consented to by the tribute we pay. For this cause pay you tribute, as an acknowledgment of your submission, and as an acknowledgment that in conscience you think it due."

The learned Scott, on Rom. xiii. 1. says—"The Jews entertained various scruples on the lawfulness of obeying heathen magistrates; and this gave occasion to many turbulent spirits to excite scandalous and ruinous insurrection: and the same spirit might creep in among christians, to the great disgrace of it; as in later times, ecclesiasticks, especially in the church of Rome, claimed the most exorbitant exemptions in this particular. The apostle, therefore, used the most decisive language on this subject: 'every soul,' or person, whether a Jewish or a Gentile convert, private christian or minister, or however distinguished by miraculous gifts, or by his station in the church, was absolutely required to be subject to the authority and edicts of those, who held authority in the state; that is, in all things lawful. The higher powers at Rome were not only heathen, but oppressive, and even persecuting powers; and Nero, who was then emperor, was a monster of cruelty, caprice, and wickedness, perhaps unparalleled in the annals of mankind: yet no exception was made on that account. Christians were to look above such concerns; and to consider God as the source of all power, and civil government as his appointment for the benefit of mankind.——It was, therefore, incumbent on all christians to render a prompt and quiet obedience to those governors, under whom their lot was cast, patiently submitting to the hardships, and thankfully receiving the benefits, thence resulting; without objecting to the vices of the constitution, the administration, or the rulers, as an excuse for refusing subjection. It is evident that the apostle did not mean to determine the divine right of absolute monarchy, or exclusively of any form of government; but to inculcate subjection to the ruling powers of every place and time, in which believers lived. But as the benefits of civil government are many and great, and it is the appointment of God for maintaining order among the apostate race of men: so any man, who set himself to oppose the established government of that nation in which he lived, would be considered as resisting the providence, and rebelling against the authority of God, who gave the rulers their authority, and will himself call them to account for the use which they make of it. Whatever be the form of the existing government, or the way by which it was established; while it continues to exist, it must be regarded and submitted to as the appointment of Providence.——Some have urged, against the interpretation here given, that if this be indeed the rule of our religion, it lays it open to the charge of abetting tyranny, and being inimical to civil liberty. But I apprehend that this is not the case: for all the crimes committed by usurpers, tyrants, and oppressors, are at least as severely condemned in scripture, as those committed by rebels and traitors. Now a religion cannot justly be regarded as abetting tyranny, or as inimical to civil liberty, which denounces the severest vengeance on those who act tyrannically, and unjustly deprive men of liberty. The apostle was not writing a treatise on politics, but teaching a company of private christians their duty.—But it should be considered, on the other hand, whether the charge of being seditious, and 'hurtful to kings and provinces,' has not, in every age, been brought against the zealous worshippers of God? Whether this has not been, and is not at this day, the main pretext of persecutors, and of those who would exclude the preachers of the gospel out of their several districts? And whether the necessity which is laid on christians 'to obey God rather than man,' is not, in many cases, likely enough to exasperate the spirit of haughty princes, without openly avowing, that there are other cases, in which we are not bound to obey them? Cases, which in fact call their right to authority in question; and directly impeach their wisdom and justice. Surely this is suited to increase that jealousy against the ministers, missionaries, and professors of the gospel, in the minds of rulers, in all parts of the world, which to this day forms one grand barrier to the propagation of christianity. A barrier insurmountable, except by the power of God. Had the primitive christians explained the apostle's doctrine, with so many exceptions and limitations, as numbers do at present, and acted accordingly; and had christianity assumed that political aspect, which it has generally borne in later ages, (arising from the circumstances of the times) nothing but a constant succession of miracles could have prevented its extirpation, by the rage of its numerous persecutors."

V. 3–5. "If the ruler abuse his authority, God will call him to an account for it; there are legal and constitutional checks upon those, who want to introduce tyranny; and, on great occasions, the people will sometimes, with one consent, arise against a cruel oppressor, and subvert his

government; (as the Romans did against Nero, who was condemned by
the senate to die, as an enemy to mankind, with the approbation of
the whole world).——The same authority which commands children to
honour their parents, commands subjects to honour their rulers: and
they should honour them in the same manner."

The Rev. Matthew Henry, from whom part of the above extracts are
taken, was the son of an eminent puritan minister, who was removed from
his congregation for non-conformity at the restoration, and paid great
attention to the education of his son, who, after being well instructed in
both divinity and civil law, chose to devote himself to the ministry of the
gospel, notwithstanding the prevailing persecution of non-conformists.
He lived, however, and published his commentaries, after the toleration
of dissenters took place. The Rev. Thomas Scott, rector, *i.e.* minister of
Aston Sanford, (London) at present of the established church of England, is well known by some practical works, as well as by his excellent
notes on the Bible. I selected the above extracts from these two eminent
divines, who wrote near one hundred years apart, but (though in different communions) taught the same doctrines, and because their works
are more generally consulted and relied on by the orthodox, than other
commentators. Extracts to the same purpose might also be taken from
the very valuable expositions of the New Testament, by Burkitt, Guise,
and Doddridge, and the very learned Dr. Gill's critical commentary.[16]

To demonstrate the uniformity of opinion between the approved
commentators of the seventeenth century, to which the Rev. Mr. Wylie
appeals, and those of the eighteenth, the perusal of the annotations of
that pious and very learned divine, Matthew Pool, rector (minister) of St.
Michael, in London, who employed ten years in composing his *Synopsis
Criticorum,* in five folio volumes, a critical work on the Bible, well known
to learned divines, and highly esteemed by them; and who, to the disgrace of the times, and the great loss of the church, was ejected for non-

16. William Burkitt (1650–1703), English Evangelical divine and biblical commentator; John Guyse (1680–1761), English dissenting minister *An Exposition of the New Testament in the Form of a Paraphrase,* 3 vols. (1739–1752), Philip Doddridge (1702–1751),
Nonconformist divine, popular hymn writer, and biblical commentator; and John Gill
(1697–1771), English Baptist minister and biblical commentator.

conformity, after the restoration of Charles II. He wrote also a book, entitled *The Nullity of the Romish Faith*, for which, finding himself in danger of being assassinated, he fled to Holland, but there did not escape the fangs of such as (with the author) believe that the legitimate method of suppressing heresy, is to kill the heretic. That great divine died at Amsterdam, in the fifty-sixth year of his age, it is still believed, by poison.

The annotations on the Bible ascribed to the assembly of divines at Westminster, but done under the direction of parliament, who employed some other divines, not members of that assembly, but in which the names of the eminently pious and learned Gouge, Gataker, Sey, &c. of the Westminster divines, are recorded.[17] Those, with other commentaries or annotations, wrote in that century, in Britain, Holland, &c. which I had an opportunity to consult in an early period of life, when, from the circumstances in which Providence had ordered my lot, it became my duty to examine the question, as a case of conscience. These works, to which I am under obligations for a share of such biblical information as I possess, I freely recommend to the perusal of others. In my review of them at that period, and comparing them with more modern expositors of the scriptures, which contain the words of eternal life, I find not only an agreement between the venerable, pious, and learned expositors themselves, but also between them and the doctrines taught, and examples set by Jesus Christ, and his divinely inspired apostles on this subject. This question relates to a plain and common practical case, in which the duty and interest of christians were deeply involved, at the time in which the apostles wrote, and in which they have been involved ever since, and probably may be hereafter. In such cases, all the protestant reformers believed and taught, that the instructions given by inspiration are so plain, and so easily understood, that he that runs may read, like the way of holiness, (Isa. xxxv. 8) in travelling which, the wayfaring

17. William Gouge (1578–1653), English Puritan minister and member of the Westminster Assembly; Thomas Gataker (1574–1654), English Puritan theologian, minister, and member of the Westminster Assembly; and William Fiennes (1582–1662), Viscount Saye and Sele, a Puritan opponent to Archbishop Laud and a member of the Westminster Assembly. In the House of Lords he was associated with the Independent faction and opposed to the Presbyterians.

men, though in other things fools, (*i.e.* simple, or men of weak capacities) shall not err or miss their way.

That ingenious and acute reasoner, Alexander Shields, highly and justly recommended in the testimony of the reformed presbytery in Scotland, more than half a century since, in his observation on the question of paying tribute to Caesar, (Hind let loose, p. 210.) treats the question of paying tribute in Mat. xvii. 24. much as the above authors have done, viz. that it was probably paid for the temple service; and that the question of paying tribute to Caesar (Mat. xxii. 21.) was a different kind; that to this question our Lord returned such an answer as might either serve to answer or to evade the question, after proving at large that the Jews, first by conquest, and afterwards by their own act, became subject to the Roman empire, he says, that the opposition to the tax for which the census was taken by Augustus, viz. when the Saviour was born, was the same—the levy of which was opposed, as afterwards mentioned by Gamaliel. He decides that tribute was lawfully due to Caesar; I am sorry that his reasoning is too long to be inserted. He appeals to several eminent authors in support of his opinion, and, among others, to the great reformer Calvin. With his quotation from that celebrated author, and from the learned Chamiers,[18] I will conclude the testimony of the sixteenth and seventeenth centuries. Calvin lived in the sixteenth, and Shields in the seventeenth century.

Shields' quotation from Calvin, is as follows: " The authority of the Roman emperors was, by common use, received and approved among the Jews, whence it was manifest that the Jews had now, of their own accord, imposed on themselves a law of paying tribute, because they had passed over to the Romans the power of the sword."

We are informed by the evangelists, that the chief priests sought for, and obtained, false witnesses against Christ; and that they, before Pilate, witnessed many things against him.—Mat. xxvii. 13. and Mark xv. 3. The most important part of *these many things* is stated in Luke xxiii. 2. "We found this fellow perverting the nation, and forbidding to give

---

18. Daniel Chamier (1564–1621), French Protestant divine, was killed in the Protestant city of Montauban when it was attacked by the forces of Louis XIII.

tribute to Caesar." The apostles have testified that this was false witness. It was a general charge, not supported by facts; when, therefore, they pressed Pilate to crucify him, he answered them, "Why! what evil hath he done?"—Mark xv. 14. and when he had maturely examined the charges, he said unto them, "Ye brought this man unto me, as one that perverteth the people; and behold, I having examined him before you, found no fault in this man, touching those things whereof you accuse him."—Luke xxiii. 14.

The chief priests and elders had added to their charge, that Jesus himself had said, that he himself *was Christ, a king,* and that *whosoever maketh himself a king, speaketh against Caesar.* This was also a false accusation. He refused to be made a king, and withdrew when they came to make him king by force; nor did he ever assume that title or character during his ministry, until after this accusation, viz. before Pilate, when he explained the spiritual nature of his kingdom so clearly and fully, as convinced Pilate that it could not interfere with the kingdom of Caesar, or any such temporal kingdoms. After this good confession, therefore, Pilate, fully convinced of his innocence, laboured the more earnestly to release him. "When the chief priests and elders cried out crucify him, crucify him, Pilate saith unto them, take ye him, and crucify him: for I find no fault in him. The Jews answered and said, we have a law, and by our law he ought to die, because he made himself the son of God." Here they give up with all the charges of the indictment before Pilate, and resorted to their former accusations before the high priest of blasphemy. John xviii. 36, 37.–xix. 6, 7, &c.

The high priests, &c. employed spies to watch him in his words, and to entangle him by questions. When the high priest asked him of his doctrine, &c. "Jesus answered him, I spake openly to the world: I ever taught in the synagogue, and in the temple, whither the Jews always resort; and in secret I have said nothing. Why askest thou me? ask them that heard me."—John xviii. 19–21. The Saviour paid the tribute to the temple, and told the people to respect the authority, and attend to the instructions of those that set in Moses' seat, and directed the lepers whom he had healed, to shew themselves to the priest, agreeable to the law of Moses. He faithfully and severely reproved the sins of those who administered the government, but he never declared the government itself (to

whom the Jews had found it expedient to submit, and under whose dominion Providence had placed them) *illegitimate* or *immoral*—nor, that
paying tribute to them was the same as compounding with a robber on
the high way.

How diametrically opposite is the practice and doctrine of the Rev.
Mr. Wylie on this subject, to the doctrine and practice of the Saviour?
and how perfectly consonant is the doctrine and practice of the apostle
Paul, &c. to that of the Saviour? Which are the most infallible authorities, every christian will decide for himself.

The chief priests, &c. who falsely accused the Saviour, were many of
them, even then, guilty of that crime. They had rebelled in the days
of the taxing, and afterwards made frequent revolts until at last, for
their rebellion, the Romans took away their place and nation. It is an
historical fact, well known, that through the influence of the Saviour's
prophetical advice, (Mat. xxiv. 16, 21.) and the teaching and example of
the apostles, the believing Jews, by separating from those who rebelled
against the Roman power, escaped the direful destruction that befel the
unbelieving Jews, of which the Saviour says, *that such had not been, from the*
foundation of the world to this time, no, nor ever again shall be. It is also a well
known fact, that the christians, whether Jews or Gentiles, never rebelled
against the Roman power, during what is called the ten persecutions,
inflicted by the heathen Roman emperors, viz. as long as Providence
had ordered their lot under that power, but served in their armies, &c.
and obeyed their lawful commands.

Having stated the exposition of the texts in question, as expressed by
approved commentators, and of reformers, supported by their example,
it is proper to give the author's glosses on it.

On the question of paying tribute to Caesar, he says, (p. 68.) "He
(Christ) split their dilemma, and left the question undecided. He, on
several occasions, thus *baffled* his adversaries." To support this assertion
he quotes several examples, which I will pass over with but few remarks.
The case of the woman taken in adultery, (John viii. 4.) and the case of
deciding on the division of inheritance, was not *baffling.* In both these
cases the Saviour instructed the parties. He convicted, in the first case
the woman's accusers, taught the woman herself to sin no more, and,
like a God, as he was, forgave her past sins. In the second case, he taught

the hearers to beware of covetousness. In both he acted agreeably to his character, and the character of his kingdom, which is not of this world. He, as on all other occasions, declined interfering with the office and duty of the civil magistrate, viz. the kingdoms of this world. He refused to accept of it from the devil, whom (John xii. 31.) he calls the prince of this world—and also from the Jews (John vi. 15.) The divine Saviour was always consistent. What a pity it is, that those who professed to believe in Jesus, did not follow his example in keeping his spiritual kingdom separate, as he did, from the kingdoms of this world.

I do not approve of the author representing the divine Jesus as a *baffler, i.e.* one who puts to confusion. Thomas Paine gave him no worse character than this. I defy the author to produce one instance in which the teacher sent from heaven, was asked for instruction with respect to moral duty, in which he evaded the enquiry, or *baffled* the enquirer. In the question respecting his own mission, he referred them to his works for testimony. With respect to the question of John Baptist's mission, the answer turned on the same ground. John Baptist had testified that Jesus *was the Lamb of God, who taketh away the sins of the world,* and the Saviour testified (John v. 36.) *The works that the Father hath given me to finish; the same works that I do, bear witness of me, that the Father hath sent me.* In this, nor any other case alluded to, was there any evasion of the question, or baffling. The divine Jesus did not come from heaven to baffle, or confuse poor sinners, but to instruct and to save them. Why does the reverend author, who professes to be a minister of Christ, treat the character of his Divine Master in such a manner? Could deists do more to dishonour him?

He says (p. 59) that if we believe and act in the manner which it is evident the Saviour, his apostles, the primitive christians and reformers have done, "then it would, on this principle, be a sin to resist the devil." In answer to this, I only recommend the author to peruse for his edification 2 Pet. ii. 10, 12. and Jude v. 8. and compare these texts with the practice of the prophets and apostles. If we have not been misinformed by our Bible, the devil is a spirit, and governs a spiritual kingdom, in opposition to the spiritual kingdom of Christ, which is not of this world. The kingdom of Christ is within believers, (Luke xx. 21) and the kingdom of the devil is within unbelievers—"*He is the spirit that now worketh in the children of disobedience,*" in the warfare with whom, christians are enjoined to *put on the whole* (spiritual) *armour of God, that they may be able to stand against the wiles of the devil*—Eph. ii. 2. and vi. 11. The devil fills the heart to lie—Acts v. iii. He is described as a roaring lion, walking about seeking whom he may devour—1 Pet. v. 8. The author has before deduced civil government from the government of angels; he now considers fallen angels as kings or emperors of this world, and not as spiritual beings or powers; they must, therefore, be corporeal beings, and can be resisted with powder and ball. Why does the author use such low sophistry to deceive the simple? Every body knows that the devil was never incarnate, nor ruled a corporeal kingdom, nor can be resisted with corporeal arms. The spirits, both good and bad, are under another law of nature than men are.

In the same page he goes on to say, that according to the doctrine of the apostles, as before stated, "then at the risk of *damnation* would tyrants and usurpers be resisted; and the justly exploded doctrine of passive obedience, would be recognized under the pain of Jehovah's high displeasure!! and, to crown all, the people of these states, who justly and valiantly *resisted* the wicked domination of the British tyrant, would have thereby rendered themselves obnoxious to damnation!!!"

I do not make this quotation in order to reply to it, but to shew how ignorant the author is of the subject on which he writes. What possible analogy could he find between the people of the United States' asserting and defending their natural and chartered rights, when they were invaded, and providing, by a moral compact, for their own happiness, and the doctrine of passive obedience and non-resistance? All people have a right to provide for their own happiness, agreeable to the moral law, and their own convenience. In what text of the scripture can he find any thing to authorise him to thunder out damnation, with treble notes of astonishment, against them for doing their moral duty? Is it because they refuse to usurp God's sovereignty over the consciences of his reasonable creatures?

In page 60, he says, "This principle is equally applicable to a people under unjust and immoral government; and to no other kind of subjection was Nero, the *monster,* at the head of the Roman empire, entitled." Whether Nero, Tiberius, or Caligula, or other emperors that might be named, to whom the christians submitted, was the greatest monster, is not necessary here to decide. Of Nero, however, it is known, that he reigned five years well, and that for his monstrous wickedness he was afterwards condemned to death by the Roman senate. But what is more to our purpose, is that Cornelius, the centurion, who enjoyed *the smiles of heaven* so much, as to have an angel specially sent to him for his direction, was under a sacramental oath of allegiance to the Roman empire, while the monster Caligula reigned. That the apostle Paul wrote the text under consideration, and, in other instances, claimed and obtained the benefit of the Roman laws, is well known. In his last trial before the Roman governor, Festus, at Cesaria, apprehensive of an unfair decision, through the undue influence of the Jews, he appealed from that subordinate court to the supreme court of the empire at Rome, in the following remarkable words: "Then said Paul, I stand at Caesar's judgment seat, where I ought to be judged: to the Jews I have done no wrong—I appeal unto Caesar." This Caesar was the monster Nero, and it is scarcely possible to combine so few words together more decisively expressive of the acknowledgment of Nero as the supreme organ of the government of the Roman empire. It was not an evasion; it was not *baffling*, as the author ascribes to the Saviour. The apostle speaks in words as decisive as human language will admit. *I stand at Caesar's judgment seat, where I ought to be judged—I appeal unto Caesar.* This was a most open and a most decisive declaration of his subjection in things lawful in themselves, to "the powers that be," perfectly agreeable to his epistles, and his conduct on other occasions, and to the Saviour's answer to the question of paying tribute to Caesar.

The author adds—"That he who has no moral right to command, can give no lawful commands;" and he speaks frequently of an immoral government, an immoral constitution, and asserts the American constitutions to be immoral, and consequently that they can give no lawful commands. While, on this principle, he overturns every government that is, or that ever was in the world, for there never has been a prefect moral government among men. It has been already demonstrated, that the national law of Israel, to be administered by sinful man, fell much short of the perfection of the moral law. He, however, in no place has defined what he means by a *moral government.* If he means a positive institution from God, there never was any such, except that given to Israel in the wilderness, whereby they were constituted a nation, and it is probable there never will be another. We believe that every man possesses the law of nature, which the author admits (p. 10.) and with him I agree, that this law is the standard of all the administrations of civil government. The law of nature indispensably obliges every man to pursue his own happiness, in connexion with that of his fellow men; consequently it is the duty of all men to form a civil society for their own protection, as soon as it becomes necessary for their happiness, or to put themselves under the protection of such governments as are already formed; every such society is a moral government—for no such society can exist, but what is founded, in a lesser or greater degree, on the moral law of nature; and though instituted by man, it is the ordinance of God, for common protection. But as God himself has a superior claim to our love and obedience, no human power has the authority to interfere with the conscientious obedience due to him; and, in as far as they do interfere, the commands are unlawful, and we ought to suffer rather than obey them. But the morality of the power or right to command, comes directly or indirectly from the people in whom the sovereignty is inherent. The author only expresses his own ignorance of the subject, when he considers this as savouring of *passive obedience and non-resistance.* It is the very reverse. It is the moral duty of the people, at all times, to pursue their own happiness; and, consequently, to change or reform the organization of their government, so as it may contribute to their greater happiness.

Governments were acknowledged by the patriarchs, in all the countries through which they sojourned. The nation of Israel, both under the most pious of their judges and kings, acknowledged the moral authority of the civil societies around them, in their incorporated character, and dealt and treated with the constituted organs of those governments as moral powers. The prophets reproved those nations for their sins, and threatened judgments, but never said they had not moral authority to command what was right, as the author tells us of our governments. He says, (p. 60, 61.) "He that has no moral right to command, can give no lawful commands." He frequently has asserted our governments to be immoral, and disowns even obedience to their lawful commands, as well as he does to Caesar's, to whose laws and moral authority the apostle Paul appealed oftener than once, and received protection.

Caesar Augustus, though he had his hands deeply stained with innocent blood, was yet, if not a much better, was a much wiser prince than

Nero. They both, however, were vested with the same imperial authority, while they continued to reign. When the sceptre departed from Judah, it devolved on Augustus, the principal organ of the government of the Roman empire. He commanded that all the world (the Roman empire being then so called) should be taxed. In obedience to this command, those who feared God went to be taxed at the places appointed by authority. It is believed they were also to be registered, with their families. The blessed virgin, the mother of the Saviour, and Joseph, her espoused husband, went to Bethlehem, the city of the family of David, to be taxed, and, if commentators are right, to be registered. At least from the time that the angel announced the miraculous conception, it is well known that Joseph and Mary acted under immediate divine direction, at least until after they returned from Egypt. We know from history, confirmed by scripture, that the wicked and irreligious Jews raised an insurrection against this tax, when it came to be collected several years after the register was taken, which could not be collected till after the return was made throughout the empire. (see Acts v. 37.) Thus God so ordered it in his providence, that *the desire of all nations should be born, who saves his people from their sins.* When his earthly parents, acting under immediate divine direction, were in the act of acknowledging the moral authority of the Roman empire; and, as a test of this acknowledgment, came of their own free will to the place appointed, to have their names registered as taxable inhabitants, under his jurisdiction, they were not forced by arbitrary power. Some of the ancient fathers say, the Saviour himself was also registered as a Roman subject. This, however, is of no importance, when we know, that no charge could be brought against him before the Roman governor, for not obeying the lawful commands of the government; he payed the tribute demanded, and taught his disciples to pay tribute to the government which they had acknowledged, and under which God had ordered their lot, and from which they received protection; in consequence of which they owed allegiance, as an equitable equivalent, agreeable to the moral law.

If the above view of the subject is supported by indubitable facts, which it is believed to be, (the patriarchs, the pious judges and kings of Israel, the pious Israelites, at the advent of the Saviour, including John the Baptist, who was greater than a prophet, and who (Luke iii. 12, 14.)

taught the collectors of public taxes, and the soldiers, to discharge the duties of their respective offices faithfully, as the condition of being admitted to his baptism, which was the intermediate and connecting link of the chain, between the dispensation of the gospel under the Sinai symbolical covenant, and what is, both by the prophets and apostles, called the *new covenant*) it perfectly agrees with the doctrine and example of the Saviour, and of his apostles, of the primitive christians, and the reformers and martyrs during the period of the reformation. With such a cloud of witnesses, I feel myself happy in concurring, from conviction, as well as from incontestable authority.

In page 61, he says, "It is farther objected here, that the apostle could not have had any other particularly in view, but Nero, or, at least, that he must be meant; because, it would otherwise render the precept useless, as to any immediate application to existing circumstances." To this he answers, "This objection is repugnant to daily experience. Were it just, then all instruction of youth, to fill the various departments of social life, to which they might be destined, when grown to maturity, would be useless and inexpedient. To what purpose, then, would God have given Israel a constitution and laws, for their kings to walk by, while they were yet in the wilderness?"

I answer, God in the wilderness constituted Israel a peculiar nation, and condescended to become their immediate king, and instituted officers to administer the government, under himself, who was always present in his sanctuary, to give them answers "in all things that they called upon him for."—Deut. iv. 7. The government was put in operation in the wilderness, and disobedience to its authority was severely punished immediately by God, their king, and provision made for its administration when they would be settled in the promised land; and also the case foreseen, *of their rejecting God as their immediate king, and choosing a king, like the nations around them.* Provision was made for tolerating this departure from the national law; provided, however, that the person should be designated by God, and exercise no legislative authority, but obey, and administer the law of Moses, agreeable to the copy thereof deposited with the priests and Levites. In the books of Moses the fortunes of Israel are also foretold to the present day, and directions given how they ought to act in their various vicissitudes. When the epistle to the Romans was wrote, they were not a peculiar nation; their government was not a the-ocracy, *i.e.* immediate government of Jehovah; nor had the Romans or other Gentiles ever been so. The Saviour and his apostles organized no new civil governments in the world, because, as he expressly declares, his *kingdom was not of this world;* and the symbolical and local theocracy was abolished by the death of Christ. As there is, therefore, no analogy between the two cases, they cannot even illustrate each other. It is the height of absurdity, to suppose, that the law of Moses, made expressly for a peculiar people, in peculiar circumstances, could repeal the laws of Christ in the New Testament, equally applicable to all nations, at all times, to the end of the world, and made 1500 years after.

The author is remarkably unfortunate in his illustrations. Who, be-sides himself, ever thought that the duty of parents to educate their children for future usefulness, has any analogy with the apostle's in-junction to obey the *powers that be*? Can words more plainly express the powers that then governed? The apostle, indeed, does not name Nero, but names *the powers that be,* viz. that then governed the Roman empire. The principal organs of government frequently changed. Nero was de-graded, and condemned to death by the Roman senate; but the power of the Roman government over the nations of whom it was composed, continued the same. Christ and his apostles taught subjection to that government, and confirmed their doctrine by their example, during the reigns of Tiberius, Caligula, Claudius and Nero. Neither Christ nor his apostles denounced the government on that account. If the author's principles are correct, the Saviour and his apostles have been very un-faithful testimony bearers for the truth in their day. The author himself must be much preferred to them.

If these practical precepts of Christ and the apostles were not ap-plicable to the church at that period, why did not the author inform us when they would become applicable, or if at any time, or if like Moore's Eutopia,[19] they were mere fanciful theories, never to be reduced to practice? I believe they were applicable, and reduced to practice at that

---

19. Sir Thomas More (1478–1535), English statesman, published *Utopia* in 1516, de-picting an ideal state.

time—and, with the apostle (2 Pet. i. 2.) that they were not of private interpretation, but equally applicable to all times of the church.

The apostle, in confirmation of the doctrine of Christ, says, "wherefore, we must needs be subject, not only for wrath, but for conscience sake. For this cause pay we tribute also," &c. The author says, (p. 66) "Simple payment of tribute never was considered as any homologation of the authority imposing it." This is mere assertion, unsupported by testimony. He has appealed to approved commentators; not only these I have quoted, but all others that I have had access to, are decidedly opposed to the author's assertion. All English dictionaries, and moral and political writers, define tribute to be an acknowledgment of the authority of the government to which it is paid. Whether paid by a tributary prince, or by a subject, the result is the same.

CHAPTER VI

The origin and obligation of the national and solemn league and covenant—Covenants, and of national uniformity in religion by human authority, considered—The great evil of divisions in the church, without scriptural authority.

Though the author of the Sons of Oil advocates in his book, what has been called the covenanted work of reformation, yet he does not make much mention of those covenants in the body of the work; until, in his concluding exhortation, page 81. He there charges us "By our covenanting obligation, you have sworn allegiance to God. After vows, dare not to make enquiry." And he has added to the work an essay solely on the subject of covenanting; in which he connects the duty of covenanting with the moral law, so as that though *distinct*, it is not *separable* from the divine law, "which (he has said in the paragraph above) suggests and commands that of covenanting as an ordinance." Again—"It is in the moral law that we are required to make them"—p. 88. But, as usual, he brings no proof for these positions from the *moral law*, only his own assertion; and what he has asserted in several instances already, shews that this proof is of no great weight. We know, however, that vows, free-will offerings, &c. were a part of the ritual service prescribed and regulated in the Sinai covenant, which is abolished. We know also, that they were again introduced into the christian church, by which means many a church was built and endowed, and many a monastery and nunnery erected, and the clergy greatly enriched—and, in return for this, many of the most scandalous and outrageous sins against God, and crimes against society, were forgiven; many a weary pilgrimage taken, and many bones of martyrs discovered and enshrined. But we have no information of it in the moral law, nor in the New Testament, that I remember of, except the covenant to kill Paul, before the parties would eat or drink.

As to the contracts, covenants, and promises, between man and man, with respect to things lawful, and within the power of the party engaging, binding to a faithful performance, so much of the knowledge of the moral law of nature remains with man, that there is no difference of opinion between christians, mahometans, and heathens, on this subject. Greeks, Romans and Turks, as well as christians, are agreed in this, except that the catholic church has, in several instances, denied its operation in favour of heretics; and, what is not much better, several protestant states have also, in their establishing or changing their national religion, broken their national covenant or contract, with such as did not approve of the change. Every *ex post facto* law is a breach of national faith. No law can take away the rights, or punish for doing what was lawful before the law was made, especially if they are natural, viz. religious rights. It is not law, but instruction, that can cure error. It belongs to law to prevent the abuse of natural rights, but not to take away such as are unalienable.

It is not my intention to follow the author through his refined distinctions on this subject; but I will take notice of a few of the examples which he substitutes for proofs (p. 91, 96). He introduces God's covenant made with Noah[1]—The Abrahamic covenant[2]—The covenant made with Jacob[3]—The Sinai covenant, called the covenant of Horeb—and the renewed engagement to that covenant by the ministry of Moses.

---

1. God's covenant with Noah and all animals promised that God would never again inundate the earth, and the rainbow was given as a sign of the covenant (Gen. 9:8–17).

2. God's covenant with Abraham promised that Abraham would be the father of nations and that his descendents would occupy the land from the Nile to the Euphrates (Gen. 15:18–21, 17:4–14). The covenant was sealed by the establishment of circumcision.

3. God's covenant with Jacob provided that Jacob's many descendents would prosper and fill the land. The covenant was sealed by giving Jacob the new name Israel (Gen. 28:10–16, 32:24–32).

These all stand on the same footing. They were all dictated by the most high God, and not by sinful man. The Sinai covenant is also very frequently, in scripture, called a law. It was, as has been shewed elsewhere, a divine law, for the peculiar purpose intended by that dispensation. It was not propounded by man, nor changeable by human authority. It engaged to confer temporal rewards for obedience, and to inflict temporal punishments for disobedience. These conditions were not dictated by man, but by God, as the peculiar king and lawgiver of that nation.

Were it not that we have before found so many examples of the facility with which the author finds analogies where they do not exist, we might be surprised at him in this instance, bringing the authority of God down to a level with his creature, man. But he has (p. 81) prepared the way. He there, in the first place, introduces the authority of *our covenants* in the superior rank of obligation. The authority of the *divine law* in the second rank, and the *law of nature* in the fifth, and our *relationship to God,* in the sixth and lowest rank of authority.

Christians of but a common measure of discernment, talents and learning, such as the reformers, approved commentators, and moral writers were, would have, in this arrangement of the grades of authority, put the last first and the first last. They would have derived all the worship, love, and obedience which the reasonable creatures indispensably owe to their Creator, from their relation to *him*—and the love and duties which creatures owe to each other, from their mutual relation to God and each other. But Mr. Wylie is not confined to common rules, and has a right to be original. I have not, however, discernment sufficient to see any analogy between the authority of covenants dictated by the most holy and wise God, and those dictated by unholy and unwise mortals, who drink up iniquity like water. I being incapable, therefore, of arguing from the one to the other, will leave the application of it to such as possess such superior discernment as the author.

His next class of examples, substituted for proofs from the moral law, are the cases of Joshua and the Gibeonite,[4] the civil practice of mankind,

---

4. During Israel's conquest of Canaan, the Gibeonites tricked Joshua into making a protective treaty with them, when the ordinary practice would have been to exterminate

in bonds and indentures, national deeds, public contracts for national
debts, binding the nations and the heirs of individuals till they are dis-
charged. It is known to every person of common understanding, that
national debts are a mortgage on the national property, and does not
follow the individuals when they cease to be a part of the nation. When
I was a subject of Britain, my property on sea might have been seized
by the government of Holland, for instance, as a reprisal for the non-
payment of debt due to her subjects, because that property was under
the protection of Britain; but my property being now under the protection of another government, is no longer liable for British debts. The
same principle applies to heirs being bound for the debts or contracts of
the parent; they are only bound to the extent of their parents' property
in their possession, unless they are otherwise personally bound.

The author employs a whole head of discourse to prove the perpetual
obligation of covenants engaged in by representation; but as the subject
is religion, viz. the faith and worship of God, I will say that nothing of
this kind can be done by representation. We cannot believe or worship
God by proxy, even if we had for that purpose given a power of attorney
to our representative. It is with his own heart that every man believeth—
and his worship, to be acceptable, must be in sincerity, agreeable to his
faith. Every believer for himself, classes with the covenant of grace in
the very act of receiving Christ, by which he becomes united to him,
and engaged in his service. Their engagement to, or covenanting with,
Christ, is evidenced by their submission to his ordinances, and having
a conversation becoming the gospel, for all the purposes necessary to
the visible church. Church or state covenants, or any new moral law
imposed by human authority, have nothing to do with this transaction
between God and the believer.

The covenants' national and solemn leagues were of human authority,
and had political objects principally in view. The first underwent various
changes, and received successive additions by the same authority which
made it; the last was prepared by a union of church and state authority

---

them. When the deception was revealed to Joshua, because he had covenanted with
them, he honored the agreement (Josh. 9:1–27).

in Scotland, amended by similar authority in England, and, as amended, ratified by both, as far as they were competent, and made a term of state and ministerial, if not of christian, communion in Scotland, and of state communion in England; and in a few days after was rescinded in both by the same authority that made them; they were afterwards considered as terms of communion by the old dissenters, not only in sealing ordinances and attending on public worship, but in private societies for prayer in Scotland, and, as such, adopted by their reformed presbytery when it was constituted. Ireland and the English colonies had nothing to do with it, as appears from record; yet their obligation has been carried, not only to Ireland, but to the United States, in which it appears to be the object of the author to enforce their perpetual obligation on the consciences of the citizens—in addressing whom, he calls them *your covenants.* This subject will be more fully explained in the following pages, wherein I will not follow the author in his essay on covenanting. In the mean time it is proper to observe, that the examples which he has produced as proofs, while they have no analogy with the subject, yet give a masterly display of the author's talents for sophistry.

When, at the revolution of the British government, on the accession of king William and queen Mary to the throne, presbytery was restored, and became the established religion of Scotland, a few of those presbyterians who suffered great tribulation during the two preceding reigns, made exceptions to the new national presbyterian constitution, and dissented from it; these considered themselves to be the real representatives of those who suffered under the former reigns, and supported their testimony against the defection of church and state. They were called old dissenters, because they were the first who dissented from that establishment; all the presbyterian ministers having joined the establishment. The dissenters were left without public ordinances for about seventeen years, viz. till the Rev. John M'Millan, in 1706, having withdrawn from the established church, joined the dissenters and became their pastor, and continued to be so without assistance, it is believed, upwards of twenty years, when he was joined by the Rev. Mr. Nairn,[5] who had with-

5. Thomas Nairn (c. 1680–1764), a Presbyterian who could not make up his mind.

drawn from the established church, and joined the associate presbytery, composed of the Rev. Messrs. Erskines, and some other ministers who had seceded from the national church at a late period.[6] Mr. Nairn again seceded from the associate presbytery and joined Mr. M'Millan, and they together constituted a presbytery under the title of reformed. I never was informed how they came to assume that designation peculiarly to themselves, which was the general name for all the churches that had separated from the church of Rome, and protested against her usurped authority—but particularly of those who adhered to the doctrine of Calvin on the sacrament. The reformed presbytery ordained the Rev. Mr. Marshall to the ministry;[7] soon after this Mr. Nairn returned to the established church. When he withdrew from the associate presbytery, he published his reasons of dissent, which occasioned a controversy between the associate and reformed presbytery, which was long carried on with unbecoming acrimony, and not without mistakes on both sides. Both maintained the truth of the gospel as set forth by the reformers, and in the Westminster Confession and Catechisms, and yet severely criminated each other.

A few of those, who had fled from the persecution in Scotland to the north of Ireland, adhered to the old dissenters in Scotland, among which were my ancestors, one of whom bore a part in the memorable defence of Derry, against king James's army. They put themselves under the pastoral charge of the Rev. John M'Millan, who, though he could not supply them with preaching, wrote them pious pastoral letters, some of which I have seen. They were afterwards supplied from Scotland by the Rev. Mr. Marshall, and again at different times by the Rev. Mr. Cuthbertson,[8] &c. About fifty-five years ago, the Rev. William Martin

6. Ebenezer Erskine (1680–1754), Scottish church leader, in 1733, along with William Wilson, Alexander Moncrieff, and James Fisher formed the Associate Presbytery. In 1740, Ralph Erskine (1685–1752), Scottish scholar and theologian, joined his brother's Associate Presbytery.

7. Alexander Marshall, itinerant preacher to the Irish Covenanters, was ordained, in 1744, into the Reformed Presbytery of Scotland by John Macmillan and Thomas Nairn, as a co-Presbyter with them.

8. John Cuthbertson (1718–1791) was sent by the Reformed Presbytery of Scotland, in 1751, to minister to the Covenanters in Pennsylvania and its vicinity.

was ordained by the reformed presbytery of Scotland, and became a
stated minister to the old dissenters in Ireland, who had been called the
Hustonites, from the name of the Rev. Mr. Huston, who had been their
minister for some time during the persecution in Scotland.[9] They had
also been called Mountainmen, their preachers, during the persecution, having, from necessity, preached on the mountains.

About this time the reformed presbytery, consisting of one minister
in Ireland, and at least four in Scotland, published a judicial declaration
of their principles, preceded by a testimony against what they believed
to be wrong in the then constitution and administration of the governments of both church and state in the three kingdoms, and against the
incorporating union of Scotland with England, by which the legislatures (parliaments) of the two kingdoms became one; but they took no
notice of the constitution or legislative administration of the English
colonies in America. They knew well that these colonies never had any
political connexion with Scotland or Ireland, nor were in any political
dependence on the parliament or internal government of England.

When I arrived in this country in 1763, I spent several months at Octarara,[10] among the covenanters, called so from their having renewed
the covenants with the drawn sword in this country, several of whom
had been the personal friends of my father—but I did not confine my
attention wholly to them. I enquired at every source where correct information could be procured, concerning the history and divisions of the
christian church in this country, and had access to those who had been
concerned in these divisions, but who are, many years since, gone to
rest. I thought I saw mistakes and extremes with all parties, but found, as
far as I could judge, pious good men among them all. I, coming certified

9. William Martin (d. 1806) emigrated from Scotland to South Carolina in 1772 and
became the first Covenanter preacher in the Carolinas; David Houston (1633–1696) was
a Reformed Presbyterian minister who preached the necessity of keeping the Solemn
League and Covenant. His followers in Ireland, called Houstonites, became the nucleus
of the Reformed Presbyterian Church in Ireland.

10. Octarara is Findley's spelling for an area along the Octoraro Creek, the bound-
ary between Lancaster and Chester counties, in southeastern Pennsylvania. Covenanters
had settled there as early as 1727. Middle Octoraro was the home and headquarters of
John Cuthbertson.

as in full communion with the reformed presbytery of Scotland, was not required to sign my approbation of the Octarara testimony, agreeable to which the covenant had been renewed, but was afterwards requested to assist, as a clerk, those new communicants that were required to sign it, in order to their admission to partake of the Lord's supper. I did so; but in the mean time was so powerfully struck with the impropriety of signing such an instrument, as a term of christian communion, that I gave notice that I would never countenance it again, and accompanied the notice with reasons. While I was still in early life, I was, with others, chosen to the eldership. We attended the session, and were presented with a copy of the questions which we were to be asked in public. I pointed out such as I disapproved, and refused to answer to any but such as were doctrinal, viz. such as my approbation of the Confession of Faith, Presbyterial church government, &c. The session, after deliberating on the reasons offered, agreed to put only such questions, and continued to do so ever after.

The Rev. Mr. Cuthbertson, their only minister, and his session, did not, in administering ordinances, require the approbation of the covenants, as national, but personal. His words were, "on the inhabitants of Great Britain and Ireland, and their posterity." He or the reformed presbytery in Scotland, as appears from their testimony, never thought of them being obligatory on the colonies in their political capacity, nor on any not descended from the British isles, nor even on those in a political capacity out of Britain.

I had a strictly religious education from my parents, assisted by religious societies for prayer and conference, to supply the want of public worship, and to them I was early introduced. My father had a larger library of church history and divinity than many of his neighbours; to these means I am under great obligations for any early religious knowledge that I possessed, or impressions that I experienced, but as I came to be capable of reflection, I could not avoid observing, that so much of the conversation in the societies were occupied about local testimonies, &c. as had a tendency to jostle out, unintentionally, the great discoveries of the gospel for the salvation of sinners, and the duties resulting from these discoveries. It was usual to pray for the revival of the covenanted work of reformation, and particularly, as some pious persons expressed it, in their mother land in Scotland. As all prayers ought to be offered in faith, and as religious faith can only look to a divine promise, I could not find a promise in favour of the church of Scotland, more than other reformed churches. I knew that professed protestants of some nations, persecuted protestants of the same doctrinal faith, more, severely there than others—for instance, in Britain than in Holland; and that a greater proportion of their clergy had prevaricated, and that a smaller number had been faithful to the death; but I did not know that there was any peculiar promise under the gospel to it, other than what equally applied to all churches.

I had not then examined the principles of the solemn league and covenant, nor the circumstances which produced it, as I have since done. Yet I know, as long as I remember, that it was in a great measure political and local, and I could find no authority for the national covenant, though chiefly religious, having any obligation on any other nation than Scotland. Nor could I ever see any foundation to believe, that God had promised, as was limited, to bring about a reformation agreeably to rules or covenants prescribed by fallen and imperfect mortals, though I saw difficulties that I could not easily surmount, and had an opinion, that those of that society were, in a more peculiar manner, the people of God, than other sects. This, and my great esteem for, and confidence in, those who prescribed these rules, and testified even to the death for them, made it long before I durst trust my own judgment in calling them in question. My early prepossessions against other denominations, as unsound and unfaithful, also discouraged my enquiry. The presbytery of Antrim, within whose bounds I resided, had separated from the synod of Ulster, because that synod required an approbation of the Westminster Confession of Faith. They openly taught Arianism and Socinianism, and, it was believed, that many of the synod itself were Arminians, in a greater or lesser degree.[11] I remember the time when the seceders came first to that part of the country, and heard them preach when it was convenient. They preached the same doctrine as the

---

11. A theology founded by Jacobus Arminius (1560–1609) within the Reformed churches that modified the doctrine of predestination.

reformed presbytery, and had likewise local testimonies; they maintained the obligation of the religious part of the solemn league and
covenant as a term of communion, but not the political, which I thought
the most essential part, being that from which it derived its name, viz.
a league, intended for the three kingdoms of Scotland, England, and
Ireland, and actually enforced, though not agreeable to the forms of
the constitution in the two former. It was, indeed, put in execution and
enforced by civil penalties in Scotland, and in part in England, but without penalties; but it was neither engaged in by the government or the
people of Ireland, nor had the representative of that kingdom any thing
to do with it. The uniformity of religion in the three kingdoms, and the
defence of what they believed to be most agreeable to the word of God,
and best reformed churches, was one great object of that covenant; but
in as far as that was intended to be the act of civil government, it was as
much political as the national league or treaty—and, therefore, if the
one was unfit to be a term of christian communion, so was the other. In
addition to this, the associate body of Scotland differed about a certain
oath, which the magistrates of certain corporations were required to
take, and they carried the controversy so high, as to separate with circumstances that gave great advantage to the enemies of real religion;
and they even carried this to be a term of religious communion to Ireland, and, as I found afterwards, to America, where I understand it is
still considered as a term of communion by one party. For these reasons,
however well I esteemed their preaching of the gospel, joining them
would not have satisfied my early scruples.

The old dissenters being long without a minister and session, and
much longer without a presbytery, conducted their religious affairs and
testimony by what they called society, corresponding and general meetings, both in Scotland and Ireland; the two last were composed of representatives from societies, but the first represented a prescribed bounds,
and the last form the whole body in each nation; sometimes delegates
went from the general meeting of Ireland to Scotland. The society meetings admitted members to the fellowship; and when they had a supply
of ministers from the presbytery of Scotland, and afterwards got one
settled among themselves, these societies certified them to the minister and session for privileges, but not unless they attended the sabbath

societies. Before they were admitted, they were examined with respect to their religious knowledge. This continued to be the practice as long as I resided in Ireland. I am not stating this to their disgrace, but to their credit. For if their testimony and separation from other denominations were justifiable, this was the most proper method of conducting it that their circumstances would admit of; and though it was attended with some evident inconvenience, yet it was conducted with a very respectable degree of decorum. When I came to this country, I found the affairs of the community were conducted in the same manner; but that from a change of circumstances and political situation, there was a difference of opinion with respect to conducting their testimony in the situation where Providence had ordered their lots, which had existed for a considerable time. At one of the general meetings, of which I was a member, a very judicious member advised to postpone the debates till they would examine more minutely the circumstances in which Providence had placed them. This was agreed to; but I thought the examination was postponed too long. In conversing on this subject with some of the most intelligent members, who had been of the longest standing, they told me, that having no presbytery, they could not decide on the question judicially; that they had, at different times, referred questions to the reformed presbytery in Scotland, without receiving satisfactory answers, and waited for a presbytery in this country, having made application for a supply of ministers; that they had been long sensible that the Octarara testimony and Mr. Craighead's reasons of dissent,[12] in which they had concurred, were not formed on due information; that they were mistaken in considering the colonies as being of the same realm with Scotland, and liable to the same national obligations, and chargeable with the same national sins—they having no political connexion with that nation. On the first perusal of that testimony and reasons, where the being of the same realm, and being responsible for the conduct of the church and state of Scotland are frequently mentioned, I objected

12. Alexander Craighead (c. 1705–1766), pioneer Irish-born Covenanter minister in Pennsylvania and Virginia, led Covenanters in a renewal of the Solemn League and Covenant, at Octoraro, in 1743.

to it as improper; and I found this was the principle that influenced the minister and session to state the obligation of the covenants as personal, and not as national.

When two very respectable ministers of the reformed presbytery arrived, but before there was time to constitute a presbytery, I observed that they, at least one of them, required, in administering baptism, a belief of the obligation of the covenants' national and solemn league, not only on the British isles, but also on the dependent colonies. On this subject I conversed with the minister, and gave my reasons in writing, in which I objected to every term of communion enacted and enforced by human fallible authority. I had a child to be baptized. He made objections to my reasons, but requested me to lay them before the presbytery, which had been then constituted. It not being convenient for me to attend at that distance, I sent them by the minister, who returned them to me with a request from the presbytery, to prepare a concise abstract of them, to lay before the next presbytery, which was to meet at a less distance. Being, from mature reflection, very averse to making new divisions, I had kept my objections very secret, till they became public through the presbytery. I was equally averse to withdrawing from the communion of brethren, in whose piety I had great confidence, without giving such reasons as I judged, on due deliberation, might probably have equal weight with them.

The subject was held under deliberation, while I withheld my child from baptism. Finally, it was discussed in full presbytery, accompanied by extra-judicial conference, in which I bore a part. The result was an agreement, that while the presbytery still continued to hold the covenants, testimonies and sufferings of those in Scotland (during the persecuting period) in respectful remembrance, they considered the scriptures of the Old and New Testament, and the approbation of the doctrines contained in the Westminster Confession, Catechisms, and Form of Church Government, as agreeable to scripture, to be the only terms of communion in their church. The above, or in words to that amount, was unanimously adopted. At a sacrament soon after administered, on public notice being given, another public conference was held, at which I assisted, and at which such general satisfaction was given, that but one communicant kept back, and he joined the next opportunity.

From 1763, the British parliament had been constantly encroaching on the rights of the colonies, till at last they proceeded even to tax them without their consent, or being represented, and contrary to their chartered rights. To this all the colonists were opposed. Besides the reasonings of the then colonists, the discussions on the British encroachments in this country, and in the British parliament, where there was a powerful opposition to these measures, headed by the great Pitt (earl Chatham)[13] and other able statesmen, and which were published in this country, powerfully called the attention of the citizens to their political rights and danger. It was a convincing argument to the meanest capacity, that if the British parliament, by a law passed in all the constitutional forms, could not constitutionally oblige the colonists to pay either a direct or indirect tax, an unconstitutional ordinance of two out of the three branches of the English legislature, passed more than one hundred years before, which never became, or was called, a law, even in England, could much less bind the conscience in the colonies. They knew that the colonies never had any political relation to Scotland— therefore could not be bound by any national laws or covenants of that nation, which had long since ceased to be a distinct kingdom. These circumstances prepared the minds of the covenanters for the revision of their terms of communion, which many of them had long before seen to be necessary.

Not long after this revision, conferences were set on foot for the union of the reformed and associate presbyteries. This was carried on amicably, and finally concluded—I believe unanimously by the associate presbytery of New-York, and by all but two ministers from that of Pennsylvania; and their reason, from what I could judge, when assisting at the most numerous conference had on that occasion, was, that they would not agree to relinquish a dependence on an associate synod in Scotland, to which they had been in the habit of carrying appeals. A member of the reformed presbytery had proposed the relinquishment of

13. William Pitt (1708–1778), English statesman and first Earl of Chatham, broke with the government over its policies toward America and urged any settlement short of independence.

dependence on foreign authority, by both parties, as a preliminary to union. I, as far as lay with me, promoted that union, not more, indeed, on its own account, than as a step towards a union of all the protestant sects which were agreed in the same faith of the gospel, and substantially in the same government and discipline, which, though they differed in some lesser things, which required the exercise of that charity, forbearance, and feeding with milk, instead of strong meat, powerfully recommended and zealously exercised by the apostles, were not justifiable grounds of separation. I have been more than half a century grieved with christians, holding the same faith of the gospel, yet biting and devouring each other; and ministers of the same gospel, making ministers of the same faith, though in another communion, offenders for a word, probably ill understood. I do not expect perfect agreement in opinion in the church militant, not even during the millennium, which I steadfastly expect, but not in my own day. There will always be room for the exercise of the graces recommended and exercised by the apostles. Some promising attempts and progress were then made in uniting presbyterians, who agreed in the same faith and worship; but they were, at least for a time, defeated. The pride, and other passions of men, have often contravened the true interests of religion, and will do so, while depraved men (and all are depraved) are employed in conducting it. It will always be the case in this state of being; but divine grace will prevent it from being exerted at all times in so high a degree.

The reformed presbytery in Scotland did not correspond with their brethren here during the revolutionary war, until after they knew that the aforesaid union was agreed on; and then they excluded us from their communion. When independence was secured, and all was peace, they sent in a Rev. Mr. Reed, whom, though I had not the happiness of being acquainted with, I was well informed, was an acceptable preacher, and a prudent man.[14] He attended decently on a sacrament administered by his former brethren, preached with them, parted in friendship, and returned to Scotland without attempting to make a party. Afterwards the

---

14. James Reid, itinerant Scottish Covenanter minister, visited societies from New York to the Carolinas during the course of a year, beginning in about 1790.

Rev. Mr. King, and, I believe, Mr. M'Geary, arrived. Mr. King I heard preach in an acceptable manner; he attacked no party, but preached the gospel. In conversation with me, in hearing of a number of his people, he said, that toleration of religion could be no charge against the American governments, because they had no religious establishments, &c. Afterwards I heard the Rev. Mr. M'Kinney preach oftener than once, and conversed with him frequently.[15] In conversation we differed about the application of his preaching to this country. I found he spoke too freely about what he did not understand. I was not surprized, indeed, that he did not understand, not having opportunity to be informed. His fault was, not waiting for that opportunity, nor looking for it where it could be obtained. This reverend gentleman really possessed talents and general information. He has been many years deceased. It remained for the Rev. Mr. Wylie to open all the batteries of declamation, misrepresentation, and slander, against the governments and laws of the United States, and the individual states, and for those who have assumed the designation of the Reformed Presbytery in this country, to patronize him in doing so.

Thus I have stated a concise, but I believe a true history of the reformed presbytery in Scotland, before the revolution, and in Pennsylvania, as far as is necessary for information on this subject. Of some professed ministers of the gospel, who in this country have assumed that designation, it remains to be enquired whether they are a branch of the same community with those of that designation in Scotland, under whose superintendance I was fifty years ago, or a new sect. In this enquiry it is to be observed, that the presbytery of Scotland had emitted no public judicial testimony till near that time; and they had not, at least before 1763, made the approbation or signing of it a term of communion. I have not heard that this has ever been required there. They acted on the principles established and carried on by the meetings which I have mentioned above.

15. James McKinney (1759–1804), graduate of the University of Glasgow, 1778, was ordained by the Reformed Presbytery of Ireland and preached throughout Antrim and Derry. Under indictment for treason, he came to America in 1793. In 1798 he reestablished the Reformed Presbytery in America, with William Gibson, and ministered to scattered Covenanters from Vermont to the Carolinas.

I was early employed in assisting to explain the practical testimony of the reformed presbytery to such as applied for admission, before they had any written testimony, and I was instructed to say that their testimony did not at all apply to the governments of either church or state; that had not made such advances in reformation as Britain had done; that the lawful commands of civil governments in France, or even in Turkey, or any other nation that had not apostatized, ought to be obeyed, while those in Britain ought not; because, in Britain the covenants were the constitutional oath of allegiance, and the departure from it was apostacy; that an advancing church, however, ought to be acknowledged—but that apostacy ought always to be testified against. That it could, therefore, be only applied to the British isles.

It is proper, however, to state some reasons why it appears, that those who have assumed the designation of reformed presbytery in this country, are a distinct religious community from the reformed presbytery of Scotland, of which, it is understood, there is a branch now in Ireland.

The old dissenters, who constituted the reformed presbytery in Scotland, testified against the civil government of Britain, because of apostacy, viz. because of the breach of the solemn league, &c. being the coronation oath, and a fundamental part of the civil and ecclesiastic constitution of the nation. It being rescinded, was an act of high national apostacy, and immoral; the government, founded on this immoral act, was in itself immoral, and, therefore, acknowledging its authority, and obeying its commands, being a breach of the moral law, was a sufficient cause of excluding from church communion those who acknowledged it.

That by this immoral government the king was constituted head of the church of Christ, thus usurping the Mediator's supremacy over his own house. That in consequence of this supremacy the civil government had established prelacy as the national religion of England and Ireland, contrary to the oath of the covenant and presbytery in Scotland, not as of exclusive divine right, but as most agreeable to the minds of the people; that this government being apostate and immoral, it was sinful to obey even its lawful commands, or contribute to its support.

On this principle they excluded from their communion all those who supported the established clergy by paying tithes and other taxes for the support of the established church, and all such as paid hearth money, or any other taxes for the support of the civil government, and all who made applications to courts or magistrates for justice, or made voluntary appearances before them; and while I continued in that country, those terms of communion were strictly adhered to. Some were imprisoned for not obeying subpoenas, or refusing to take the book oath, and some had their goods taken in distress. This, however, had a good effect on their morals. I never knew one of them sued for debt, trespass or damage, and many of them suffered loss and damage, rather than become plaintiff in any suit. In renting land (the landlords generally being desirous to have such sober, peaceable tenants) included the tithe, and other stated dues, in the rent. With respect to sueing for debt, &c. some made transfers to a third person—but these were looked upon as very slippery testimony-bearers, by their brethren. They had not learned the refined ideas, since acquired in this country by the Rev. Mr. Wylie and his people, who have contrived to receive every protection and facility to acquiring property, even to obtain patents for land, the granting of which is one of the highest governmental acts, and, at the same time, testify that we have no lawful government. Granting patents is a royalty. In all republics it is an act of the commonwealth; and deeds of conveyance, or transfer from citizens, receive their validity solely from the law of the government, and must be recorded by an officer of government. This is not the case with goods and chattels, renting houses and lands, for a limited time, as Mr. Wylie supposes. This case, however, has been examined before, and is only introduced here to demonstrate, that this new reformed presbytery does not hold the same testimony with the reformed presbytery in Scotland.

This, indeed, seems evident, on the first impression. The colonies have never apostatized, in either religion or politics, unless the rescinding of the exclusive establishment of prelacy, by the legislatures of the southern states, whose predecessors had enacted it, can be called apostacy. This Mr. Wylie will not do, because it was accomplishing one object of the solemn league and covenant. The other states, with respect to religion, stand nearly as they were on their first colonization. We have no king, to whom the supreme headship of the church of Christ has been transferred; neither have our state or federal governments been invested by the citizens with any such sacrilegious power, as to enable them to usurp it. Christ's kingdom, which is not of this world, has not been permitted by the people of this country to be, by carnal antichristian wisdom, dragged into an unnatural incorporation with the kingdoms of this world—consequently, neither citizens nor aliens are called upon to pay tithes, *i.e.* every tenth shock of their grain, &c. before it is taken from the field, or to compound for it, and to pay a tax for keeping the church in repair, purchasing the sacramental elements, and marriage money, christening money, burying money, church clerks' dues, &c. nor are we obliged to serve as church wardens or vestrymen to a church, with which we do not communicate. In addition to the above, the old dissenters testified against the book oath, administered, not only by courts and magistrates, but by petty collectors of customs at fairs, many of whom could not read, but had either a New Testament or common prayer, bound up in the form of a cross, presented to those who brought in cattle for sale, to testify by kissing the book, whether they had sold or bought. Not only the old dissenters, but many others, preferred paying the impost, to taking the oath so administered, and for so small an object.

The union of church and state in that country being established on Mr. Wylie's principles, but not accommodated to his mind, the old dissenters and reformed presbytery in Scotland testified against even the establishment and the administration of the presbyterian church of Scotland, for various causes, which they assign. None of those causes exist in this country. We have no political establishment of religion. We have no patronage, whereby ministers are intruded on congregations, not only without their consent, but contrary to their remonstrances, and sometimes with an armed force. We have no connexion with, and partake of none of the guilt of the alleged unfaithfulness or partiality in discipline of the church of Scotland, stated in their testimony.

None of the objects of the testimony of the reformed presbytery of Scotland, applying to this country, and that judicature, though they had one of their number residing here as a missionary for a limited time, never having applied their testimony to this country, it is clear, to a demonstration, that those assuming that designation here, are a new sect, imposing themselves on the people under a disguised character. I have some further reasons for this opinion.

When the Rev. Mr. Reed, before mentioned, came from the reformed presbytery of Scotland, he found no ground for applying the local

testimony of Scotland, &c. to this country, and prudently returned without attempting, or, as far as is known, advising the application of it.
When the Rev. Mr. King arrived, I enquired if he designed to apply
the testimony of the reformed presbytery of Scotland to this country?
He answered no: that the circumstances were very different. I advised
him to examine well before they would introduce a new presbyterian
church, lest they should not find scriptural ground on which to erect
their standard, so as to be justified in keeping separate from all others. I afterwards put the same question to the Rev. Mr. M'Kinney. He
answered as Mr. King had done, that the testimony of Scotland would
not apply to this country; but that he and his colleagues had authority
from the reformed presbytery to exhibit a testimony, and require terms
of communion in this country, adapted to circumstances. I was, indeed,
so astonished at this answer, that I made no more enquiries. The apostle
Paul planted churches where other men had not laboured, expressly by
the authority of Christ. Mr. M'Kinney, &c. came to plant a church in
the United States; they came not expressly by his authority, where other
servants of Christ had planted and watered before they were born; but,
if my information be correct, they came by the authority of a presbytery in a foreign country, not with the Bible in their hands, for it was
here long before them in the hands of other christian sects, not even
with the local testimony of the reformed presbytery of Scotland in their
hands, but with authority from that presbytery to make such other local
testimonies and conditions of holding communion with Christ in his
ordinances, as their own caprice might suggest. They cannot say with
the apostle, that the Spirit expressly speaketh the terms they propose, or
that he gave them a special commission to prescribe local terms of communion to every nation under heaven, as he did the apostles to preach
the gospel—but even to them he gave no authority to preach local terms
of communion, to establish political national churches, to interfere with
national leagues, nor to exclude any from communion that approved
of the terms of communion prescribed by the Saviour himself, and
explained and applied by the apostles.

That they are a new sect of religious adventurers come to avail themselves of the christian liberty secured and protected in the United States,
agreeably to the moral law, spying out our liberty that we have from

Christ, in order to make themselves conspicuous, by availing themselves of circumstances and prepossessions, to support a party in the church of Christ, is to me evident. I do not say that along with this view, they do not preach the gospel. If they do, it is so far well; but we know that some, even in the apostles' days, preached the gospel out of envy, while their principal view was to add affliction to the great apostle himself, and to excite animosities and divisions in the church of Christ.

I have already stated, that when the Rev. Mr. Reed came from the reformed presbytery of Scotland, to behold our order, he decently countenanced it, and returned without complaint or exciting division; that afterwards, when the Rev. Mr. King arrived, and still at an after period, when the Rev. Mr. M'Kinney arrived, they both declared that the terms of communion prescribed by the reformed presbytery of Scotland, did not apply to this country. I enquired at those who I found were about to join them, on what terms they were to be admitted. I was answered, that that was not yet decided. Thus, for a number of years, they have been engaged in finding some plausible foundation on which to found a new sect; in the mean time, using their own discretion, from which they may retreat or vary, according to circumstances.

This was not the case with the apostles and disciples of Christ, who enlightened the world with his gospel. They had always the same terms of communion to offer to sinners, of all nations, kindreds and languages. If the peculiar terms of the reformed presbytery of Scotland were only those prescribed by the Saviour and his apostles, they were equally applicable to all nations; if they were not applicable to the United States, they were not the terms prescribed by the church's Head. If, as is certain, the sect that has assumed the designation of the reformed presbytery in this country, had to wait to examine circumstances and feel pulses, before they could prescribe the terms of holding communion with Christ, in his ordinances, they are at least, in so far, not a church of Christ, whose terms of communion are wholly contained in the New Testament. If they have this authority from the reformed presbytery of Scotland, not only to preach the gospel, but to prescribe such conditions of holding communion with Christ in his ordinances, arising from circumstances, such as in their own caprice they think proper. They are, without doubt, a new sect, not founded on the authority of Christ, nor, (at least as far as relates to terms of communion with him, in his ordinances,) ministers of Christ, but sect-makers, and of a peculiar character. When the methodists, moravians, and other sects came into this country, they had their terms of church communion ready to propose, and whether they were right or wrong in themselves, they were in so far like the gospel of Christ, that they were equally applicable to all countries, and all people, whether they were masters or slaves, without regard to the nature of the civil governments or laws of the respective countries. So was the gospel of Christ, but the terms of this new sect have not been offered in the same unshackled manner. It is understood they are not yet fully developed, nor their rules of discipline established. The apostles, wherever they came, declared the whole council of God without reserve or delay, and it was the same with respect to every country, whether the people were Jews, Greeks, or barbarians, except a temporary and limited toleration granted to the Jews; consequently, the terms of communion taught by this new reformed presbytery, is not the gospel of Christ, nor taught by authority derived from him, but, as is pretended, from a foreign local presbytery.

With respect to the opinion strangely entertained, that these covenants are personally binding on the posterity of those who took them, which was long acquiesced in without examination, little need be said. These covenants, particularly the solemn league, being proposed and enjoined by national authority, with a view to national objects, have no relation to those who have no connexion with the nation. Besides, it is absurd to suppose, that parents have authority to enact new, unchangeable, moral laws for their posterity. But it is said by some, that it is only to the moral, and not the political or changeable part of the league and covenant, posterity are bound; and, in support of this, they refer to the baptismal engagements of parents.

These engagements have their authority wholly from the moral law, obliging the parent to instruct his child as the scripture directs. This is equally obligatory on the parent, whether he engages before the congregation or not. Hence it is that we sustain the baptism received in all christian churches, even in the church of Rome, without examining into what obligations the parents come under, or whether any at all. It is certain, that Christ and his apostles have prescribed none, and that if they are perpetually obligatory, by the same reason we must at this day

have been all in the Roman Catholic communion. Our ancestors, for
many ages, have been engaged to receive human tradition, the decrees
of councils, and of bishops, as articles of faith.

My father, I believe, when presenting me to baptism, and my brothers
and sisters, engaged, among other things, to bring us up in the knowledge and belief of the binding obligation of the solemn league and covenant on Britain and Ireland, to the latest posterity. They even then had
too much good sense to include the colonies. But after he came into this
country, where he was very respectfully received, though in an advanced
age, he, on deliberation, was convinced that these covenants had no obligation on the colonies, and from thence concluded, that being local, and
not equally applicable to people of all nations, could not be imposed as
a condition of communion with Christ in any nation; Christ's conditions
of holding communion with himself being equally applicable to all nations. He regretted that the principle had not been sooner examined.

The Saviour has (Mark xvi. 16.) connected teaching with baptism;
instruction ought, therefore, to accompany it, and this ought to be as
public as circumstances will admit. But ministers have no authority
to add new terms of admission to those which the great Head and lawgiver of the church has already prescribed. This the divinely inspired
apostle of the Gentiles has declared (1 Cor. i. 24.) "not that we have dominion over your faith, but are helpers of your joy," &c. If this is the language of the great apostle Paul, by what authority did the emperors or
councils (such as the Rev. Mr. Wylie introduces as having dominion over
our faith) or two parts out of three of the English legislature 170 years
ago, come to have dominion over the faith of a people above 2500 miles
distance, and not subject to their laws? and by what authority does the
author of the Sons of Oil come forward, at this time of day, to enforce
that claim? Not certainly by the authority of Christ, or of his apostles. It
does not, however, appear, from any records I have examined, that the
parliaments of either England or Scotland imposed the league and covenant as a term of christian communion, but as a condition of enjoying
civil privileges. In Scotland the taking of it was enforced by severe civil
penalties; in England no civil penalties were annexed to the ordinance
of parliament for taking the covenant. It was in both, however, made a
condition of admission into the ministry of the established church, viz.

to the enjoyment of the established emoluments. This is consistent with all political establishments of religion, because the ministers of such churches are in so far officers of government; but this is not founded on the authority of Christ or his apostles, but on the authority of Constantine the Great, and other political governments. Yet neither these nor the English parliament ever attempted to extend their ecclesiastic jurisdiction beyond the extent of their civil authority. This right is, for the first time, asserted by those assuming the name of reformed presbytery in this country.

Ecclesiastic authority has made a great noise in the world. It has not been the church of Rome *only* that has engaged the sword of the civil magistrate to execute its decrees, or to support them by penal laws, viz. persecution. But this power is not derived from Christ. He could have converted and employed kings and emperors to be ministers, as well as fishermen, if it had been his will. The power committed by Christ to his apostles and ministers, is, *to teach all things which he hath commanded them, and to administer his ordinances, and to do those things in decency and order, that his worship may be a reasonable service, i.e. a declarative and ministerial,* or, as some choose to express the last, executive power; a power for edification, and not for destruction; not for revenge, or for the aggrandizement of churchmen, to which purpose it has been so often applied. The highest censure exercised by the apostles, for the most aggravated offences, was exclusion from the communion of the church, viz. from the kingdom of God then erected in the world, under the new covenant dispensation, to the kingdom of satan, who is by the apostle called the God of this world for edification, that the soul might be saved in the day of the Lord. It went no further among the Jews than exclusion, or casting out of the synagogue. It has been carried much further by christians. It consigned the body to death, without allowing time for repentance. From the time of Constantine and the council of Nice, down to the council of Trent. viz. for more than 1200 years, it had this result. Unhappily it did not stop there. It has been practised in protestant states; so that even protestant, as well as popish churches, have preferred the example, in this instance, of the heathen druids (the priests of human sacrifices) to that of the apostles of Christ. The Saviour not only refused to call fire from heaven, at the request of his apostles, to consume the

Samaritans, who refused to receive him, but *turned and rebuked them, and said, ye know not what manner of spirit ye are of*—which that learned and evangelical divine (Dr. Owen) explains to mean: *Ye know not the spirit of the dispensation ye are under; it is totally different from that under which Elias was.* Under that dispensation, they were authorised to destroy the idolatrous nations of Canaan and apostate Israelites; but the Saviour says, *he came, not to destroy men's lives, but to save them;* therefore, with great propriety he is called the Prince of Peace. This is quoted from memory.

As the above reasons apply against all terms of christian communion, prescribed by human authority, a few observations further may be necessary, with respect to local terms of communion depending wholly on the credibility of human tradition. Of this kind are the solemn league and covenant, and all the testimonies in its support, such as the testimonies and declarations of Sancques, Lanerk, Rutherglen, &c.[16] However suitable they were to the then time and occasions, they were not intended by those who made them, to be terms of church communion. Their intention makes no difference. They had no authority for that purpose. The question is, are they prescribed by the Saviour as terms of enjoying communion with him in the ordinances of his own institution? If they are, christians are equally obliged to subscribe to the testimonies of every church, from that of Jerusalem and Antioch, where the disciples were first called christians, down to the present day. Certainly any other, at least any earlier converted church, has an equal right to have their local testimonies made a term of communion, as the church of Scotland.

Protestants have generally agreed in rejecting human tradition as a rule of faith, and in making the maintaining of it one principal ground of separation from the Roman Catholic church, as well as the instituting terms of communion by human authority. The covenants were ordained by human authority, and several of the testimonies in support of them, by only individuals, neither acting in a political or ecclesiastic capacity, nor designed by them as terms of communion in the church of Christ; but only as a declaration of the causes for which they suffered, and all of them handed down to us by human, and much controverted, tradition.

---

16. Scottish towns at which Covenanters, at various times, issued manifestos, most notably at Rutherglen (1679), Sanquhar (1680), and Lanerk (1682).

I ask, therefore, with what consistency protestants can condemn the authority of tradition in the church of Rome, and, at the same time, oblige protestants to receive the human tradition respecting the solemn league, &c. as an article of divine faith, viz. as a condition of communion with Christ in his ordinances. Were they not the work of fallible and erring man, and the tradition uncertain?

That the tradition respecting those things is much controverted, is well known to all who are acquainted with the histories of these times. The reformed presbytery of Scotland, indeed, in their testimony (p. 201.) assert, "that the national covenant of Scotland, and the solemn league entered into by the three nations, for reformation and defence of religion, &c. are moral, and so perpetually binding upon the nations, and every individual of them, to the latest posterity." This opinion was also entertained by some of the sufferers during the tyranny of the two last of the Stuarts, and appears to have been countenanced by the intelligent Mr. Shields, in his *Hind let loose,* and to have been handed down without due enquiry, and implicitly received, certainly without other authority than that the name of Ireland is put in the title, which proves no further than that those who framed it had a view or expectation, that Ireland would engage in it; but this never took place, as I have shewed elsewhere, and also that it never became a national law in England.

I equally reject human tradition, if it was ever so certain, and human authority, if it was ever so constitutionally exercised, as conditions of holding communion with Christ in his ordinances; but how much more objectionable are they, when the tradition is so uncertain, and the authority is exercised without the constitutional forms, and when they relate to things changeable in their own nature. Scotland and England, by their own act, have ceased to be distinct nations above one hundred years ago, and Ireland has ceased to be a distinct nation about ten years since. The national covenant was taken more than two hundred years since, and the solemn league and covenant near one hundred and seventy years ago. Thousands of the posterity of the covenanters in this and other countries, do not know whether their ancestors took them or not; and many thousands, not having access to the history of those times, do not know that such an instrument ever existed, and I believe that, notwithstanding this, they having the Bible, may receive Christ as he is freely offered in the gospel, and be entitled to the ordinances of his house.

It is not easy to free the mind from prepossessions early imbibed and deeply impressed. It requires some fortitude to bear the reproach of apostacy and backsliding, from those who have more zeal than knowledge, and perhaps do not know the meaning of the terms they make use of. There can be no backsliding or apostacy in drawing closer to the pure word of God, or in rejecting such terms of communion as are not prescribed therein to the people of every nation or language under heaven, nor in rejecting local and traditionary terms of christian communion, when enjoined by protestants, more than when they are enjoined by papists. Indeed the church of Rome cried out apostacy against the reformers, but they were not deterred by this. They took up the New Testament as containing the religion of christians, and Christ, the prophets, and the apostles, for their guide. *They loved not their lives unto the death.* They did not make self or party aggrandizement the object of their pursuit, as has been since done in the greater and the lesser apostate and apostatizing churches. I sincerely believe, that all the superstition and will-worship introduced in the primitive church, before it became united to, and governed by, the kingdoms of this world, were introduced with the purest intentions; and that the promoters of them believed that they were reformers. I have the same opinion of those, who, with ill-informed zeal, put a stop to advances in reformation at the threshold, by promoting anew the great footstep of antichrist to his throne, viz. the union of the church of Christ, which is not of this world, with the kingdoms and politics of this world, and thereby erecting a barrier against advances in reformation. From that time reformation, not only in theory, but in practice, has declined. Many of the successors of those who promoted and protected the reformation in its beginning, have been reconciled to the Roman Catholic church. The territories possessed by protestants, and their number, have been greatly contracted, and the tents of the Pope and Mahomet greatly enlarged. For the truth of this, I appeal to history. These proofs are too numerous to be inserted in this place. It is true that those powers are coming down, but by other means than the protestant reformation. It is well known to all who are acquainted with the controversies between the Roman Catholic and protestant doctors, since the union of protestant churches with the civil state, viz. since numerous national political churches grew out of the reformation, and exerted themselves in persecuting or tolerating, according to their own caprice, such as did not approve of their political terms of communion, formed and changed agreeable to their own interests or caprice, that the ingenious Bosuet,[17] and others, taking advantage of this circumstance, have demonstrated, to the conviction of numbers of all ranks, that there is no essential difference between the protestant national churches, and the church of Rome; that though there might be more instances of superstition in the course of dark ages, crept into the church of Rome, than into the newer churches, yet the human authority by which they both were governed, was the same; that much of the rest was a difference only in name, &c. and those doctors of the Roman Catholic church, fortified themselves by extracts from the able writings of the protestant doctors, especially in Britain, in favour of political religious establishments, and the persecution of non-conformists. It is well known, that, with exception of occasional revivings, the protestant churches have been losing ground, both in purity and power, ever since they were connected with, and governed by political influence. I will appeal to every true protestant acquainted with church history, for the truth of the following fact, viz. that no political church has ever reformed itself, further than contributed to its own temporal aggrandizement, including the civil government with it, to whose tyranny the clergy of such churches almost always became subservient.

One most valuable advantage, indeed, those protestant churches politically established, have over the Roman Catholic church, as established by Constantine and Theodosius, and further modified by successive emperors, councils, and Popes, viz. in all the protestant states, the laity are permitted to read the scriptures in their mother tongue. This was not the case in the Roman church; and I believe, with the apostles, that the scriptures contain the whole will of God necessary to salvation. The church is built upon them (Eph. ii. 20.) They are able to make wise to salvation, through faith in Jesus Christ (2 Tim. iii. 15.) They are able to

---

17. Jacques-Bénigne Bossuet (1627–1704): French bishop and defender of the French church against papal authority.

save our souls (James i. 20.) And with Luther, and other reformers, that neither tradition, the opinions of the fathers, nor of councils, nor any thing founded on human authority, ought to be brought in competition with them. Those who are acquainted with the writings of Luther, Calvin, and other reformers of that age, know that, next to preaching the gospel for salvation of sinners, and connected with it, their object was, overturning tradition and human authority, in matters of conscience. I admit also, that though all the national churches differ from each other, in what they require, under penalties less or more severe, to be believed and practised, and that, though the Roman Catholic church, as well as those protestant churches, retain the true principles of the christian religion in their creeds; that, yet she has perverted those principles in a much greater degree, and disfigured and disgraced religion with a much greater amount of absurd superstition, than the protestant national churches. This, however, must be admitted, that the church of Rome has not enjoined local terms of communion; she has, from the council of Nice down, prescribed for the whole catholic church, and considered and punished as schismatics, those who did not obey. It is true, protestants have done the same thing. Such as adhered to the national faith of the protestant states of Switzerland, were persecuted in Britain; and such as adhered to the national faith of Britain, were persecuted in Saxony, Denmark, &c. Even in the present more moderate times, such as adhere to the national faith of Scotland, are excluded from some civil privileges in England, though both are governed by one king and parliament. This state of things was not prescribed by Christ, the christian church's sole Head and Lawgiver.

I have already shewed, that, in the reformation period, no such doctrine was advanced by the reformers. All of them, Mosheim informs us, asserted the right of submitting religious truth to private judgment. This, indeed, was the fundamental principle of the reformation itself. All the reformers had some shades of difference of opinion. Not only Luther laboured under a mistake about the real presence in the sacrament, but Calvin, Zuinglius, &c. differed from each other on that subject; though they all differed from Luther, yet they all held communion with each other, till the idol of uniformity in the national churches was introduced.

That the principle of expedience, viz. being agreeable to the opinions of the majority of the people to be governed, and to the interest of those in whom the powers of the government were vested, was the foundation on which all the political establishments of religion, in the protestant states of Europe, were founded, might be easily evinced from the history of the union of church and state in each of them. That this was the foundation of the unhallowed union which first commenced during the reign of Constantine the Great, in the fourth century, has already been demonstrated. I shall only, in this place, add a concise statement of the political reformation, as established in the United Provinces, more generally in this country known by the name of Holland, the principal province, the churches of which, in this country, are known by the name of Low Dutch.

The seventeen provinces of the Netherlands had been formerly so many different states, subject to their respective sovereign dukes, earls. &c. in all of which, however, the people, the nobles, and the clergy, retained a vote in making their own laws. All these small sovereignties, through the means of intermarriages, successions, &c. became subject to the dukes of Burgundy, each of them, however, still retaining their own laws and privileges. Under this government they prospered so greatly, that their cities became the manufacturers and marts of commerce for all Europe. By intermarriages, the dominions of Burgundy became transferred to the house of Austria, and, eventually, both came to be united under the crown of Spain. Charles V. the first who came to possess that vast empire, was also elected emperor of Germany, about the commencement of the reformation. He persecuted the Lutherans in Germany, and his powerful and persecuting rival, Francis I. persecuted the disciples of Calvin, &c. in France, while Henry VIII. did the same in England, and James V. in Scotland. Charles, while he persecuted the reformers in his other extensive dominions, did not infringe on the constitutional rights of the states of the Netherlands (Burgundy) which was his native country, and which had assisted him greatly in his wars; consequently, these states, even while they remained in the profession of the Romish religion, as ten out of the seventeen continued to do, yet they received and protected the persecuted protestants of all nations, who, though they all agreed in renouncing popery, human inventions, and the authority of human tradition, in the worship of God, yet differed in many other points of inferior importance.

When Philip succeeded to Charles, in the possession of Spain, the low countries, &c. he deprived the states of Burgundy of their ancient rights, governed them by foreign troops, forced on them fourteen additional bishops, and supported these by an infernal court of inquisition, formerly unknown to that country, and exacted the most exorbitant taxes. The blood of the protestants was shed, without regard to age or sex, till much of the country was laid desolate. When oppression and tyranny were at an unexampled height, the people in the province of Holland stood on their own defence, and soon after seven of the provinces united in declaring themselves independent of Spain, which, with occasional assistance from queen Elizabeth of England, some of the princes of Germany, and the protestants of France, after sixty years war, from being exceedingly weak and poor, had their independence acknowledged even by Spain, whose overgrown power they had contributed greatly to reduce, and were become themselves rich and powerful.

When they constituted an independent government, they left as much of the ancient civil privileges in the possession of provinces and cities, as was consistent with their federal union, but made an essential alteration in the established religion. Having been before oppressed by bishops, and their ecclesiastic courts, and by their voice in the government of the states, they abolished the order. They not only declined the protestant hierarchy admitted in England, but the less exceptionable episcopacy of the Lutheran states, and admitted of no higher order than presbyteries, and even those they restrained from any share in the civil government, or from any power of oppressing other sects, by levying tithes or other church dues, as is done in Britain. They are paid a moderate salary by government, and are severe reprovers of vice, but never interfere with the principles or the measures of the government in their administrations. They profess the same doctrinal faith of the other reformed churches, and maintain the presbyterian church government and discipline of Geneva. This is the established form of religion in the United Provinces, called formerly in Scotland, &c. Netherlands.

But as the great cause of their revolt was persecution, on account of difference of religion, and oppression, the great care of these states, since their establishment, has been to guard against those evils, and favour, by civil authority, no peculiar or curious inquisition into the faith or religious principles of any peaceable men, who come to live under the protection of their laws, and to suffer no violence or oppression on any man's conscience, whose opinions break not out into *expressions* or *actions* of ill consequence to the peace of the state. Having, at a great expense of blood and treasure, contended for these rights themselves, they thought it unreasonable to refuse them to others. With respect to any new sect, however, commissioners are appointed to examine whether or not their principles are consistent with the peace of the country, before they are permitted to hold public assemblies; but no inquisition is held on the worship in private families.

The Roman Catholic religion alone, was at first excepted from the common protection of their laws, on the opinion that their acknowledgment of a foreign and superior jurisdiction (of the Pope) had a tendency to make men worse subjects; and that by their religion, they seemed to represent, and were probably attached to the Spanish government, the great *patron* of popery and persecution. They have never, however, persecuted the Roman Catholics for not renouncing the faith of their ancestors; the states did not attempt to bribe or force them to become hypocrites, and they having proved themselves to be peaceable citizens, were permitted to enjoy equal protection as other sects, except that they are disqualified from holding offices of trust. The constitution and administration of the churches of the United Provinces, have continued without any change from the time of the reformation, and without persecution, which, it is believed, cannot be said of any other protestant establishment.

For an account of the reformation of the churches of the United Provinces, I might refer to different histories; but the above is an abstract of what is stated by the very intelligent sir William Temple, in his observations on the United Provinces, and, as far as convenient, in his own words.[18] He was long resident minister from the court of London to the

---

18. William Temple (1628–1699), English diplomat, *Observations upon the United Provinces of The Netherlands* (1672).

government of the United Provinces; and, on his return, refusing to be minister of the state in the corrupt court of Charles II. he retired to private life, and wrote his *considerations,* a statement of his negociation, &c. at the same period when the persecuted presbyterians of Scotland were in communion with the churches of Holland.

I have selected the account of the reformed establishment of religion in the United Provinces in preference to that of other protestant states, because the reformed church of Scotland always held communion with it, and through it with the Swiss and Palatinate churches, and the persecuted protestants of France; with them those who were banished by James VI. and Charles I. of Scotland, took refuge during the struggles for power between the civil and ecclesiastic authority in that nation during those reigns, and some of them became ministers of congregations, and teachers in the universities of these states. It was to this church that the persecuted presbyterians, during the establishment of episcopacy and persecution in Scotland by Charles II. and James II. resorted. It was in the seminaries of the United Provinces that their students received education for the ministry, and also ordination from their churches. The Rev. Mr. Renwick,[19] the last who suffered death as a presbyterian, under James II. in Scotland, and many others, who became afterwards shining lights in the gospel ministry in that church, were ordained by the Low Dutch presbyteries, there called classes, and they having made no change, still are in communion with the presbyterian church of Scotland, as restored and established at the revolution; and as they were before that period with the same presbyterians when they suffered persecution under episcopal tyranny. The old dissenters, however, seventeen years after the restoration of presbytery in Scotland, formed a worshipping congregation, and several years afterwards constituted the reformed presbytery, separate from the presbyterian national church, and, therefore, separate from the churches of Holland, and consequently from the persecuted presbyterians during the reign of the Stuarts, thus they became a new church, separate from all other reformed churches.

---

19. James Renwick (1662–1688), Scottish Covenanter minister, was hanged February 17, 1688.

That the presbyterian national churches of Holland themselves considered it in this point of view, and declined holding communion with the old dissenters in their state of separation from the presbyterian church, as restored in Scotland, is admitted in the judicial testimony of the reformed presbytery of Scotland. Certainly the same reasons which they apply in support of their separation, would equally apply against every other national reformed church, as none of them have established their forms of church government, as of exclusive divine right, but as expedient. The famous protestant churches of France have supported their government and order under such bloody scenes of persecution, as has produced a more numerous list of martyrs than any other nation can shew, without ever thinking of the civil magistrates' power, *circa sacra*. All they claimed, or plead for, was protection in worshipping Almighty God agreeably to the discoveries of his will to their own understanding and judgment, viz. conscience. In this they are in perfect unison with the presbyterians of the United States, at least with the general assembly and associate reformed synod, and the persecuted protestants of France have always held communion with the other reformed churches, where Providence ordered their lot in their dispersions. If we look for a divine form of church government and discipline, we must seek for it in the New Testament, and not in the imperfect decrees of states, or of church and state united; and in receiving it with a divine faith, we must receive it as dictated by divine, and not by human authority. The church of Rome, for many ages, assumed divine authority, both in spiritual and temporal concerns. They disposed of and dictated laws to kingdoms, as well as to churches, and claimed the exclusive right of doing so. The civil governments of the protestant states have not gone quite so far. They have only dictated to their own subjects, and permitted other sovereign states to dictate to theirs agreeably to their own interests. Supposing Mr. Wylie, and the new church in this country, of which he is a minister, to be right, they must admit that they are so on original ground, for they can claim no example as their model from the reformed, nor from the primitive apostolic churches, nor from the saints during the Old Testament dispensation. They have the testimony of no approved commentators, nor of martyrs, in their favour. None ever suffered martyrdom under such civil governments as those of the United States; and no commentators, to which I have had access, have dared to pervert the plain grammatical language of scripture in such manner as to support the system which he advocates. Where, then, is the great cloud of witnesses and approved commentators, to which, in order to deceive the uninformed, he has appealed, without even naming or making quotations from any of them? Those who presume, whether clothed with the purple robes and other regalia of supreme civil authority, the red hat and scarlet robes of the vatican, viz. the sacerdotal conclave of Rome, or the more decent and modest garb of a protestant minister of the gospel, to dictate to poor guilty sinners, as all the sons of Adam are, what doctrine they shall believe, or what worship they shall offer to God, in order to obtain salvation, viz. in what sense or on what authority of church or state they shall receive the scriptures—Such teachers are, in so far, Antichrists, of which an apostle testifies, that there were many even in his own time.

The creeds or confessions of all the reformed churches renounce the authority of church or state to prescribe articles of faith; but those of the English church support the authority of the church to prescribe rites and ceremonies not contrary to the word of God, and of the state to enforce their observance. That the church has authority from scripture to prescribe rules for the decent and orderly administration of divine ordinances, is fully admitted; and also that, as the exercise of this authority must depend much upon human discretion and circumstances, they may vary in different times and places, is admitted; but these can never be objects of divine faith; therefore, as great personal liberty should be permitted in the use of them, as could be done without evident confusion. This was all that was plead for by the puritans. This necessary authority has, indeed, been carried so far by some protestant churches, as to approach to superstition, and they have been enforced as if they were articles of divine faith; but the obligation of national and local covenants are not even plead for as rules of decency and order in the worship of God, but as articles of faith and of unchangeable local obligation on some churches, and not on others, and require a divine faith in uncertain human tradition, and a knowledge of the history of a particular nation, or else implicit belief respecting it. This neither the scriptures, the primitive church, nor the reformers required. They do not, therefore, as terms of religious communion, belong to the christian church, but are solely the invention of fallible men. That they contain part of the moral law is admitted, and so do the articles of the church of Rome, and every other sect; but the obligation to obey this does not depend on human authority; it has the same infallible authority at all times, and in all nations.

To the advocates of persecution I wish to address a few thoughts. All the arguments of Bellarmin[20] and Bossuet, assisted by all their army of popish doctors; all the sophistry of Bolingbroke,[21] Hume, Voltaire,[22] Gibbon, and the whole phalanx of deists, even with the assistance of the Socinians, cannot injure the cause of christianity so much, as one instance of persecution by real protestants, in support of their divine religion. Pure christianity depends on other authority than the gallows, or the faggot, fines or forfeitures. Having recourse to these in its support is, in fact, giving up the cause. It is an open acknowledgment, that it cannot be supported by scripture and reason. If so, it is not of God, and ought to be given up.

The first reformers, except Zuinglius, were opposed to civil government making laws for the church. Calvin contended against it; so did the reformers of Scotland—but unhappily, that church called on the state to support its censures by civil penalties; this soon after turned against their successors with severity. The doing so was inconsistent with the doctrine on which the reformation was built, which was the scriptures, addressed to the consciences of individuals.

The division of presbyterians into numerous sects, especially in Britain, and from thence carried into this country, all of them holding the same faith, and, at the same time, as far as in them lies, unchurching each other, originated, as I have said, with political tests, enforced by civil authority; every new test became a new snare, and source of end-

---

20. Roberto Francesco Romolo Bellarmino (1542–1621): cardinal, Roman Catholic theologian, and defender of the Roman Catholic Church against the Reformation.

21. Henry St. John (1678–1751): Viscount of Bolingbroke, English Tory politician, historian, and political propagandist.

22. François Marie Arouet de Voltaire (1694–1778): French philosopher, historian, and dramatist.

less division and animosity. I speak here of those sects who profess
to adhere to the Westminster Confession of Faith, and Presbyterian
Church Government. The old dissenters separated from the established
presbyterian church of Scotland, and instituted the reformed presbytery. That presbytery, more than fifty years ago, separated into two reformed presbyteries, who wrote and testified against each other. In this
country, within a few years past, two reformed presbyteries have started
up, who not only refuse to hold communion with each other in sealing
ordinances, but in *social* prayer. I have known two praying societies held
in different apartments of the same house, occupied by the father and
the son, who would not, in prayer, hold communion with each other.
Both these reformed presbyteries, it is understood, make the covenants
of Britain and persecution, as they believe, authorised by the judicial
law of Moses, terms of communion, both separate from, and unchurch
all other sects but their own. I have understood that they only differed
about the application of their testimony to the civil governments of this
country. Such a question was never agitated by the apostles, nor by the
early reformers.

After the well known secession of the divines from the established
church of Scotland, who instituted the associate presbytery, that presbytery soon divided into two associate presbyteries, I believe now synods,
who censured and excluded each other from communion, viz. as far
as it was in their power, unchurched each other. They did not assign
the defectiveness of the constitution of the established church, as the
ground of their separation, as the old dissenters had done; but some instances of unfaithfulness and tyranny of its administration, and errors
in doctrine not duly opposed. These sects (since called seceders) both
when they separated from the established church, and from each other,
adopted the obligation of the national covenants as terms of communion,
but not to the same extent that the reformed presbytery had done; they
did not apply them so as to justify disowning the civil government of the
country, or disobeying their lawful commands. This occasioned a lasting controversy between these two bodies and the reformed presbytery,
in which christian charity and moderation were not prominent features.

The seceders divided about an oath required in the royal burghs
(incorporated towns) in Scotland, to maintain the true religion, as by

law established. Strange it is indeed, that such a local question should
have been made a condition of holding communion with Christ in his
ordinances, but still more strange, that it should have been promoted as
such in Ireland and America, among a people, who, many of them probably, did not know that such a place as Scotland existed, and where, it is
at least probable that few of them were acquainted with the laws or powers of the royal burghs of Scotland. Though it is the country of my ancestors, I am not acquainted with those laws. Those who objected to making
this oath a condition of christian communion, among whom we find the
respectable names of some eminent gospel ministers, such as the Rev.
Messrs. Erskines, Fisher, &c. took the designation of burgher seceders,
and the others of antiburghers.[23] I can remember, though then almost
a child, the time that these hard names were introduced in the north
of Ireland as terms of communion, and was not a little surprized, soon
after coming to this country, to find these distinct terms of communion
and separation, injurious to christianity itself, transferred to America.

In a few years after, both parties were so much convinced of the impropriety of such conduct, in the church of Christ, that they formed a
union; but this union the antiburgher synod in Scotland dissolved by
an authoritative decree. Such is the result of protestant churches assuming the authority of the church of Rome. The reformed presbytery
having in this country, agreeable to the plainest dictates of scripture
and reason, renounced all human authority and local testimonies, as
conditions of holding communion with Christ in his ordinances, and as
wholly inapplicable to the circumstances of this country. On this ground
the seceders and reformed presbytery united, with the exception of two
antiburgher seceding ministers. The ground of their opposition was,
that a member of the reformed presbytery moved, as a preliminary resolution, that both parties should renounce all subordination to foreign
jurisdiction, against which the two members voted, and on this ground
dissented from the union. I was a member of that conference. It is not

23. James Fisher (1697–1775), minister of Kinclaven, Scotland, formed the Associate Presbytery, in 1733, along with Ebenezer Erskine, William Wilson, and Alexander
Moncrieff.

necessary to detail all that followed, but it was not conducted without the opposition of low intrigue. Of one thing I am certain, that in the opinion of those pious and disinterested ministers of the gospel who promoted that union, it was not their object to stop there. It certainly was not mine. I thought I saw a promising opening for uniting all the christian sects in this country, who professed the same faith, in the same communion. This I had long revolved in my mind, and sincerely rejoiced at the probability of its confirmation. It was attempted, with promising circumstances, but failed in the issue, from the passions and caprice of men. It will yet succeed, though I may not live to see it. It will do so when the authority of God in the scriptures is taken as the sole rule, and the examples of the apostles and reformers are followed; and local testimonies, national covenants, &c. discarded from the christian creed.

The result of the facts I have stated above, is, or has not long since been, that the presbyterians in Scotland, five different sects, all of them unchurching each other—that is to say, excluding each other from church communion, existed, viz. The presbyterian church by law established, two reformed presbyteries, and two associate synods, all at war with each other, and, as far as lay with them, excluding each other from the kingdom of Christ in this world, in which I have no doubt that his sincere worshippers, from all these sects, will be admitted into the kingdom of heaven. I do not, however, suppose, that the church of Christ is to be found only among presbyterians; but because the divisions among that body are more singular than what has taken place among other christians, I speak particularly of them. They all agree in professing to take the scriptures as the alone perfect rule of faith and manners, and also in professing, that the doctrines of the gospel, as stated in the Westminster Confession of Faith and Catechisms, are agreeable to scripture; they all have the same form of church government and order of worship. This Confession, &c. must be very imperfect indeed, or else their differences must be about things comparatively small.

I know well that the old dissenters, who, perhaps, were the most strict of all the sects, against occasional communion, did not mean thereby to unchurch other sects, or that their ministers were not the ministers of Christ. They believed that many of them preached the gospel truly, and they read their sermons freely when they were printed, though they would not hear them preached. They made the attendance on praying societies, when they had not their own ministers to hear, a condition of communion; and hearing the most orthodox minister preach, even the sermon that they would read in their societies, when published, a ground of exclusion and censure. This they called faithful testimony bearing for the glory of God. They considered all other presbyterians as having, in a lesser or greater degree, apostatized from the covenanted work of reformation, and that it was their duty, and for the glory of God, to testify against that defection, by keeping separate from those who were chargeable with it. Stated testimonies, in the church of Scotland, originated from the conflicts that were occasioned by the addition made to the national covenant, and the solemn league, soon after enforced; but the testimonies emitted during the tyranny of the Stuarts, which were numerous, and not always consistent, were certainly never intended by the pious and oppressed authors, as a term of communion for the church, even at that time of tyranny, and much less for posterity in times of peace—they were only intended for the vindication of the sufferers. Yet they have been not only used as terms of communion, but even given as authoritative examples for a continued emission of such testimonies, and the approbation of these testimonies again made terms of church communion; and the support of the covenanted work of reformation has been made the great object of them all. However, after persecution for religious opinions ceased, and protection was extensively afforded to all who live peaceably, even to those who made it a part of their religion to disown the authority of the government itself. Stated testimonies were still emitted, to shew on what principles the new church, or sect, was founded, and the grounds on which they kept separate from other sects. Of this kind was the judicial testimonies of the associate and reformed presbyteries of Scotland, and such is the judicial testimony of the new reformed presbytery of this country, to which Mr. Wylie's Sons of Oil was the precursor. These, as a matter of course, became terms of church communion with the sect to which they belonged. Though the local testimonies, during the persecution in Scotland, varying according to the occasion, were not then emitted as terms of communion in the church of Christ, yet they have been adopted as such in the testimony of the reformed presbytery, &c. This has introduced a habit of stated testimonies to such a degree, that, ever since I remember, many zealous people of that society were calling for them before they were thought necessary, or could be agreed upon by their ministers; and they were often offended at their ministers if they neglected, at least in the application of their sermons, to give a testimony against the sins and defections of the times, viz. of the civil magistracy, and the ministry of other sects, always considering their own sect as the pure church of Christ, and their own opinions of civil magistracy as the only perfect model. There is something, indeed, pleasing to human nature, in discerning the faults of all around us, and not seeing our own. Yet that disposition is the source of many of the religious and political parties, and of the party spirit, that has perplexed both church and state in modern times.

It long since gave me pain to hear, frequently, the misapplication of scripture texts, in support of those stated local testimonies. Such as, "bind up the testimony"—"To the law and to the testimony, if they walk not according to this word, it is because there is no light in them." The term testimony is above fifty times mentioned in the Bible, but in no one instance is it applied to instruments or laws made by human authority. In the Old Testament it is frequently applied to the Sinai covenant, and the two tables containing the moral law; to the ark in which they were deposited; to the tabernacle, &c. In the Psalms it is frequently put for the whole revealed will of God. In the New Testament it frequently means the gospel of Christ, and the miracles that bear testimony to the truth thereof, and the testimony of our consciences. Among men in civil affairs, it means the testimony given on oath to the truth of a fact within the knowledge of the witnesses. "It is written that the testimony of two men is true"—John xviii. 17. None of those will apply to such testimonies as have been, by some sects, made the evidences of a true church of Christ for 150 years past.

But, besides this, I am equally opposed to additional terms of communion, to those which the scripture prescribes, as I am to any other popish corruption. I know nothing about such a christian church as prescribes peculiar conditions of communion for one nation, that are not equally binding on all nations. Such was the commission given to the apostles. (Mark xvi. 16.) The national covenant, after the last addition made to it, and the solemn league and covenant, brought persecution in their train, and persecution brought, and always did bring, hypocrisy into the church. National covenants could not be enforced without this aid. The knowledge of these covenants and testimonies, depending, as they do, on human and much controverted tradition, are not objects of divine faith. The reformation being solely founded on the scripture, had nothing to do with human authority or human tradition; these belong solely to the apostate Roman Catholic church, or to such as coalesce with her. Not only so, but they are the foundation on which that church is built. The reformed presbytery of Scotland, I believe, did not mean so, but their intention did not change the principle. With respect to the presbytery, which has assumed the name of reformed in this country, if Mr. Wylie speaks their sentiments, which there is sufficient ground to presume he does, they will admit the charge. He having declared himself in unison with the political christian church in the fourth and fifth centuries, he has not only admitted, but proposed as a model for imitation, human authority and tradition, but what went hand and hand with these, prelacy in its highest grades and most numerous ramifications, when bishops sat on princely thrones, &c. but also actual regeneration by baptism; the efficacy of the sign of the cross; of the bones (relics) of martyrs, not only to cure the soul, but the body, and a thousand other such things. So many superstitions, and, in my opinion, idolatries, that, on reading his book, I was astonished at finding, that he was not in communion with the present church of Rome, and still the more astonished at his making the not burning, hanging, or banishing such of them as were in this country, a reason for not acknowledging the moral authority of the civil government in this country.—The presbytery of Scotland did not recognize these catholic councils as their model.

The principle being admitted, why does he declaim and rail against the superstructure raised upon it. I am equally opposed to the foundation and the superstructure. I wish to build on a more sure foundation—A foundation not laid by man. I wish to be a member of the church of Christ, enlisted under the commission given to his apostles, and not of any political church. Yet if we withdraw from all churches that are in some degree corrupt, we must withdraw from the whole visible church of Christ.

It was the doctrine of the reformers, and is the doctrine of our Catechism, that the faults or errors of those who administer the ordinances,
do not corrupt them to the worthy partakers—therefore, in obedience
to Christ, whose the ordinances are, I would partake of them even in
a national church, if I had not access to one more pure, and if that
national church did not exclude me from her communion, by obliging
me, in order to enjoy it, to believe or practice what I could not do with
a good conscience.

In all the views I have been enabled to take of the church of Christ,
I think the period since the reformed churches have become political
churches, is the most singular. In the primitive church, and till after she
apostatized, schism, viz. separation, was esteemed a sin of a very deep
dye. Since that period, it is not even esteemed a venal sin, except that
in the seventeenth century the civil authority punished as a civil crime
the not attending on the worship established by political authority. I still
think separating, without very sufficient cause, is a sin, and that wilfully
neglecting Christ's ordinances, without such causes as will justify us before his judgment seat, is rebellion against his authority. Human creeds
and confessions are only rendered expedient from circumstances, viz.
from the divisions that have taken place in the church. They were not
introduced till after the church had greatly apostatized; and even then,
Dr. Owen, one of the highest human authorities, thinks they did harm
by leading christians from the study of the scriptures themselves, to human authority. It was by these means that the grand apostacy was consummated; and by the same means, when enforced by human authority,
the progress of the reformation was checked.

As to myself, I approve of the doctrines of the gospel, as laid down in
the Westminster Confession of Faith and Catechism. I approve also of
presbyterian church government, as the most agreeable to the word of
God, of any form now existing; but would not persecute such as thought
otherwise. I certainly, with full persuasion, agree with all that the apostles prescribed on that subject, as far as I understand them, and, weak
as my understanding is, I will say, as Luther did about the judicial law
of Moses, that "their understanding shall not govern mine." Blessed be
God, he has given me the scriptures, addressed to my own conscience,
as he did to the Jews, and as the apostle Paul did to the Romans, with

certification that I should answer for myself for the improvement of it. I dare not trust to Mr. Wylie to answer for me at the day of judgment, nor would he be admitted; nay, none of the standard general councils, nor emperors, who, agreeable to his principles, have ratified and added sanctions to the laws of the most high God, will be admitted as advocates or mediators in that awfully solemn day.

We have heard much about judicial and stated testimonies. I ask, what does the additional terms *judicial* and *stated* add to the authority of these testimonies? Does it give them more authority than arises simply from the information they convey? It is my opinion it does not. My opinion has long been, that synods had authority to emit synodical testimonies against the errors which endangered the body over which they had oversight; but though this united testimony might, and ought to have more general influence, it had no more authority than the declaration of an individual minister to his congregation. In short, that the ministers of the gospel had no authority to make laws; that the change of a meeting from two or three, to a thousand meeting together at one place or time, made no addition to their authority, because nothing is submitted to their legislative discretion in the New Testament—but that they should provide that every part of the worship of God should, under their direction, be conducted with decency and order. Such, however, has been the effect of the application of this reasonable and necessary authority, that many of Christ's children have been prevented from eating of his bread, by the exercise of it. I have here only to add my sentiments, in the words of an eminent reformer.

"First let us hold this, that if we see in every fellowship of men, some policy to be necessary, that may serve to nourish common peace, and to retain concord: if we see that in doing these things there is alway some orderly form which is behoveful for public honesty, and for very humanity not to be refused, the same ought chiefly to be observed in churches, which are both best maintained by a well framed disposition of all things—and, without such agreement, they are no churches at all. Therefore, if we will have the safety of the church well provided for, we must altogether diligently procure that which Paul commandeth, that all things be done comely and according to order—1 Cor. xiv. 40. But forasmuch as there is great diversity in the manners of men, so great variety in minds, so great disagreement in judgments—neither is there any policy steadfast enough, unless it be established by certain laws; nor any orderly usage can be observed, without a certain appointed form: therefore, we are so far off from condemning the laws that are profitable to this purpose, that we affirm, when those be taken away, churches are dissolved from their sinews, and utterly deformed and scattered abroad."—*Calvin's Institutions, Book iv. chap.* 10. *sec.* 27.

Having shewed that neither by the primitive church, nor by the reformers, was there a perfect agreement in religious opinions, or uniformity in the rules of decency, and order of performing the worship required, in order to enjoying communion with Christ in the ordinances of his own institution; that a belief of the fundamental principles of the gospel, and a corresponding practice, and a submission to such rule of decency and order as did not affect the substance of religion, was all that was required by the church at the before mentioned periods, and all that the ministers of Christ's church, in any nation, or any age of the world, had, or have a right to require—Having, with the reformers, admitted, that rules of decency and order may differ in different particular churches, according to circumstances; and that particular churches may differ greatly in purity, in doctrine, and discipline, and be very defective in both, and yet be worthy of communion, as is evident from the case of the seven churches of Asia, to whom John the divine wrote his epistles, and the churches of Corinth, Gallatia, &c. to whom Paul wrote, and from the opinion of the learned Durham, and other approved commentators on these epistles; and that the apostles called these churches to repentance, and gave instruction with respect to doctrine, discipline, and order, but did not call on them to separate from each other in the same church, nor on the more pure churches to separate from the less pure, but reproved such divisions—Having shewed also, from the examples of the reformed and associate presbyteries, who, after having separated from the established church of Scotland, separated from each other, while they were under no restraint from civil government; to which I could have added numerous other examples, to prove that perfect uniformity is not attainable in the visible church, and cannot be attained, while all know but in part, and while every man must account unto God for his own knowledge of divine truth, and his use of the means to attain that knowledge—Having, however, admitted that the ordinances being Christ's, that, therefore, the unworthiness of those who administer them, does not corrupt the ordinances to the worthy partakers; but that where any particular church so far separates herself from the church of Christ, which is one through the whole world, and whose signs are, as Calvin saith, the pure preaching of the word and ministration of the sacraments; and, as he adds, wheresoever these signs are, we ought not to depart from that fellowship; that though some faults creep in, we ought not to cast off that communion, because those ministrations are always attended with some profit. I say, having stated these particulars—

I now ask, and ask it with the utmost seriousness, on what authority the numerous sects of presbyterians, who not only profess to adhere to the scriptures as the only infallible rule, but also to the Westminister Confession and Catechisms, as a sound exposition of scripture, do refuse to hold communion with each other in the ordinances instituted and enjoined by their common Lord, and divine prophet, and king over his own house? Not only so, but why do they forbid those who adhere to them, even to hear the gospel preached, or be present at the administration of the sealing ordinances of his institution, by ministers of the gospel lawfully called and duly qualified? Not because of error in the doctrines of the gospel; not because of superstition or idolatry in the worship; not because of any qualifying conditions enjoined by human authority—but because they do not approve of the terms which they themselves have enjoined by human authority, supported by human and fallible tradition, thus putting their church on the very same foundation on which the church of Rome is built. Every qualifying condition, added to those which Christ has himself prescribed, is an usurpation of his authority, and is the same in principle, though differing in degree, with the church of Rome. The beginnings of the grand apostacy were small, and believed to be beneficial. When they were introduced, all were believed to receive benefit by them, and made their own opinion of the benefits they received the rule for further additions of their own inventions; and even now, when those inventions in the worship of God have become innumerable, the members of that church believe they receive benefit from them, that they are followed by the blessing of

Christ, &c. The reformers believed this to be a delusion, and that Christ never conferred his blessing but with ordinances of his own institution, and for the purposes of his own appointment. Our own opinion of receiving benefit is a very deceitful rule, because we are very liable to be self-deceived.

The present divided state of the church of Christ, even of such sects as profess the same faith, the same worship, discipline, and government, has, for half a century, exercised my mind with serious reflections, notwithstanding my early prepossessions, from education, in favour of local terms of communion instituted by human fallible authority, and only known to me by human tradition. I could not silence my convictions so far, but what I saw that those things were not calculated for the edifying of the body of Christ, which is one in every nation under heaven, where the good seed of the word has been planted, but to impair the unity of it; that if christians in one nation had authority to institute peculiar terms of communion, every other nation had the same authority; that, consequently, Christ would have many mystical bodies, instead of one. Nor could I avoid observing, that all those exertions to promote the union of national churches, not having the authority of Christ, did not receive his blessing, but became the source of new divisions and subdivisions, and of hatred, strife, and debate, instead of promoting the unity of the spirit in the bond of peace.

The old dissenters, greatly agitated by persecution and tyrannical oppression, which Solomon says will render wise men mad—and being, on the revolution which was introduced by king William, left for seventeen years without a minister of the gospel, had to grope their way in the dark—they kept societies, and excluded from their societies all who would hear presbyterian ministers preach, or be married by them— when they got a minister in Scotland, their people had to go to Scotland to get married, just as if marriage had been a gospel ordinance. On this I need make no further remarks.

I have been informed, and I have reason to believe it is true, that Mr. Wylie, and the sect to which he belongs, hold all their people censurable for even hearing the gospel preached by a minister of another presbyterian sect. The consequence is, that as their people are few in number, and much dispersed, many of them do not see nor hear their ministers more than once or twice a year. In this situation, the pastoral duties of visitation, catechising, &c. cannot be performed, nor the characters of the people known to the minister; the people, afraid of church censure, stay at home, and undoubtedly, on this principle, are encouraged to believe, that all who attend the public worship, from which they, by the rules of their church are restrained, are on the high road to hell; or otherwise, that their own testimony for the glory of God, in their intention, is of greater importance than the salvation of their own souls; to the appointed means of which, they prefer their own testimony, founded on human authority and fallible tradition.

I do not mean to charge all the presbyterian sects in this country with unchurching all other churches who do not agree with their own particular order. The German, the Low Dutch presbyterians, and general assembly, formerly the synod of New-York and Philadelphia, and the associate reformed synod, do not censure their people for attending on the ministrations of gospel ordinances, by lawfully called ministers of other sects; nor, as far as I know, for partaking in Christ's sealing ordinances, administered by them. I well know that it is not esteemed censurable by the two last, for I have frequently, as opportunity offered, communicated with both, and still do so. The ordinances are Christ's, and not theirs, and neither of them put any bars of human invention in the way.

In doing so, I am not intimidated with the charge of being a latitudinarian, for I take the scriptures for my alone rule of orthodoxy; and protestant creeds, &c. only as they are, a sound exposition of the scriptures. Nor am I afraid of the frightful name, sectarian. This term is, like toleration, relative to political church establishments. In some of the testimonies, and other writings of the seventeenth and eighteenth centuries, the reader would be induced to believe, that sectarians were abominable heretics; whereas, the name includes all such as differed from the politically established church. All the dissenters from the established churches in England and Scotland, whether they be orthodox presbyterians, or heterodox Socinians, are equally sectarians; formerly they would have been called schismatics. The reformers were so called by the dominant apostate church, but the name sectarian has no meaning, as applied to this country, because no national establishment of one religious sect over another exists in it. Schisms, *i.e.* divisions of the church of Christ, without sufficient scriptural foundation, no doubt abound. Most of these divisions, however, have been imported from Europe; but to decide on these, no high commission courts, star chambers, or other courts of inquisition, are in this country constituted by civil government. They are left to the proper tribunal—the judgment seat of Christ.

I conclude, by declaring my wish to reject, as excrescences, all conditions of communion depending on political ecclesiastical establishments, and to be a member of the church of Christ, founded on the doctrines of the prophets and apostles, agreeable to the rules prescribed in the New Testament, which contains the religion of christians. On this ground, I know nothing of sufficient importance, to perpetuate a separation between the different sects of presbyterians in this country, including the New England churches, from communion with each other, and in this happy situation, strengthening each others hands in the work of the Lord, instead of making each other offenders for a word. There is reasonable ground to believe, that they all endeavour to walk according to the truth of the gospel, the pillar and ground of truth. Who, or what is he, that censures or reproves christians for seeking for edification from other quarters, than from the demagogue who wishes to keep him in bondage? He must be more than an apostle. The apostles did not do so. Christ commanded to search the scriptures, and so did the disciples, and commended such as did so.

The great object of the important doctrine taught them, was, to fortify the christian converts against will-worship (called the rudiments of the world) and against implicit faith in human authority and human tradition, which, as was foreseen by the divinely inspired apostle (Acts xx. 29. 2 Thess. ii. 3, 12. 1 Tim. iv. 1, 3. 2 Tim. iii. 9. and 2 Pet. ii. 1, 3.) soon defaced the purity and beauty of the church. Implicit faith in human authority and tradition became the handmaid of superstition, ignorance, tyranny, persecution, licentiousness, and even of atheism.

Mr. Wylie, however, does not consider these covenants, the knowledge of which we receive only by human, doubtful, and much controverted tradition, as of human invention. In the Sons of Oil (p. 91–93.) he puts them on an equal footing with God's covenants with Noah, with Abraham,

with Jacob, with Israel at Mount Sinai, and the renewal of that covenant, under the direction of Moses, by immediate divine inspiration,
in the plains of Moab, &c. The difference, however, is this—The covenants which he introduces as examples, were expressly dictated by
Jehovah, and are handed down to us by infallible inspiration. Those
which Mr. Wylie puts on an equal footing with them, were the invention
of fallible, short-sighted, and self-seeking men, and the knowledge of
them to us depending on the same authority with the Jewish and popish
traditions. I have been often astonished, when I reflected on the subject,
to think how it ever came into the minds of pious and zealous christians,
who contended against popery, to assume the very foundation on which
the grand apostacy was erected. Trusting in the promise of the church's
divine Head, that he will be with it to the end of the world, and that
the gates of hell shall not prevail against it, I have the same confidence
of the accomplishment of this divine promise, that I have of the promises for our own salvation, through the righteousness and atonement of
Jesus, who came to save sinners, and to destroy the works of the devil.
I rejoice, and am thankful, that my lot was cast among the reformed
churches—however imperfectly they have been hitherto reformed, it
was a happy and a blessed reformation. I trust and believe, however,
that it was only a prelude to a reformation much more advanced, yet
not perfect—perfection will not be attained by the church militant. I
am far from complaining of the day of small things; the reformation,
compared with what had been enjoyed for more than a thousand years
preceding, was a day of great things, for which I am sincerely thankful.

I conclude with a quotation from the very learned and orthodox
Dr. Witsius:

Vol. iii. p. 346—"But there is a king, who has power over conscience,
and God only is such a king: and there is a king who has power over the
body, and such are the supreme rulers of this world." Speaking of christian liberty, in five particulars, he says, (p. 368.) "Freedom from human
empire, or constraint, with respect to divine worship, and the actions
of religion, as such: for God alone has dominion over the conscience—
James iv. 12. Nor is it lawful for the sons of God, who know themselves to
be bought with a price, to become the servants of men—1 Cor. vii. 23.
Mat. xv. 9. Col. ii. 18, 22, 23. Though formerly the scribes and pharisees

sat in Moses' chair, yet God never gave them a power to load the conscience with new institutions, beyond and besides the law of God, to which all were equally bound—Deut. iv. 2. and xii. 34. All the authority of the doctors of the law tended to keep the people to the observance of the law of Moses; Christ justly rebuked them, when they went beyond that. Whatever man has devised from his own invention, in matters of religion, has ever been displeasing to God. Freedom from the obligation to things indifferent, which are neither good nor bad in themselves, and which God has neither commanded nor forbidden. When the knowledge and sense of this liberty is wanting, the conscience, in that case, is disquieted, and superstition has neither measure nor end—Rom. xiv. 5, 14, 23. The possession, however, is to be distinguished from the use; the right, from the exercise of it: the former ought ever to remain inviolable to the conscience, the latter to be circumscribed by the rules of prudence and charity, to avoid giving offence to weak brethren—1 Cor. vi. 12, 2 Cor. x. 13. Rom. xiv. 19."

FINIS

INDEX OF BIBLICAL CITATIONS

Old Testament

New Testament

INDEX

The typeface used for this book is ITC New Baskerville, which was created for the International Typeface Corporation and is based on the types of the English type founder and printer John Baskerville (1706–75). Baskerville is the quintessential transitional face: it retains the bracketed and oblique serifs of old-style faces such as Caslon and Garamond, but in its increased lowercase height, lighter color, and enhanced contrast between thick and thin strokes, it presages modern faces.

This book is printed on paper that is acid-free and meets the requirements of the American National Standard for Permanence of Paper for Printed Library Materials, z39.48–1992.⊗

Book design by Erin Kirk New, Watkinsville, Georgia

Typography by Newgen

Printed and bound by Worzalla Publishing Company, Stevens Point, Wisconsin